# ADAPTING INSTRUCTION FOR THE MAINSTREAM

## A Sequential Approach to Teaching

### Judy W. Wood

Virginia Commonwealth University

With Contributions by Betty B. Englebert

Charles E. Merrill Publishing Company
A Bell & Howell Company
Columbus   Toronto   London   Sydney

Published by
Charles E. Merrill Publishing Company
A Bell & Howell Company
Columbus, Ohio 43216

This book was set in Serif Gothic and Palatino.
Production Coordinator: Sandra Gurvis
Copy Editor: Beth Rigel Daugherty
Cover Designer: Tony Faiola
Cover Photo: Ginny Padgette

ISBN: 0-675-20129-2
Library of Congress Catalog Card Number: 83-062727
1  2  3  4  5—89  88  87  86  85  84
Printed in the United States of America

*To my sons
Eddie, Scott, and Jason*

# Preface

This book emerged out of pleasant and unpleasant personal experiences that influenced me to explore working with the mildly handicapped student—specifically, with adapting instruction for the mainstreamed student. Since I presently train special education teachers and have spent many years in regular and special education public school systems, I know how much needs to be done for both mainstreamed students and their teachers. Betty Englebert spent numerous years counseling handicapped students and their parents and providing instructional assistance for mainstreamed students. She worked daily with the problems of adapting instruction for handicapped youth.

As these needs became more clearly defined, I designed and implemented, with Betty's assistance, a model for mainstreaming the whole child. This model focuses on providing an appropriate education for the mildly handicapped student and includes all the components of a handicapped student's environment: parents, peers, and school. These components greatly influence not only how much and how quickly the mildly handicapped student learns but also what kind of self-concept he or she develops. The first phase of the trial model emphasizes counseling and providing information to parents; the second phase focuses on peers within the school environment; and the third phase addresses the school through the administrators, through the teachers, and, most importantly, through instruction itself.

This book focuses on the instructional part of the overall model for mainstreaming. The instructional model is illustrated on p. vi; each chapter covers one component of this illustration. As teachers gain knowledge of each of the components, they can easily adapt the instructional process for all mildly handicapped students. The model also provides a continuum for instruction in the regular classroom, and slow learners can benefit also. Each chapter is designed to provide a sequence for educators in these classrooms. In addition, teachers can apply the basic design to all grade levels and subject areas.

The reader can use this book in several different ways. Some suggested uses follow:

1. Teachers and students needing an overview of mainstreaming can begin with Chapter 1. However, those already having general information about mainstreaming may want to begin with Chapter 2.
2. Teachers welcoming a mainstreamed student for the first time will be most interested in Chapter 2 because it shows how to understand and interpret the data collected on a student.

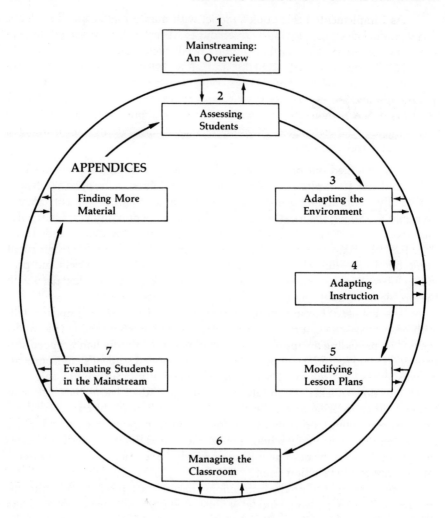

3. Teachers may also begin with the chapter that deals with their particular problems in instructing mildly handicapped students.
4. Teachers who see that a mildly handicapped student is not succeeding in the regular class should pinpoint the problem and then consult the chapter dealing with that problem.
5. Teachers can refer to any point of interest in the book and develop a sequential continuum for adapting each phase of their instruction. Numerous alternatives are offered for mainstreaming more smoothly within a flexible curriculum. Readers are encouraged to test the ideas and select those most applicable to them and their students.
6. Both undergraduate and graduate students can use this book as a resource on the process of teaching mildly handicapped students in the mainstream.

As I implemented this book's model with mildly handicapped students, I saw gradual changes: previously discouraged, defeated mainstreamed students developed self-assurance as their unique needs were met.

Mildly handicapped students and slow learners can succeed in the mainstream if teachers use this model. When teachers have a way to adapt the instruction and the content of their classes to meet the unique needs of these students, teachers develop more positive attitudes about instruction and about the students. And as teachers' attitudes change, students begin to learn, enjoy school, and feel good about themselves.

# ACKNOWLEDGEMENTS

To all mildly handicapped students, may your educational trials and frustrations lessen through this endeavor of love.

Appreciation is extended to my colleagues, especially Paul Wehman, who helped me see the possibilities in myself and in my work; to Nancy Fallen and Ada Hill, who never stopped believing in me; to Rosemary Lambie, who provided assistance with Chapter 6 in addition to sharing her support; and to Barbara Fuhrmann, who devoted many hours patiently editing the manuscript and who never stopped encouraging me. Many thanks to Dean Charles Ruch, Dr. John Oehler, Dr. Gay Whitlock, and Dr. William Bost.

Ginna Dalton and Marjorie Loya provided the research for the Appendices. Pam Wright and Helen Hartford assisted with the indexing. Sheila Tyler Scott and Reginald Tinsley provided expert typing for the manuscript and Steve Ware assisted with the original ideas for the artwork. Carol Scearce O'Brien shared ideas for Chapter 6. To each of you, thank you.

To all of my friends and colleagues at the University of Southern Mississippi in Hattiesburg: Gary Rush, Carolyn Reeves, Beth Arnold Richardson, Mark Richardson, Harold Knight, and the faculty of the Department of Special Education, thank you for always remembering and supporting.

I am also grateful to my good friends and neighbors, especially Vivian and Griff Griffin, Nancy and Jerry Finch, Alan Cambell, Cheryl Cross, Sandy Warlick, Dean and Tom Bain, Maureen and Bob Jarvis, Sharon Dodson, Bob and Patsy Glover, Joe and Art Kilgore, Martha and Harold Ervin, Daryll and Brenda Brickey, Ann Norris, Peggy Foster, Nancy Holfhimer, Nancy Owen, Laura Finch, Wendy Fugett, Ginny Brandon, Donna DuPue, and Jerry Aldridge. You gave me support, encouragement, and endless love through the long months of work.

To the teachers in the field and to that unique population, my students, thank you.

I am indebted to my original administrative editor, Marianne Taflinger, who had faith in my work; to my present administrative editor, Vicki Knight;

to my production editor, Sandra Gurvis, and to my copy editor, Beth Rigel Daugherty. To the staff at Charles E. Merrill, thank you.

I wish to acknowledge Ginny Padgette for her love, friendship, and assistance in taking the picture for the book's cover. A special thanks to Debra Gibson who assisted my family through many long months and who provided endless encouragement. To Jack Corazzini, for his guidance, thank you. For their never fading faith, love, support, and encouragement, I thank my sister, Sandra Foutz, and my mother, Ercyle Walker.

Betty Englebert has always supported me and my dreams. Additionally, she assisted in the development of this manuscript. For your faith, love, and expert assistance, I thank you. I also extend sincere appreciation to Lynn Englebert for his support and graphic work on the project.

To my sons and earthly treasures, Eddie, Scott, and Jason Wood, thank you for sharing your mother so that other children might experience success in learning. You helped my dream become a reality and I love each of you dearly.

Judy W. Wood
Virginia Commonwealth University

# Contents

# FIVE
## Modifying Lesson Plans

# SIX
## Managing the Classroom

# SEVEN
## Evaluating Students in the Mainstream

# APPENDICES
## Finding More Material

# ADAPTING INSTRUCTION FOR THE MAINSTREAM

A Sequential Approach to Teaching

# Chapter One

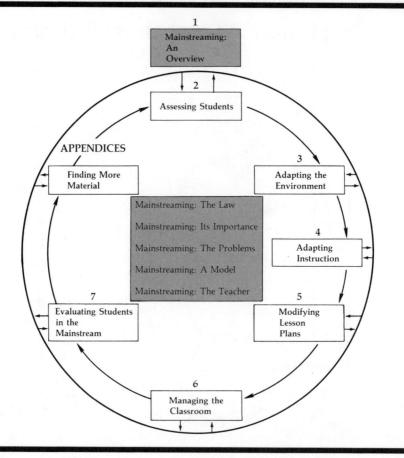

# Mainstreaming:
# An Overview

Mainstreaming, educating handicapped children with their nonhandicapped peers in the least restrictive environment possible, is no longer a dream of far-sighted parents and educators, but a reality. This book was developed in response to that new reality, to what Hawisher and Calhoun (1978) call "the integration of mildly handicapped students into the general educational program of the public school" (p. 1). It will focus on adapting instruction for the *mildly handicapped*, that is, the educable mentally retarded, the emotionally handicapped, and the learning disabled, in the mainstream. (See Table 1.1 for information about these groups of students). Although this text emphasizes the mildly handicapped, its guidelines for instruction can be applied to all children in the classroom, especially to slow learners. However, before teachers can adapt instruction, they need to understand how we arrived in this new era of mainstreaming, what mainstreaming hopes to accomplish, what problems sometimes accompany mainstreaming, what alternative placements are available, and what new teaching roles have emerged as a result of mainstreaming. The rest of Chapter 1 will deal with these concerns.

## MAINSTREAMING: THE LAW

Mainstreaming has two basic purposes: to protect the rights of handicapped children and to make life as normal as possible for them. Concern for the rights of handicapped children began to grow in the early 1950s.

## RIGHTS OF HANDICAPPED INDIVIDUALS

Our nation has always taken pride in our guarantee of basic freedoms for all persons. For example, the Constitution clearly states that all human beings are created equal. But at one time the fundamental freedoms shared by most American citizens were not enjoyed by the handicapped. The movement to establish the individual rights of handicapped persons gained force when the National Association for Retarded Children (presently known as the National Association for Retarded Citizens [NARC]) was formed in 1950. The public schools began to feel pressure from parents who had organized to support and nurture the educational rights of their children. Parents advocated programs for the moderately retarded in public schools and expansion of other special educational services.

Also, by the early 1950s civil rights movements pursuing equal opportunities across racial boundaries had entered the arena of public education. The 1954 U.S. Supreme Court decision in *Brown* v. *Board of Education of Topeka* ruled that school segregation violated the Fourteenth Amendment, thus setting a precedent for equality in education for handicapped children.

In 1958, the Council for Exceptional Children (CEC) began to support the NARC in seeking legislation for training of special education personnel. These two groups proposed a reorganization of the U.S. Office of Education in order to meet special education demands and to seek more appropriate services for the handicapped. The Office of Education created the Division of Handicapped Children and Youth in 1963, thus meeting the demands of advocacy groups. The Division later became the Bureau of Education of the Handicapped and is now the Office of Special Education.

The Elementary and Secondary Education Act (ESEA) of 1965 further supported the movement for services in special education by providing federal monies to the states for economically disadvantaged children and for the handicapped. Federal services began to expand rapidly when in 1970 Public Law 91-230, The Elementary and Secondary Education Act Amendments, became law and recognized handicapped and exceptional children as a special needs target population. Society was beginning to acknowledge that humane treatment and educational opportunities were necessary for handicapped children (Haring, 1978).

At the same time legislation supporting handicapped persons was passed, several major suits brought by dissatisfied parents were decided. For example, in the 1967 landmark decision of *Hobson* v. *Hanson*, Judge Skeely Wright ruled that the tracking system used to place children was discriminatory. In 1972 the Pennsylvania Association for Retarded Citizens (PARC) filed a class action suit concerning the right to education for handicapped children against the Commonwealth of Pennsylvania. The PARC charged that the state was violating the equal protection and due process rights of mentally retarded children when it allowed a school psychologist to recommend that a child be excluded from school based on the inability of the school to serve the child. In the consent agreement a three-judge federal court ruled that all retarded children must receive a free public education and appropriate training. Additionally, the judges ruled that all previously excluded children had to be identified and evaluated by local school districts, a re-evaluation of all children in special education had to be initiated every two years or when change of placement was considered, and parents who were dissatisfied with their child's placement had a right to a hearing. Also in 1972 *Mills* v. *Board of Education* was decided in favor of handicapped children's rights: the judge ruled that handicapped children had the right to an education and that the term handicapped included all physical, mental, or emotional handicaps, not just mental retardation.

Attention to the individual rights of the handicapped continued to grow. Section 504 of the Rehabilitation Act of 1973, Public Law 93-112, made provisions to disallow the exclusion of any handicapped person from vocational programs receiving federal funds, and in 1974 Section 111a of Public Law 93-516 amended the Rehabilitation Act to require *any* recipients of federal funds to provide equal employment services for the handicapped.

From 1950 to 1975, then, litigation brought about by advocacy groups built a framework for the educational future of the handicapped. As laws were passed, educational opportunities began to open for handicapped children and

TABLE 1.1
Comparison of Mildly Handicapped Categories

| Category | Prevalence in School | General Characteristics |
|---|---|---|
| Educable Mentally Retarded | 1–2% | Ability level lower than norm. |
| Emotionally Handicapped | 1% | Inability to learn that cannot be explained by intellectual, sensory, or health factors; Inability to build or maintain satisfactory interpersonal relationships with peers and teachers; Inappropriate types of behaviors or feelings under normal conditions; A general, pervasive mood of unhappiness or depression; A tendency to develop physical symptoms, pains, or fears associated with personal or school problems. (Bowers, 1970, pp. 22–23) |
| Learning Disabled | 3–4% | Disorder in learning that usually involves processes related to language usage (either spoken or written). (Gearheardt & Weishahn, 1980, p. 159.) |

the basic individual rights of handicapped children soon became a major national concern in public education. As litigation continued, the need grew for a federal mandate that would have significant ramifications for the education of handicapped children. This movement culminated in Public Law 94-142, The Education for All Handicapped Children Act, which President Gerald Ford signed into law on November 29, 1975.

TABLE 1.1 (continued)

| School Placement | IQ Range |
| --- | --- |
| Placement can range from total special class placement, through mainstreamed into regular classes, to total regular class placement. | 50–70% |
| Placement can range from total special class placement, through mainstreamed into regular classes, to total regular class placement. | Ranges from above average to slightly below average. Could be in gifted range. |
| Placement can range from total special class placement to total regular class placement. Placement generally combines part-time special class placement with part-time regular class placement. | Must have average I.Q. Could be in the gifted range. |

# PUBLIC LAW 94-142

Soon recognized as a landmark in legislation for education, The Education for All Handicapped Children Act basically provides a free public education for handicapped individuals. Public Law 94-142 has four major purposes: to insure all handicapped children a free appropriate public education that includes special education and related services to meet their unique needs; to insure the protection of the rights of handicapped children and their parents; to assist states and localities in providing for the education of all handicapped children; and to assist in and insure the effectiveness of efforts to educate those children.

## MAJOR COMPONENTS OF THE LAW

Five components of Public Law 94-142 directly affect the classroom and instruction. A brief discussion of each major component will provide a better understanding of the law.

RIGHT TO A FREE APPROPRIATE PUBLIC EDUCATION   By law all children are guaranteed a public education at no expense to parents or guardians, but historically, many handicapped children were denied this basic freedom and either received no education, were charged tuition for private services, or were unable to obtain any type of services. The passage of Public Law 94-142 established the fundamental right of a free appropriate public education for handicapped children.

NONDISCRIMINATORY EVALUATION   According to Public Law 94-142, testing and evaluation materials and procedures used for the evaulation and placement of children defined as handicapped must be selected and administered so as not to be racially or culturally discriminatory (Federal Register, Vol, 42, pp. 42496–42497). The law requires that, at the minimum, all state and local educational agencies insure that:

1. Trained personnel administer validated tests and other evaluation materials and provide and administer such materials in the child's native language or other mode of communication
2. Tests and other evaluation materials include those tailored to assess specific areas of educational need and not merely those designed to provide a single general intelligence quotient
3. Trained personnel select and administer tests to reflect accurately the child's aptitude or achievement level without discriminating against the child's handicap
4. Trained personnel use no single procedure as the sole criterion for determining an appropriate educational program for a child
5. A multidisciplinary team assess the child in all areas related to the suspected disability

PROCEDURAL DUE PROCESS   Due process, a right extended to all U.S. citizens by the Constitution, guarantees handicapped children and their parents fairness during educational evaluation and placement by providing certain procedural safeguards:

1. Written parental permission is necessary before a handicapped child can be evaluated for special education services.
2. Written parental permission is necessary before special education placement, and this permission may be withdrawn at any time.
3. Parents have the right to examine and question all relevant records on their children, and they have a right to an independent evaluation.
4. Confidentiality must be maintained.
5. Parents and school authorities have the right to a hearing, have the right to present evidence, call and confront witnesses, and have a lawyer.
6. Parents and school authorities have the right to an appeal.

INDIVIDUALIZED EDUCATION PROGRAM (IEP)   The individualized educational program refers to a written education plan that must be developed annually for all handicapped children receiving special education services. Actually a road map for the instruction of a handicapped child, the IEP is the one safeguard parents have to insure that their child receives instruction designed to meet the child's unique needs. Prior to placement of a handicapped child, a selected committee composed of a representative of the school system, the child's teacher, one or both of the child's parents, the child, if appropriate, and other individuals (at the discretion of the parent or school system) hold an IEP meeting at which they write and sign the IEP. Even though the IEP is written every year, a complete assessment of the child is required at least every three years.

From state to state and locality to locality, the format of the IEP may vary. However, certain basic components appear on all IEPs. A fundamental understanding of these components will assist the regular classroom teacher not only in instructing the handicapped child in the mainstream, but also in understanding the total special education program. Table 1.2 contains basic information about, and examples of, all the components common to IEPs.

TABLE 1.2
Components of an IEP

| Component | Description | Example |
|---|---|---|
| Present level of educational functioning | Information obtained from norm or criterion referenced tests. Gives actual level and skill at which a child is functioning. | Student can add number facts from 1 to 20 with 100% accuracy. |
| Annual or long-range goals | Projection of how far teachers think child can progress during school | Student will be able to add two digits, one addend without |

TABLE 1.2 (continued)

| Component | Description | Example |
|---|---|---|
| | year. Each present level of educational functioning will have a projected annual goals. | regrouping with 95% accuracy. |
| Short-term instructional objectives | An objective, written in behavioral terms, listing the intermediate steps between the present level of performance and the annual goals. | Student will be able to add zero as addends with 95% accuracy. Student will be able to add three or more digits in a column with 95% accuracy. |
| Beginning and ending dates | Projected dates for initiation of services and anticipated duration of services. | September, 198X to May, 198X. Student will be evaluated each six weeks. |
| Objective criteria and evaluation procedures for short-term objectives | Statement of criteria and evaluation procedures for completion of short-term objectives. | Criterion checklists, teacher made tests, work samples. |
| Special education services | Type of specific service child is receiving. | EMR resource. |
| Related services | Any service outside of special education required for appropriate education. | Speech therapy. |
| Regular classroom participation | Curriculum areas and amount of time each day handicapped child will spend in regular classroom. | Art, 30 minutes twice a week; PE, 30 minutes each day; Music, 30 minutes once a week. |
| Projected dates for assessment | IEP must be reviewed at least annually by IEP committee to determine whether short-term instructional objectives are being achieved. | May, 198X. |
| Committee members present | IEP must be signed by all committee members. | |
| Parental signature | Parents present at IEP meeting are asked to sign IEP. | |

LEAST RESTRICTIVE ENVIRONMENT   The least restrictive environment clause of Public Law 94–142 places responsibility on the school district to educate, to the maximum extent appropriate, handicapped children with nonhandicapped children. The child's needs, as indicated on the Individualized Education Program, determine placement in the least restrictive environment. The concept of the least restrictive environment is based on the premise that many creative alternatives exist to help the regular educator serve children with learning or adjustment problems within the context of a regular class setting.

Thus, since the 1975 passage of Public Law 94–142, mildly handicapped children have moved from being almost totally excluded from regular classrooms to being almost totally included. Although the budget-minded Reagan Administration sought to revise the law's regulations in 1981, pressure from advocacy groups soundly defeated such attempts. Again, in 1982, Reagan's efforts to amend and weaken the law were strongly opposed. The handicapped child's right to a free and appropriate education in the least restrictive environment remains guaranteed by law.

# MAINSTREAMING: ITS IMPORTANCE

Mainstreaming, of course, means more than obeying the letter of the law. Simply putting handicapped children in the regular classroom will not necessarily fulfill the *intent* of the law, which is to place handicapped children in the least restrictive educational environment so that they can have lives that are as normal as possible.

## NORMALIZATION

For handicapped children to be properly served in society, schools must accept and serve them in an environment that is as normal as possible by providing settings common to all children and by adjusting to the needs of each child, handicapped or nonhandicapped. Wolfensberger (1979) defines this basic principle of normalization as "utilization of means which are as culturally normative as possible, in order to establish and/or maintain personal behaviors and characteristics which are as culturally normative as possible" (p. 28). Since 1969, the term *normalization* has provided the philosophical basis for the concept of the least restrictive environment (Kugel & Wolfensberger, 1969). However, as early as 1962, Reynolds had enunciated this principle:

> The prevailing view is that normal home and school life should be preserved if at all possible. When a special placement is necessary to provide suitable

care or education, it should be no more "special" than necessary. . . . children should be placed in programs of no more special character than ab-
solutely necessary. There should be continuing assessment of children in
special programs with a view toward returning to more ordinary environments as soon as possible. (Reynolds, 1962, pp. 368–370)

Educators, then, want to provide handicapped children with an everyday life similar to that enjoyed by nonhandicapped children. They hope that
integrating the handicapped into the educational arena will help society inte-
grate them into businesses and social occasions more easily.

## POSITIVE SELF-CONCEPTS FOR THE HANDICAPPED

Gaining individual rights and normal environments has an important effect on
mildly handicapped children: they develop competence and long lasting positive self-concepts. Mainstreaming helps the handicapped child to develop
academically and, thus, to develop feelings of self-worth.

From birth, all children begin to develop a relative sense of worth. During children's early years, numerous factors influence this development of the
self. For example, success or failure during preschool correlates with many different social and developmental factors. Once in school, however, the pressure
to achieve and to progress academically affects self-esteem the most. Robbins
and Harway (1977) see the school age period as crucial in the child's development of self and further explain that because the learning disabled child usually
experiences a wide variety of successes and failures in school, he or she may
have more difficulty developing a sense of identity. Similarly, Chapman and
Boersma (1979) point out that although most professionals believe learning problems can be remediated, such efforts are hindered when students with a history
of failure in school develop negative affective characteristics. Calhoun and Elliott
(1977), working with mentally retarded and emotionally disabled children, agree
that a positive relationship between self-concept and academic achievement
exists.

In comparing academic outcomes and self-concept, Chapman and Boersma
(1979) identify three constructs that influence a child's success in school: academic
locus of control, academic self-concept, and self-expectations for future achievement. Academic locus of control reflects the way in which the student explains
successes and failures. Those students who tend to attribute their successes and
failures to themselves and who feel that they have the ability to achieve generally do obtain higher levels of achievement and have an internal locus of control. Those students who attribute success and failure to others or to chance
achieve at a lower level and have an external locus of control. Learning disabled students, on the other hand, often accept responsibility for failures but
cannot take credit for their successes. Thus, these students view success in school
only partly as a measure of effort and ability while at the same time they view
failure as a *lack* of effort and ability. According to Chapman and Boersma,

the learning disabled child also has a significantly lower academic self-concept and demonstrates a lower level of self-expectation than does the normal student. Because learning disabled students confuse effort and outcome, they tend to question their own abilities and then give up. Then they think so little of themselves and their abilities that they are pessimistic about their future performance. Since, as Chapman and Boersma point out, school learning requires the students' belief that they can complete a given task and will succeed, educators must try to restore learning disabled students' confidence in themselves as they work to remedy the students' cognitive deficits.

Usually mildly handicapped children begin the educational process in a regular classroom. At this point, unless teachers adjust instruction, the children fail academically and their self-concepts begin to deteriorate. But no mildly handicapped student need experience failure in our schools. In the mainstream, teachers can adjust instruction immediately and preserve students' self-worth as a result. If mainstreaming produces mildly handicapped adults with both positive self-esteem and the skills to function as normally as possible in adult society, it has succeeded. Educators cannot expect all children to learn the same material or the same amount of material at the same rate. But teachers can encourage all children to feel good about themselves.

Legally, then, mainstreaming requires that schools place handicapped children into regular classes with support from special class teachers when needed. Mainstreaming's importance to society goes beyond legal rights, however, because it attempts to help mildly handicapped children grow into adults who can function normally within that society. In practice, regular class placement of a handicapped child may or may not help that child reach the goal of living a normal life. If the teacher does not adapt regular class instruction to the instructional level of the handicapped student, for example, and the handicapped child loses educational opportunities and self-esteem as a result, the law has actually done the opposite of what it intends. Therefore, for educators to fulfill the true intent of the law, they must not only provide instruction for the handicapped student within the regular classroom, *they must also adjust that instruction to meet the emotional, physical, and educational needs of the student.*

## MAINSTREAMING: THE PROBLEMS

Because the era of mainstreaming arrived as the result of a federal mandate to provide the least restrictive environment for all handicapped children, educators had to comply with new regulations rapidly. No matter how receptive to both the letter and the spirit of the 1975 law, many regular educators were perplexed about how to meet their responsibilities to the growing numbers of mildly handicapped children entering their classrooms.

Struggling to implement mainstreaming quickly, schools often faced, and continue to face, some or all of the following difficulties:

1. The emphasis on least restrictive environment pushes mildly handicapped students into already overcrowded regular classes.

2. Regular educators trained prior to mainstreaming frequently do not know how to adapt and modify instruction to meet special needs.
3. The introduction of mainstreaming without proper preparation often creates negative attitudes about special education and mainstreamed students.
4. Students ruled ineligible to receive special education and related services and labeled "slow learners" remain in regular classes and place another demand on the teacher to adapt instruction.
5. Administrators burdened with paperwork must also manage special education with all of its procedures and technicalities.
6. Universities and colleges have a new responsibility, the training of both regular and special education teachers to accommodate the mainstreamed student.
7. Parents, expecting mainstreaming to meet all their children's needs, see that some needs go unmet even with mainstreaming.
8. The general public complains that mainstreaming overworks special and regular educators, wastes the taxpayer's money, represents a federal intrusion into public education, and is ultimately a futile effort.

Only by honestly confronting the problems connected with mainstreaming can educators hope to solve them and thus correct the public's misconceptions.

## MAINSTREAMING: A MODEL

Many of the problems growing out of educators' attempts to adjust to mainstreaming will be solved as teachers learn to adapt their regular instruction to the needs of the mildly handicapped. But before they can do so, they need to know the options available for serving handicapped students. The following discussion will clarify such instructional alternatives.

Models for the integration of the handicapped into regular class settings or for reentry into the mainstream fill educational literature. The basic assumption that a handicapped child placed in a model can move either up or down the scale depending on the severity of the handicap underlies all such models. Figure 1.1, an adaptation of Deno's cascade model (1973), presents a continuum of instructional alternatives available to the handicapped. Regular class placement with adaptations and modifications, Step 2, has been added to show the handicapped child served in the regular classroom by adapting instruction to meet the individual needs of that child. The model also shows degrees of labeling. The further down the model, the more labeled the student. Thus, the insertion of Step 2 in Deno's model decreases the number of children labeled as handicapped.

School districts are mandated to serve the handicapped student in an array of alternative placements. Some educators think that as students move from one alternative to another, they must become more or less restricted. However, the student's placement cannot be called restrictive when it meets the individual's needs. For example, a regular class setting would restrict a severely mentally

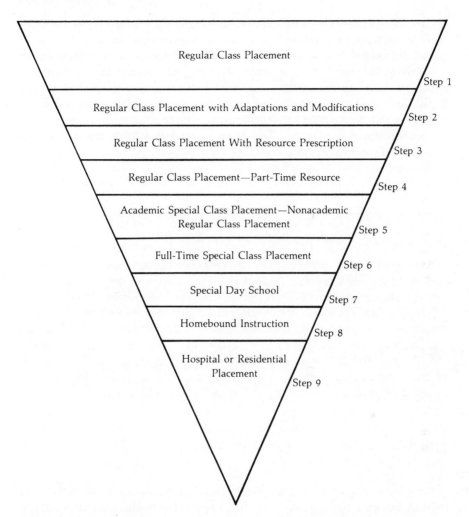

Regular Class Placement

Step 1

Regular Class Placement with Adaptations and Modifications

Step 2

Regular Class Placement With Resource Prescription

Step 3

Regular Class Placement—Part-Time Resource

Step 4

Academic Special Class Placement—Nonacademic
Regular Class Placement

Step 5

Full-Time Special Class Placement

Step 6

Special Day School

Step 7

Homebound Instruction

Step 8

Hospital or Residential
Placement

Step 9

FIGURE 1.1 Instructional Alternatives Available to Handicapped (Note, From "Special Education as a Developmental Capital" by E. Deno, *Exceptional Children*, 1970, 37, 229-237. Copyright 1974 by The Council for Exceptional Childen. Reprinted by permission.)

retarded student, but a full-time special class placement within a public school might not restrict the same student as long as it met his or her individual needs and instructional demands. A brief discussion of each step in Figure 1.1 will show the placement options available for handicapped students and the implications of those options.

## STEP 1—REGULAR CLASS PLACEMENT

A mildly handicapped student may be served in the regular classroom where children receive instruction daily. Certainly, most mildly handicapped children begin school in the regular classroom. Unfortunately, the self-esteem of many mildly handicapped students begins to deteriorate in this placement when no one identifies their handicaps. Society expects all students to learn like everyone else and at the same rate, and when handicapped children cannot learn new concepts, get frustrated at being presented material too far above their instructional level, and develop behavior problems, they are often classified as immature or different. Often, students remain in these situations for years before proper adjustments are made. Thus, to recognize immediately that a child may have a handicap may protect the child from the failure that often transfers into adult years.

## STEP 2—REGULAR CLASS PLACEMENT WITH ADAPTATIONS AND MODIFICATIONS

In the second step of the continuum, the student still receives educational instruction in the regular classroom. However, at this point the regular class teacher adapts instruction for the handicapped student. Frequently, adaptations of teaching techniques or material within the regular classroom provides all the adjustments a mildly handicapped child needs. As teachers make Step 2 a natural component of their instruction, they will need to identify fewer and fewer mildly handicapped students as such and place them in special education. The remainder of this book amplifies Step 2—providing a continuum of alternative services to mildly handicapped children within the regular classroom.

## STEP 3—REGULAR CLASS PLACEMENT WITH RESOURCE PRESCRIPTION

In the third step, the special needs student receives regular class instruction with nonhandicapped students. This step *does not* involve resource room placement. However, when the regular class teacher has instructional or behaviorial problems with the handicapped student, that teacher can summon the special education resource teacher for instructional adaptation and modification suggestions. The special education teacher "prescribes" educational alternatives to regular class instruction. Thus, the handicapped student receives services without being moved to a special class.

The clear advantages of resource prescription include less obvious labeling of students, less stress on teachers, and less crowding of special education classrooms. For example, even though handicapped students must be screened, evaluated, and placed for special education prescription services, they remain more "like" than "different" because they are still integrated with their peers in the regular class setting. In addition, the overworked regular classroom teacher has a support teacher to assist in the instructional modifications. And finally, keeping handicapped students on prescription keeps special class space available for those students who really require it.

## STEP 4—REGULAR CLASS PLACEMENT—PART-TIME RESOURCES

Other situations require that a handicapped student, although still in a regular class setting, receive part-time services in the resource room. For example, a student may need special assistance in reading or require extra time for social studies. The adaptations and modifications in the appropriate instructional program for these students require a more concentrated effort by the special resource teacher. In this step on the model the student may go to resource room for as little as one class period a day or for as much as half a day. The student's IEP dictates the amount of time to be spent as well as the subject(s) to be studied in both the resource room and the regular classroom. The main difference between Step 4 and Step 3, then, is that in Step 3 the student never leaves the regular classroom for instructional purposes, whereas in Step 4, the student may leave for one to several periods per day.

## STEP 5—ACADEMIC SPECIAL CLASS PLACEMENT— NONACADEMIC REGULAR CLASS PLACEMENT

This point in the continuum reflects the change in emphasis from the mildly handicapped student to the student with more severe difficulties. Students served at this step need a more concentrated effort in a special academic program because the regular class setting, even with modifications and adaptations, fails to meet the instructional needs of the student. In Step 5, the special needs student is served primarily in the special education class, going to the regular class only for nonacademic courses, such as physical education, art, music, home economics, industrial arts, and vocational placements.

## STEP 6—FULL-TIME SPECIAL CLASS PLACEMENT

For many reasons, academic and nonacademic, some handicapped students need a full-time special class placement to receive appropriate individualized instruction. The assessment of the student and the degree of the handicap's severity will determine whether or not the school places a handicapped student in a full-time special education class, sometimes referred to as a self-contained class.

## STEP 7—SPECIAL DAY SCHOOL

As severity in handicap increases, another type of placement may more appropriately serve the handicapped. Some school systems maintain a variation of the special day schools designed for a total handicapped population. Such programs may be in a separate building or wing. Although the movement from segregation to integration means fewer special day schools exist, many states have schools for the deaf and blind that serve handicaps unlikely to be served appropriately in the public setting.

## STEP 8—HOMEBOUND INSTRUCTION

Sometimes, children need to receive school services at home. A child recovering from surgery may need such services for only a short period of time, whereas a more seriously ill child may require homebound instruction for an extended period of time. In any case, a visiting teacher usually travels to the student's home and provides instructional services; occasionally, a school uses a two-way communication system when services are required for an extended period of time. This approach, if used during school hours, provides contact between child and classroom, between child and teacher, and between child and peers, thus providing a simulated educational environment for the handicapped student.

## STEP 9—HOSPITAL OR RESIDENTIAL PLACEMENT

The hospital or residential placement is the oldest form of special educational placement. Historically, this alternative simply removed the handicapped child from society and offered little or no treatment and remediation. However, the trend toward placing the handicapped child in the least restrictive environment has changed the size and nature of the population in residential placements: because public schools now serve mildly handicapped students, only severely handicapped students are placed in a residential setting. Also, residential placement now emphasizes treatment, remediation, vocational skills, self-help skills, and a comprehensive 24-hour-a-day program.

Thus, schools now offer various instructional alternatives to their handicapped students. Regular classroom teachers planning to adapt their instruction can see that they will work in the area of Step 2 through Step 5 on the mainstreaming model.

## MAINSTREAMING: THE TEACHER

As facilitator of learning, vehicle for change, and model for future adults, the teacher ultimately determines whether or not mainstreaming succeeds. Teachers' attitudes—the way they feel about the mainstreaming process and the degree to which they accept the handicapped student in general—contribute significantly to that success. A survey of the relevant research shows, however, that such attitudes vary widely. For example, nonteaching school personnel (administrators and school psychologists) often view mainstreaming more positively than teachers do (Overline, 1977; Barngrover, 1974), and many teachers see emotionally disturbed children as more threatening than mildly retarded, learning disabled, or physically impaired students (Casey, 1978; Vance & Kirst, 1977). Special educators and regular educators alike have the responsibility to obey the law and to fulfill the instructional needs of each handicapped child. To develop more positive attitudes about mainstreaming, to decrease their anxieties and frustrations, and to meet their responsibilities to handicapped students, teachers may need to learn more about adapting and planning curriculum for the mildly handicapped and about their new roles within mainstreaming.

## CHANGING ROLES FOR TEACHERS

Passage of Public Law 94-142 has changed the roles of special and regular educators dramatically. Both groups have had to adjust to the new demands mainstreaming has placed upon them by developing new skills.

THE SPECIAL EDUCATION TEACHER   Before mainstreaming, universities and colleges trained special education teachers to work closely with handicapped children. But with the passage of Public Law 94-142 a new role for special educators emerged, that of working closely with regular educators. Special educators now have to seek new and innovative ways to support regular classroom teachers who work with handicapped children. To be successful in this new capacity of consultant to regular classroom teachers, some special education teachers may have to develop skills that were not part of their formal education. Special education teachers need to know what teaching characteristics may contribute to their success in mainstreaming handicapped students. Recent research (Wood & Carmean, Note 1) focuses on what primary characteristics regular education teachers see in successful special education teachers. A successful special education teacher, according to this survey, has genuine concern for educational, social, and emotional needs of handicapped students; the ability to work with other professionals in identifying handicapped children's strengths and weaknesses; the ability to meet each child's specific needs through the development of effective IEPs; the competence to handle a wide variety of situations; the ability to communicate effectively with regular classroom teachers, administrators, and parents; the ability to insure some success for all handicapped children; the knowledge and training to deal with the scholastic and emotional problems of handicapped children; the ability to influence regular classroom teachers about special education programs; the ability to coordinate the instruction of special and regular classes; and the ability to relate to handicapped students.

In addition, like many excellent teachers, the successful special education teacher usually possesses patience; the desire to help students; flexibility; dedication; reliability; organization; imagination; energy; initiative; enthusiasm; the ability to provide a secure environment; the ability to motivate; self-understanding and a positive self-concept; and an awareness that all children are human beings with human feelings.

Special education teachers should try to incorporate as many of these characteristics into their teaching as they can. Clearly, their new role in mainstreaming requires that special education teachers communicate effectively not only with mildly handicapped students but also with regular education teachers.

THE REGULAR EDUCATION TEACHER    Mainstreaming has produced a new role for the regular classroom teacher as well, the responsibility of educating the handicapped child. Prior to passage of Public Law 94-142 universities trained regular educators to teach only those children who presented no obvious learning difficulty. The child with learning problems was quickly and quietly scurried off to the special class. But with the pendulum swinging from segregation to integration, the regular class teacher must now exhibit competencies required for special instruction as well as those required for regular class instruction.

Wood and Carmean (1982) show that special education teachers call regular classroom teachers successful in mainstreaming handicapped children if they possess the following characteristics. A regular education teacher successful in mainstreaming loves children and is concerned about their individual needs; understands special education and its goal of helping students to reach their full potential; has a positive attitude about special education and mainstreaming; understands the mildly handicapped child's capabilities; wants to help students learn to cope with everyday problems; enjoys teaching children regardless of their abilities or disabilities; interacts with the special education teacher to provide a well-balanced program; adjusts to new situations and is receptive to new ideas; incorporates mainstreamed children into the activities of the regular classroom and makes them feel comfortable; recognizes the importance of social acceptance to the handicapped child; sees special students as more normal than different and accepts them as such; can identify and motivate special students; can individualize instruction; is sensitive to the handicapped child's feelings; has patience, flexibility, and organization; and strongly wants to help mildly handicapped children.

Thus, successful mainstreaming requires that regular educators learn more about the instructional needs of mildly handicapped children.

According to Crisci (1981), the essential mainstreaming skills for both regular and special educators fall into nine major categories: assessment, diagnosis, prescription, analysis, behavior management, motivation, communication, evaluation, and human relations. Other authors (Lilly, 1974; Shotel, Iano, & McGettigan, 1972; Alberto, Castricone, & Cohen, (1978) have presented similar categories of skills. Shifting roles and increased responsibilities make communication between regular and special educators the most crucial mainstreaming skill.

## COMMUNICATION

Communication, the transmitting of ideas, information, and suggestions, is crucial to establishing a good working relationship between the special education teacher and the regular education teacher. Because the regular educator faces the task of adapting instruction in the mainstreamed classroom, the special educator bears more, though not all, of the responsibility for making the communication process easier. To communicate better, special education teachers must understand themselves; realize that others see and respond to them as they project themselves; be able to listen; demonstrate an understanding of other's concerns by acting in positive ways; respect the problems and concerns of their colleagues; and respond quickly to the needs of others.

Understanding one's self leads to good communication. Also, knowing and internalizing one's role as special educator and then projecting that role in a positive way provides others with guidelines by which to communicate. Others see us as we project ourselves. If special educators project confidence in their abilities, others trust that competence. However, the reverse is also true: if special educators project a lack of confidence in their abilities, others may see them as incompetent. Thus, projecting one's positive qualities facilitates good communication among colleagues, which in turn opens instructional doors for handicapped children.

Listening is the basis of any communication. Many times we listen to what is being said without actually hearing what is being communicated. Special educators must not only listen, but also hear the concerns of regular educators. One shows one has heard by reacting to a colleague's needs in a positive manner. For example, special education teachers who quickly provide the appropriate instructional material, suggest an alternative teaching technique, or assist in designing a behavior management plan for a mainstreamed student show that the problems of others are major concerns of theirs. Once regular educators feel the door of communication is open, effective mainstreaming becomes a reality. Special educators cannot always respond immediately, but collaboration among teachers can generate many instructional alternatives.

Thus, the development of a positive working relationship between regular and special educators has a significant effect on the handicapped child. For mainstreaming to succeed, the special class teacher and the regular class teacher must communicate. To promote effective communication, special and regular educators should:

1. Establish a communication system
2. Discuss each placement together
3. Assist each other in individualizing instruction
4. Work together to adapt subject matter
5. Share materials
6. Assist each other in adapting evaluation procedures

7. Exhibit characteristics of flexibility, dedication, reliability, organization, imagination, energy, initiative, and enthusiasm
8. Involve others by sharing plans and ideas
9. Seek support and suggestions from others
10. Set realistic goals
11. Work to improve interpersonal relations
12. Be happy and proud about working with handicapped students
13. Remember that presenting a positive attitude will change attitudes about mainstreaming both inside and outside the school

## SUMMARY

This chapter presents an overview of mainstreaming. Mainstreaming's history, importance, problems, model, and effects on teachers have all been discussed. Using this basic understanding of mainstreaming, teachers can begin to modify and adapt instruction according to the model presented in the following chapters. Chapter 2 will cover the process of assessing handicapped students.

## REFERENCES

Alberto, P. A., Castricone, N. R., & Cohen, S. B. Mainstreaming: Implications for training regular class teachers. *Education and Training of the Mentally Retarded*, 1978, *13*, 90–93.

Barngrover, E. A study of educators' preference in special education programs. *Exceptional Children*, 1971, *36*, 754–755.

Bowers, E. M. *Early identification of emotionally handicapped children in school* (2nd ed.). Springfield, Ill.: Charles C. Thomas, 1970.

Calhoun, G., & Elliott, R. W. Self-concept and academic achievement of educable retarded and emotionally disturbed pupils. *Exceptional Children*, 1977, *43*, 479–480.

Casey, K. The semantic differential technique in the examination of teacher attitudes to handicapped children. *The Exceptional Child*, 1978, *25*, 41–52.

Chapman, J. W., & Boersma, F. J. Self-perceptions of ability, expectations, and locus of control in elementary learning disabled children. San Francisco, Calif., 1979. (ERIC Document Reproduction Service No. ED 169 738)

Crisci, P. E. Competencies for mainstreaming: Problems and issues. *Education and Training of the Mentally Retarded*, 1981, *16*(3), 175–182.

Deno, E. (Ed.). *Instructional alternatives for exceptional children*. Reston, Va.: The Council for Exceptional Children, 1973.

*Federal Register*. Washington, D.C.: Department of Health, Education, and Welfare, Office of Education, August 23, 1977.

Gearheardt, B. R., & Weishahn, M.W. *The handicapped student in the regular classroom*. St. Louis, Mo.: C. V. Mosby, 1980.

Haring, W. C. (Ed.). *Behavior of exceptional children.* Columbus, Ohio: Charles E. Merrill, 1978.

Hawisher, M. F., & Calhoun, M. L. *The resource room.* Columbus, Ohio: Charles E. Merrill, 1978.

Kugel, R., & Wolfensberger, W. *Changing patterns in residential services for the mentally retarded.* Washington, D.C.: President's Committee on Mental Retardation, 1969.

Lilly, M. S. *Classroom teacher competencies for mainstreaming.* Duluth, Minn.: University of Minnesota, 1974.

Overline, H. M. *Mainstreaming—making it happen.* Sacramento, Calif.: California State Department of Education, 1977. (ERIC Document Reproduction Service No. ED 149 514)

Reynolds, M. C. A framework for considering some issues in special education. *Exceptional Children,* 1962, *28,* 367–370.

Robbins, R. L., & Harway, N. I. Goal setting and reactions to success and failure in children with learning disabilities. *Journal of Learning Disabilities,* 1977, *10*(6), 356–362.

Shotel, R., Jr., Iano, R. P., & McGettigan, J. P. Teacher attitudes associated with the integration of handicapped children. *Exceptional Children,* 1972, *38,* 677–683.

Vance, W. A., & Kirst, W. Emotionally disturbed children and regular classroom teachers. *The Elementary School Journal,* 1977, *77,* 307–317.

Wolfensberger, W. *The principle of normalization in human services.* Toronto, Canada: National Institute on Mental Retardation, 1969.

Wood, J. W., & Carmean, M. A profile of a successful mainstreaming teacher. *The Pointer,* 1982, *27*(1), 21–23.

## ADDITIONAL READING

Anthony, W. A. The effects of contact on an individual's attitude toward disabled persons. *Rehabilitation Counseling Bulletin XII,* 1969, *12,* 168–171.

Bradfield, R. H., Brown, J., Kaplan, P., Rickert, E., & Stannard, R. The special child in the regular classroom. *Exceptional Children,* 1973, *39,* 384–390.

Chow, S. H. B. *Effects of a mediated training course on teachers and students in mainstreaming programs.* Washington, D.C.: Bureau of Education for the Handicapped, 1976. (ERIC Document Reproduction Service No. ED 123 822)

Clore, G. L., & Keffrey, K. M. Emotional role playing, attitude change, and attraction toward a disabled person. *Journal of Personality and Social Psychology,* 1972, *23*(1), 105–111.

Dunn, L. M. Special education for the mildly retarded—Is much of it justifiable? *Exceptional Children,* 1968, *35,* 5–24.

Evans, J. H. Changing attitudes toward disabled persons: an experimental study. *Rehabilitative Counseling Bulletin,* 1976, *19,* 572–579.

Gearheardt, B. R., & Weishahn, M. W. *First annual report of the National Advisory Committee on Handicapped Children*. Washington, D.C.: Office of Education and Welfare, 1968.

Harasymiw, S. J., & Horne, M. D. Integration of handicapped children: Its effect on teacher attitudes. *Education*, 1974, *96*(2), 152–158.

Johnston, W. *A study to determine teacher attitude toward teaching special children with regular children*, 1972. (ERIC Document Reproduction Service No. ED 065 950)

MacMillan, D. L., Meyers, C. E., & Yoshida, R. K. Regular class teacher's perceptions of transition program for EMR students and their impact on the students. *Psychology in the Schools*, 1978, *15*, 99–103.

Ringlahen, R. P., & Price, J. R. Regular classroom teachers' perceptions of mainstreaming effects. *Exceptional Children*, 1981, *47*, 302–304.

Trotter, E. A. *Teacher encouragement to activate mainstreaming*. Sacramento, Calif.: California State Department of Education, 1977. (ERIC Document Reproduction Service No. ED 149 496)

Tyler, R. W. In-service education of troubles: A look at the past and future. In L. J. Rubin (Ed.), *Improving in-service education: Proposals and procedures for change*. Boston: Allyn and Bacon, 1971.

Wilson, B., & Sapir, S. G. The selection of special educators and learning disability specialists. *Journal of Learning Disabilities*, March 1982, *15*, 166–172.

Yates, J. A. Model for preparing regular classroom teachers for "mainstreaming." *Exceptional Children*, 1973, *39*, 471–473.

# Chapter Two

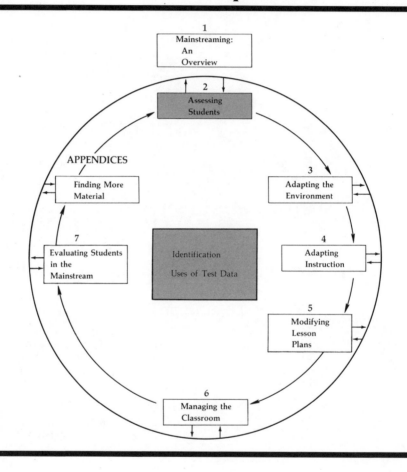

1 Mainstreaming: An Overview

2 Assessing Students

APPENDICES

Finding More Material

3 Adapting the Environment

7 Evaluating Students in the Mainstream

Identification

Uses of Test Data

4 Adapting Instruction

5 Modifying Lesson Plans

6 Managing the Classroom

# Assessing Students

Educators too often envision assessment only in terms of state or locally mandated standardized achievement tests or only in terms of comprehensive assessments for placement of students into special education programs. While assessment does include these purposes, it also has a broader meaning. Vergason (1979) defines assessment as "a process of employing observation, task analysis, and testing to arrive at learning characteristics for educational, vocational, and social decision making about individuals" and points out that "such decisions are at the heart of instruction" (p. 3). Thus, since the goal of educational programming is to meet the unique needs of each student so that learning may take place, teachers must use a multitude of assessing and instructional strategies.

Every school includes students with definite learning problems. These students may already be diagnosed as mildly handicapped, or they may just appear to be slow learners or problem students. Regardless of their classification, these students often challenge the regular classroom teacher. For this select group of students, traditional approaches or single-method teaching techniques yield unsuccessful results—inadequate achievement and unacceptable behavior. Although comprehensive assessment may prove necessary in the long run to determine a student's specific strengths or weaknesses, the teacher should try the strategies outlined in subsequent chapters—adapting the learning environment, adapting instruction, modifying lesson plans, modifying classroom management procedures, and using alternative evaluation techniques—before referring a student for a comprehensive assessment. If the regular teacher thus meets a student's educational needs through instructional modifications, the school can eliminate comprehensive assessment and special education placement for that student.

Special education is necessary and beneficial for certain students, but it is also costly. In 1980, the National School Board Association found that the annual cost per pupil for educating a handicapped child was twice as much as the expense of educating a nonhandicapped pupil—$3,638 versus $1,819 ("The rude reality. . . ," 1980). Total expenditures in education also continue to increase. In only one year, educational expenditures in the nation grew from the 1980–81 total of 181 billion to the 1981–82 figure of 198 billion (Grant, 1982). As the public demands accountability in the classroom and accountability for its taxes, educators must develop strategies that increase student achievement without adding financial burdens to the school system. If the teacher can accommodate students' needs more effectively in the regular classroom, everyone benefits: the regular teacher, from helping a student with a learning problem achieve; the problem learner, from achieving academically and thus improving self-concept; the other students, from increasing their awareness of individual differences; and the school system, from keeping specialized classes to a minimum and thus saving money.

If the strategies discussed in Chapters 3–7 do not achieve the desired results with a particular student, however, the regular teacher may then consider

TABLE 2.1
Classroom Teacher's Role in Assessment Process

| Assessment Process | Regular Classroom Teacher's Role |
| --- | --- |
| Identification of Handicapped Student | • Recognize those behaviors and/or characteristics of handicapped students so that these students can be identified, evaluated, placed, and served. |
| Referral to Placement Process | • Be aware of handicapping conditions in order to refer for special educational services.<br>• Investigate alternatives to labeling, such as using community resources, adapting within the classroom, using instructional interventions.<br>• Prepare teacher narrative.<br>• Orally present detailed information about nature of student's problem to child study committee.<br>• Communicate with parents about resources and alternatives available during evaluation process.<br>• Participate during development and implementation of IEP. |
| Uses of Test Data | • Use IQ Tests appropriately.<br>• Be aware of tests/categories.<br>• Carefully read test interpretations. |

a comprehensive assessment. To participate successfully in such an evaluation, teachers need to understand their roles within the total process. Chapter 2 therefore focuses on the three major components of the whole assessment process: identification, referral to placement, and uses of test data. (See Table 2.1.)

# IDENTIFICATION

Students with specific handicaps exist in every school. Table 2.2 presents information about the nine major handicaps affecting students. The term mildly handicapped includes educationally handicapped, learning disabled, and emotionally handicapped students.

Mildly handicapped students are the largest group within the total population of handicapped students, as Table 2.3 shows, and are also the students most likely to be mainstreamed into regular classrooms. Regular education teachers need to know the characteristics of mildly handicapped students so that they can identify students needing further testing for possible special education placement and can plan appropriate instruction.

TABLE 2.2
Definitions of Specific Handicaps

| Handicap | Definition |
| --- | --- |
| Educationally Handicapped | Has significantly subaverage intelligence along with deficits in adaptive behavior and in academic performance. |
| Educable Mentally Retarded (EMR) | EMR—between 2 and 3½ standard deviations below mean of test administered. |
| Trainable Mentally Retarded (TMR) | TMR—between 3 and 4 standard deviations below mean of test administered. |
| Severely Mentally Retarded (SMR) | SMR—Between 4 and 5 standard deviations below mean of test administered. |
| Profoundly Mentally Retarded (PMR) | PMR—more than 5 standard deviations below mean of test administered. |
| Emotionally Handicapped | Exhibits some of the characteristics shown below over a long period of time and to a marked degree; the following characteristics adversely affect educational performance: Inability to learn cannot be explained by intellectual, sensory, or health factors; Inability to build/maintain satisfactory interpersonal relationships with peers or teachers; Inappropriate types of behavior or feelings; General pervasive mood of unhappiness or depression and/or a tendency to develop physical symptoms or fears associated with personal or school problems. |
| Hearing impaired | Includes both deaf and hard of hearing persons whose impairment adversely affects educational performance. Deaf means hearing impairment so severe that child has difficulty processing linguistic information with or without amplification. Hard of hearing persons have sufficient hearing to process information through the auditory channel. |

TABLE 2.2 (continued)

| Handicap | Definition |
|---|---|
| Language/speech | Communication disorder, such as stuttering, impaired articulation, language problem, or voice impairment, that adversely affects educational performance. |
| Visually impaired | Has visual impairment that, even with correction, adversely affects educational performance.<br><br>Partially sighted means visual acuity between 20/70 and 20/200 in better eye and able to read either regular or large print.<br><br>Legally blind means visual acuity of 20/200 or less in better eye after correction and/or peripheral field limited to 20 degree or less area.<br><br>Blind means so little remaining vision that braille must be used to read. |
| Physically handicapped[a] | Has orthopedic or other health impairments that adversely affect educational performance.<br><br>Examples of orthopedic impairments: club foot, absence of one or more members, poliomyelitis, and cerebral palsy.<br><br>Examples of other health impairments: heart condition, tuberculosis, asthma, sickle cell anemia, epilepsy, diabetes, and hemophilia. |
| Multihandicapped[b] | Has combination of disabilities causing such a severe educational problem that cannot be accommodated in special education program designed for one of the disabilities. |
| Deaf-blind | Has combination of auditory and visual handicaps causing such severe communication and other developmental and educational problems that cannot properly function in a special education program for the hearing impaired or the visually impaired. |

TABLE 2.2 (continued)

| Handicap | Definition |
| --- | --- |
| Specific learning disabilities[c] | Disorders in one or more of the basic psychological processes involved in understanding or using spoken or written language.<br><br>Manifests itself in an imperfect ability to listen, think, speak, read, write, spell, or do mathematical calculations.<br><br>Includes perceptual handicaps, brain injury, minimal brain dysfunction, dyslexia, and developmental aphasia.<br><br>Does not include problems that are primarily the result of visual, hearing, or motor handicaps, mental retardation, emotional disturbance, or environmental, cultural, or economic disadvantages. |

[a]Children who make normal progress without special education, even though with a physical disability, must be called physically handicapped.

[b]Term does not include deaf-blind children.

[c]No learning disabled child will exhibit all the characteristics indicated, nor will one of these characteristics mean a child has a learning disability.

*Note.* From State of Mississippi Referral to Placement Guidelines, 1982. Reprinted with permission.

## EDUCATIONALLY HANDICAPPED

Comprising approximately 2 percent of the population, educationally handicapped students fall into four distinct categories: educable mentally retarded, trainable mentally retarded, severely mentally retarded, and profoundly retarded. Only the characteristics and learning problems of the educable mentally retarded student fall within the category of the mildly handicapped, so the following descriptions of the more severely retarded are offered solely for comparison purposes.[1]

PROFOUND RETARDATION  Psychologists diagnose individuals profoundly retarded "when intelligence testing scores are more than 5 standard deviations

[1]In some states, the term *educationally handicapped* includes all mentally retarded, learning disabled, and emotionally disturbed children. In this text, however, the term educationally handicapped will include only the four categories of mentally retarded children.

TABLE 2.3
Percent of School Age Children Served, by
Handicap, 1982-1983

| Handicap | Percent of School Age Children |
|---|---|
| Educationally Handicapped | 1.70 |
| Learning Disabled | 3.80 |
| Emotionally Handicapped | .76 |
| Speech Handicapped | 2.47 |
| Visually Handicapped | 1.60 |
| Multihandicapped | .14 |
| Physically Handicapped | .12 |
| Hearing Impaired | .08 |
| Deaf/Blind[a] | |

[a]Data not available.

*Note.* From "Report of handicapped children receiving special education and related services as reported by state agencies under PL 94-142 and PL 98-313. School year 1982-1983" by the U.S. Department of Education, Special Education Program, September 7, 1983. Copyright by the U.S. Department of Education. Adapted by permission.

below the norm—Stanford Binet IQ of 19 and below and a Wechsler IQ of 24 and below" (Grossman, 1977, p. 149). Although motor development may be present, profoundly retarded individuals generally develop minimal self-help skills and therefore require total support throughout their lifetimes.

SEVERE RETARDATION  Severe retardation means that "intelligence testing scores range more than 4 and up to 5 standard deviations below the norm—Stanford Binet IQs of 20 to 35 and Wechsler IQs of 25 to 39" (Grossman, p. 149). Severely retarded individuals can learn to talk and communicate, and they may learn to perform simple tasks, but usually under close supervision.

TRAINABLE MENTALLY RETARDED  The trainable mentally retarded have intelligence testing scores that "range more than 3 and up to 4 standard deviations below the norm—Stanford Binet IQs of 36 to 51 and Wechsler IQs of 40 to 54" (Grossman, p. 149). Trainable retarded individuals acquire communication and social skills, and they generally benefit from simple occupational and vocational training. They are limited academically, although they may acquire basic functional academic skills.

EDUCABLE MENTALLY RETARDED  Educators classify students as educable mentally retarded "when intelligence testing scores range more than 2 and up to

3 standard deviations below the norm—Stanford Binet IQs of 52 to 67 and Wechsler IQs of 55 to 69" (Grossman, p. 149). To be classified as educable mentally retarded, such children must also demonstrate deficits in adaptive behavior. Kirk (1972) says that generally, educable mentally retarded students exhibit:

1. Normal height, weight, and motor coordination
2. An inability to perform well on verbal and nonverbal intelligence tests
3. The social and attitudinal values of the community
4. A short attention span and/or lack of ability to concentrate for long periods of time
5. A delayed maturation of such specific intellectual functions as memory for auditory and visual materials, generalizing ability, language ability, conceptual and perceptual abilities, and imagination and creative abilities
6. A lack of readiness for reading, writing, spelling, and arithmetic at age 6 because of delayed mental development
7. A mental development rate of approximately ½ to ¾ that of an average child
8. A preference for concrete presentation of concepts
9. An academic potential that does not exceed the sixth grade level of performance
10. The potential to participate in unskilled and semiskilled work as adults

For all practical purposes, educable mentally retarded students have needs and aspirations similar to those of other students—the same physical and emotional needs, the desire for an education, the desire for some vocational preparation, and the desire for marriage and family life. Since educable mentally retarded students whose IQ falls within the upper limits of the retardation range, 60–70, have the potential of acquiring jobs within the semiskilled range and becoming self-supporting and contributing members of society when they reach adulthood, they need to participate in as many "normal" school activities, classes, and vocational training programs as they can. Such nonsheltered training prepares these students to participate normally in society.

## LEARNING DISABLED

The prevalence of learning disabled students within the school population has not been clearly established. Whereas some studies in the field estimate that anywhere from 1 to 30 percent of the school population is learning disabled, others more conservatively estimate that the total school population contains from 1 to 3 percent learning disabled students (Lerner, 1976, p. 11). By definition, a child with a specific learning disability

> has a disorder in one or more of the basic psychological processes involved in understanding or in using language, spoken or written, which may manifest itself in an imperfect ability to listen, think, speak, read, write, spell or to do mathematical calculations. The term includes such conditions as

perceptual handicaps, brain injury, minimal brain dysfunction, dyslexia, and developmental aphasia. The term does not include children who have learning problems which are primarily the result of visual, hearing, or motor handicaps, of mental retardation, of emotional disturbance, or of environmental, cultural, or economic disadvantage. (State of Mississippi, 1982, p. 67)

Determining whether a student does or does not have a learning disability generally requires proof that a discrepancy exists between achievement and aptitude. Educators usually find such a discrepancy by comparing standard scores of intelligence and aptitude tests or by using learning quotients. Learning disabilities frequently occur in one or more of the following areas: oral expression; listening comprehension; written expression; basic reading skills; reading comprehension; mathematics calculation; or mathematics reasoning. (State of Mississippi, 1982)

The regular teacher needs to develop the ability to recognize behavior and/or characteristics common to learning disabled children so that these students can be properly identified, evaluated, placed, and served. The learning disabled child will exhibit anywhere from one to a composite of the following traits:

1. Average to above average intelligence
2. Discrepancy between aptitude and achievement
3. Hyperactivity
4. Distractibility
5. Inability/difficulty processing visual information
   a. Difficulty interpreting written directions
   b. Difficulty transferring information from blackboard to notebook
   c. Inability to separate figure from background
   d. Difficulty remembering what has been seen or read
   e. Difficulty relating parts to the whole
6. Inability/difficulty processing auditory information
   a. Difficulty following verbal directions
   b. Difficulty remembering the order of items presented orally
   c. Difficulty discriminating between similar sounds
7. Difficulty concentrating for long periods of time
8. Lethargy, apathy, indifference
9. Poor organizational abilities
10. Difficulty with concept of time
11. Difficulty with concept of direction, such as with left/right, up/down, and over/under
12. Inconsistency in performance
13. Poor motor coordination, such as a lack of rhythm or problems with balance
14. Easily frustrated
15. Tendency to perseverate
16. Limited vocabulary

17. Loses place while reading and uses a finger to follow along
18. Reverses letters and/or words when reading and writing
19. Difficulty associating letter or syllable sounds with the printed letter or syllable
20. Experiences problems with writing mechanics such as spacing, staying on the line, and size distortions
21. Experiences problems with basic number facts such as addition, subtraction, multiplication, and division
22. Experiences problems with language expression

Because a large percentage of these students have the potential for normal academic development—participation in regular academic programming throughout elementary and secondary school, graduation from high school, participation in post secondary vocational programs, college, and even professional school—teachers must identify learning disabled students *early*. Learning disabled students generally possess average to above average intelligence; their overall potential exceeds that of the educable mentally retarded student and as a rule compares with that of the average student. However, educators must teach these learning disabled students to compensate for their particular learning difficulties so that they can reach their potential. When these students are not identified early and taught appropriate compensating techniques, they often develop inappropriate behavior patterns and poor self-concepts. As a result, many learning disabled students fail to achieve satisfactorily and become school dropouts unnecessarily. Therefore, regular teachers must aim to recognize the characteristics of a learning disabled child as early as possible.

## EMOTIONALLY HANDICAPPED

Comprising a smaller percentage of the total school population than either educationally handicapped or learning disabled students do, emotionally handicapped students still total approximately 1 percent. As with learning disabled students, teachers find emotionally handicapped students difficult to identify, and often incorrectly refer them to special classes because of behavior difficulties in the regular classroom. To be classified as emotionally handicapped, a student must show:

> an inability to learn which cannot be explained by intellectual, sensory, or health factors; an inability to maintain satisfactory interpersonal relationships with peers and/or teachers; inappropriate types of behaviors or feelings under normal circumstances; and a general pervasive mood of unhappiness or depression and/or fears associated with personal or school problems. (State of Mississippi, 1982, p. 63)

In addition, the Mississippi guidelines suggest that unless these characteristics exist over a "long period of time and to a marked degree," and "adversely affect educational performance" (p. 63), they cannot be called an emotional handicap. However, teachers need to be aware of the specific behavioral symptoms common to emotionally handicapped students. They often cry a lot, have temper tantrums, threaten teachers or students, exhibit withdrawn behavior, demonstrate an inability to make friends, appear continually depressed, injure themselves, attempt or threaten suicide, have delusions or hallucinations, and seem out of touch with reality.

Since an emotional handicap is not necessarily a function of intelligence, emotionally handicapped students can range from the mentally retarded to the gifted. Also, since the span of problems within this handicap ranges from easily correctable problems to counseling and appropriate classroom interventions to conditions necessitating institutionalization, educators find it difficult to predict academic potential. However, a large percentage of these conditions are correctable, especially if detected early, so for the good of the students, and the school, a teacher should learn the traits of emotionally handicapped children.

# REFERRAL TO PLACEMENT PROCESS

As part of following the mandate of Public Law 94-142, schools have had to develop guidelines to cover the referral to placement process of handicapped students. Although individual state guidelines differ slightly in terminology and/or procedure, the general pattern remains similar in all fifty states. Regular teachers need to understand their state's guidelines on the referral to placement process, because although parents, principals, or counselors can and do identify children needing special help, it is usually the regular teacher who makes such a referral.

The referral to placement process can be divided into five stages—alternatives prior to referral, the child study process, comprehensive assessment, placement procedures prior to initial placement, and initial placement procedures. This text uses Mississippi's guidelines as the basis of its discussion about the referral to placement process. Guidelines from other states may vary slightly. Copies of guidelines are generally available from the school district's Director of Special Education or from the State Department of Education.

## ALTERNATIVES PRIOR TO REFERRAL

The classroom teacher has most of the responsibility for attempting different alternatives prior to referral. Figure 2.1 identifies several of the alternatives a teacher should consider before recommending a student for a comprehensive evaluation. Although teachers may easily identify students who experience difficulty in school, they face a complex task in ascertaining the basis for such problems. Usually, no single cause exists; more frequently, a combination of factors contributes to a student's inability to achieve in school.

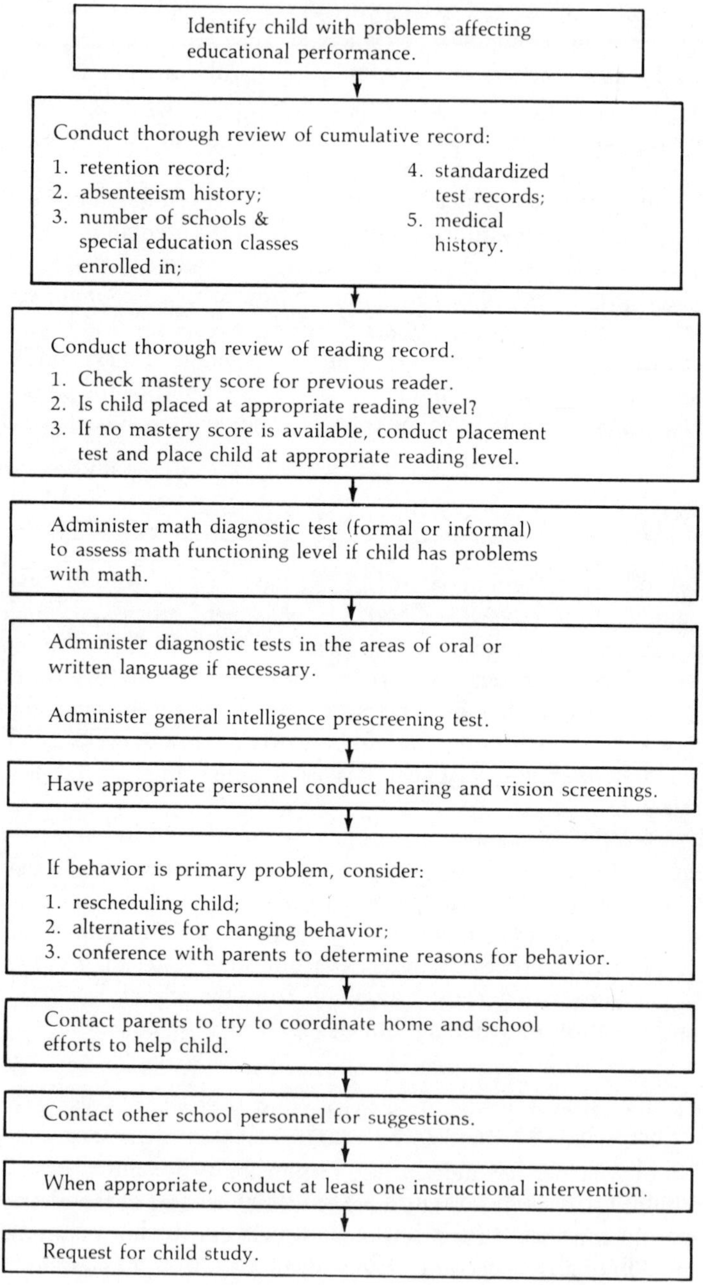

Identify child with problems affecting educational performance.

Conduct thorough review of cumulative record:

1. retention record;
2. absenteeism history;
3. number of schools & special education classes enrolled in;
4. standardized test records;
5. medical history.

Conduct thorough review of reading record.

1. Check mastery score for previous reader.
2. Is child placed at appropriate reading level?
3. If no mastery score is available, conduct placement test and place child at appropriate reading level.

Administer math diagnostic test (formal or informal) to assess math functioning level if child has problems with math.

Administer diagnostic tests in the areas of oral or written language if necessary.

Administer general intelligence prescreening test.

Have appropriate personnel conduct hearing and vision screenings.

If behavior is primary problem, consider:

1. rescheduling child;
2. alternatives for changing behavior;
3. conference with parents to determine reasons for behavior.

Contact parents to try to coordinate home and school efforts to help child.

Contact other school personnel for suggestions.

When appropriate, conduct at least one instructional intervention.

Request for child study.

FIGURE 2.1. Alternatives Prior to Referral

First, the teacher should review the student's cumulative record. The student's previous grades, previous standardized test scores, previous placement in remedial classes or special education, number of years retained, attendance records, medical problems, communications between parents and teachers, marital status of parents, whether the mother or father is deceased, the name of the child's present guardian, any recent traumatic events in the child's life, and the number of schools the student has attended and the frequency of changes— any one of these bits of information from a child's cumulative folder may explain the student's present difficulties.

The elementary and junior high teacher especially need information about the student's reading and comprehension ability. The teacher should place the student in an appropriate reading program if achievement scores indicate deficits in reading recognition or comprehension. Information about reading ability is equally important for the secondary teacher, but because secondary remedial programs frequently are not available, other alternatives, such as special education placement or tutorial assistance, may be necessary for the student to achieve in the regular classroom.

Similarly, the teacher should note the student's overall ability in mathematics and suggest placement in an appropriate math remedial program, if necessary. If the teacher discovers significant discrepancies between achievement scores and aptitude in either math or reading, the teacher should consider special education evaluation and placement.

The student may also encounter problems in language. Teachers may need to assess strengths and weaknesses in either oral or written language expression or both to plan more effective instruction for the student.

If the student has trouble in all academic areas and progresses at a rate *considerably* below that of peers, the teacher should assess overall intelligence. The student may not possess the aptitude necessary to achieve successfully in the regular classroom. The student may need alternative placement and/or resource assistance to proceed at an individualized rate on the appropriate grade level.

Any time a student has trouble in school, and particularly when a student is being considered for a comprehensive evaluation, the appropriate district personnel should conduct vision and hearing screenings. If abnormalities do exist, the school should notify the student's parents. Frequently, students' academic difficulties disappear or decrease when they acquire glasses or hearing aids. Comprehensive assessment cannot begin until these problems are corrected.

In addition to academic deficits, a student sometimes demonstrates inappropriate or disruptive behavior in the classroom. A teacher may solve such problems by moving the student to a new location within the classroom or by changing the student's schedule, but occasionally, the teacher may need to use more extensive measures. Chapter 6 discusses some of the alternatives teachers can use to modify a student's behavior and/or environment. A teacher should definitely have a conference with the student's parents or guardian because parents may offer reasons for the student's behavior or may confirm similar behavior patterns at home. Only when the teacher cannot correct the student's behavior problems in the classroom, should he or she consider alternatives such as counseling or evaluation for placement into an emotionally handicapped program.

Most school and/or districts provide specialists such as counselors, school psychologists, reading and math supervisors, and curriculum coordinators, any one of whom can suggest other valuable alternatives. For example, the school psychologist might refer the student and/or entire family to some community agency for individual or group counseling.

If, after investigating these alternatives, teachers still think a handicap may exist and that a student may be educationally handicapped, learning disabled, or emotionally handicapped, they should document at least one instructional intervention, complete a teacher narrative (a brief description of the student's educational performance and behavior), and request a child study by the local survey committee in the school. Instructional interventions include individual instruction as opposed to group instruction, instruction using peer tutors, oral instead of written administration of tests, and the use of tape recorders and other auditory means as opposed to visual presentation of information.

## CHILD STUDY PROCESS

An official child study begins with the submission of a written request, usually the teacher narrative, to the chairperson of the school's local survey committee. The local survey committee is usually composed of the student's teachers, one or more administrators, a guidance counselor and/or appropriate school personnel (school psychologist, school nurse, speech therapist, or audiologist). Figure 2.2 outlines the steps of a child study.

The local survey committee then meets to review the vision and hearing reports, the teacher narrative, and any available information from previous parent conferences. If the committee decides that the teacher has attempted adequate alternatives and that the student's problems warrant further investigation, it can recommend that comprehensive assessment procedures begin. If, on the other hand, the committee decides that either the teacher should try additional alternatives or comprehensive assessment should not begin, the committee can recommend that the child continue in regular education until the need for comprehensive assessment can be more fully demonstrated. Thus, the regular teacher, in daily contact with the student, primarily keeps other members of the local survey committee informed about the exact nature of the student's difficulty. Since forms alone cannot present a complete picture of the student in question, the committee should welcome the teacher's perspective.

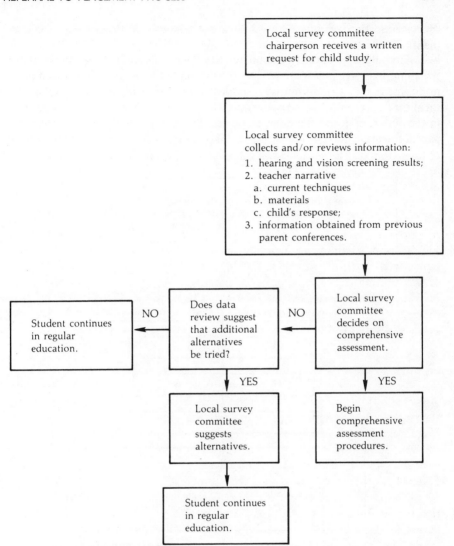

FIGURE 2.2. Child Study Process

# COMPREHENSIVE ASSESSMENT

After the local survey committee completes its initial child study and decides to evaluate a student for a handicap, comprehensive assessment begins. A comprehensive assessment determines the nature and degree of a student's handicap, an evaluation that is then used to determine whether or not a student needs special education services. Figure 2.3 traces the steps in a comprehensive assessment.

First, the appropriate personnel notify the child's parent or guardian about the comprehensive assessment. The notification letter includes the written prior notice for initial evaluation that provides parents with information used by the local survey committee to make its decision; options or alternatives attempted in the classroom; and the date, time, and location for the parent conference. The notification letter also includes the parent information pamphlet and a copy of the school district's procedural safeguards policy and procedures. These two

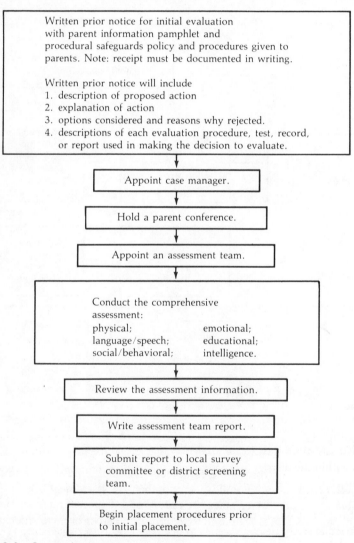

FIGURE 2.3. Comprehensive Assessment

documents outline parents' rights as parents and their children's rights. Examples of these documents can be found in Appendix D. Proof that the parent has received the written prior notice must be obtained in writing either through the return of the notification signed by the parent, through the use of registered mail, or at the parent conference.

To further protect the student's rights, a case manager is appointed to supervise each step of the comprehensive assessment. The case manager certifies that the committee conducts each step of the comprehensive assessment appropriately and promptly, from initial parent conference to the development of the IEP for placement. After a case manager has been appointed and the parent receives written prior notice for initial evaluation, a parent conference can be scheduled. The parent interviewer, "an individual designated by the school district who has been specially trained to interview and work with parents" (State of Mississippi, 1982, p. 56), conducts the conference. This individual can be a regular classroom teacher, a special education teacher, a guidance counselor, or an administrator. The student's teacher or teachers, the guidance counselor, the chairperson of the local survey committee, and others, as needed, also attend this initial conference. During the interview, these committee members explain the parent information booklet and procedural safeguards policy and procedures, document receipt of these two documents, and make sure the parent understands both the problems the child experiences in the classroom and the alternatives available to the parent and child at this point. If the parent consents to the comprehensive evaluation, the committee obtains that permission in writing and then the parent completes a parent questionnaire. (See Appendix D.) While the parent is at the school, the adaptive behavior inventory (a measure of the student's independent functioning skills), is also completed if the committee suspects mental retardation or if adaptive behavior is pertinent to the evaluation.

If the parent consents, the comprehensive assessment continues with the appointment of an assessment team. This team then evaluates the student's physical development, language development, social and behavioral development, emotional development, educational achievement, and intelligence. After the team completes its testing, it writes a report and submits its finding either to the local survey committee at the school or to the district screening team.

During the comprehensive assessment the regular teacher communicates the student's problems to the parent. Since the regular teacher sees the student daily, he or she can give the parent firsthand rather than secondhand information. Also, aware of the difficult handicaps and the available special education services within the district and the school, the regular teacher can be invaluable in convincing a parent that a child needs a comprehensive assessment. Unfortunately, misconceptions about special education still exist. Parents frequently believe their child will be removed from regular classroom participation and/or extracurricular activities as a result of special education placement. When the regular teacher, along with other school personnel, can communicate intelligently about handicaps, probable learning problems, and available resource programs, parents may understand and accept more readily the services being offered to their child.

## PLACEMENT PROCEDURES PRIOR TO INITIAL PLACEMENT

After the assessment team completes the assessment report, the school district has two main options. The school district may request that the assessment team return the assessment report to the local survey committee at the school (Option 1) or that the team submit their report directly to the district or regional screening team for an eligibility ruling (Option 2). See Figure 2.4 for an outline of the possible steps under each option.

If the school chooses Option 1, it returns the assessment report to the local survey committee. The committee then reviews the report, and if a handicap seems to exist, makes its recommendations on the Pupil Personnal Data Sheet (PPDS) and submits the report to the district screening team for an eligibility determination. If no handicap seems to exist, the local survey committee notifies the parent, and the child continues in regular education.

However, if the school selects Option 2, it forwards the assessment report directly to the screening team with recommendations from the assessment team. Thus, under Option 2 the screening team sees all evaluations.

After the screening team decides whether or not the child is eligible for special education services, it returns the report to the local survey committee at the school. If the child is ineligible, the local survey committee has two options. First, if the committee agrees with the ineligible ruling, the committee notifies the parent and the child continues in regular education. Second, if the committee disagrees with the ruling, it either resubmits the report because a different handicap may exist or recommends that the child needs further assessment. Prior to resubmitting or conducting additional tests, the committee must obtain the parent's permission. If after obtaining permission and gathering more information, the committee thinks a handicap exists, it resubmits the report to the screening team.

During these placement procedures prior to initial placement, the regular teacher still serves as a valuable source of information to the local survey committee. For example, if the screening team rules the child ineligible, the teacher can observe the student and recommend to the committee what additional information it might gather. Thus, the teacher remains a key figure in the overall eligibility determination.

## INITIAL PLACEMENT PROCEDURES

The final stage of the assessment process involves initial placement procedures. See Figure 2.5. When a screening team rules a student eligible for special education services, three important steps must be taken prior to placement. First, the

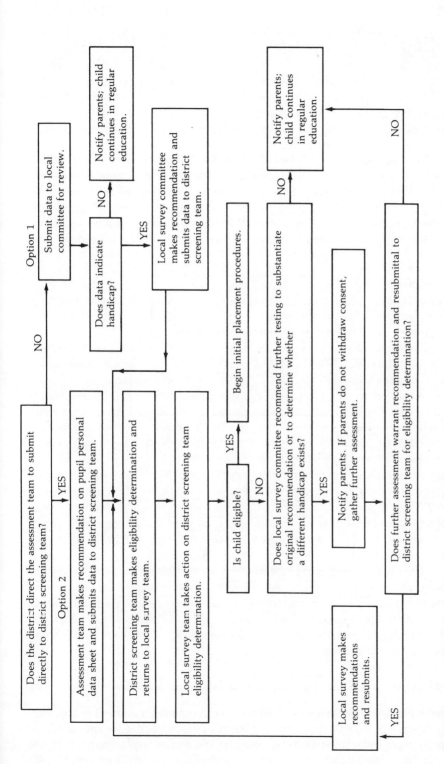

FIGURE 2.4. Placement Procedures Prior to Initial Placement

45

school must send the parent written prior notice for initial placement, a letter that specifies type of a placement, basis for placement, other alternatives attempted, and time and location of a proposed conference. Second, the parent must verify receipt of the written prior notice. Third, the parent meets with the IEP or placement committee to review the assessment team's report, to give written permission for placement, and to develop the child's IEP, which is then signed by the parent and school personnel. However, the parent still can accept or refuse placement for the child at this stage.

Thus, with initial placement, especially if the student participates in regular classroom activities in addition to special education classes, the teacher comes full circle from trying alternatives before referral, to informing the child study and assessment committees about the child's difficulties, to participating in the development and implementation of the IEP. Working with the student's parents, the special education teacher, and other members of the IEP committee, the

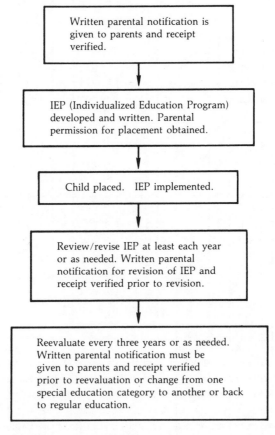

FIGURE 2.5. Initial Placement Procedures

teacher helps establish realistic goals and objectives for the handicapped student, goals that will enable the student to achieve within the classroom according to his or her own abilities.

If the student remains in the regular classroom for any part of the day at all, the regular teacher should use the data collected during the assessment process to gain insight into the student's problem and to develop an ongoing classroom process for assessing that student. When the student stays in the regular classroom, the teacher can continue to assess the student by following these suggestions: carefully read all previous test data collected; read the detailed report accompanying the educational and psychological evaluations for test interpretations and classroom suggestions; consult with the special education teacher about possible instructional adaptations; break the skill being taught into small parts, sequencing the small parts (More information on sequencing can be found in Chapter 4.); observe how the student performs and adjust both the amount of work and the type of skill taught accordingly; and continuously observe—for example, if a student has difficulty writing sentences, the teacher may learn through observation that the student does not know the parts of speech or cannot read the words.

Psychological evaluations, although providing the regular and special teacher with an abundance of information, do not usually contain detailed instructional activities or *specifically* pinpoint skills the student does or does not possess. However, the data in psychological reports, collected to define a student's handicap and used to formulate that student's IEP, include information about intelligence, adaptive behavior, emotional development, physical development, learning style, and achievement and have continued classroom use. Most achievement scores are reported in terms of grade equivalents, age equivalents, standard scores, or percentiles, and they provide the regular teacher with only a general indication of where to place the child on the instructional continuum. But the teacher can use the other information in the reports to find out more about the student's functioning level.

The following section discusses the information available in most psychological evaluations. Teachers should understand the tests used in their districts so that they can make full use of the scores reported in the respective categories.

# USES OF TEST DATA

As mentioned earlier, assessment can make instruction more effective. Yet teachers frequently do not use the extensive information about a student found in a comprehensive assessment because they have only a limited knowledge of testing in general or they are more familiar with group intelligence and achievement tests than with the individualized tests used in comprehensive evaluations. But teachers must learn how to use such a wealth of material: in addition to reporting how much a given student deviates from the norm, into what broad intellectual range the student falls, and what grade equivalent scores in reading, math, and spelling the student has, tests in a comprehensive evaluation also provide the teacher with specific information about a student's skill development in key areas.

The numerous tests used within any one psychological evaluation generally fall into such categories as intelligence, academic achievement, perceptual motor development, language development, and behavior. This section provides information about each of these categories so that the teacher can plan more effectively for the mildly handicapped student.

## INTELLIGENCE

To assess intelligence, most examiners and/or psychologists select either one of the four Wechsler Intelligence Scales or the Stanford-Binet Intelligence Scale. The Wechsler Scales include the Wechsler Preschool and Primary Scale of Intelligence (WPPSI) for children between 4 and 6½ years of age (Wechsler, 1967); the Wechsler Intelligence Scale for Children (WICS) for children 5 to 15 years of age (Wechsler, 1949); the Wechsler Intelligence Scale for Children—Revised (WISC-R) for students between 6 and 16 years, 11 months of age (Wechsler, 1974); and the Wechsler Adult Intelligence Scale (WAIS) for adults (Wechsler, 1955).

Schools use the WISC-R to assess intelligence more often than they use the other tests. Swanson and Watson (1982) say the WISC-R features a verbal and a performance scale, each containing five subtests and one alternative test. Scores on the WISC-R subtests are reported as standard and may be converted to deviation IQ scores for each scale. "The deviation IQ scores have a distribution with a mean of 100 and a standard deviation of 15, making results comparable for all ages. A scaled score of 10 indicates average ability" (Swanson & Watson, p. 135).

In addition, Swanson and Watson outline the skills measured by each subtest. The verbal scale subtests measure information (acquired from experience and education); comprehension (of practical knowledge and social judgment, particularly the ability to judge the consequences of a behavioral situation); arithmetic (both concentration and arithmetic reasoning); similarities (the ability to recognize and describe essential relations between objects or ideas; verbal concept formation); vocabulary (the quality of language used; reflects cultural environment); and digit span (attention, auditory memory, and sequencing). The Performance Scale Subtests measure picture completion (visual alertness, organization, and recognition of essential details); picture arrangement (nonverbal judgment; responsiveness to interpersonal relations, social alertness, and common sense); block design (visual motor perception, coordination; and logical insight into space relationships); object assembly (visual motor coordination and the ability to see the relationship of parts to a whole); coding (speed of visual motor reaction and association of symbols and the ability to learn unfamiliar tasks); and mazes (visual motor planning). (p. 135)

When analyzing a student's WISC-R scores, the teacher should first ascertain the student's overall intellectual ability by using WISC-R classifications and corresponding population percentages. See Table 2.4. Next, the teacher should compare verbal and performance scores. Generally, a higher verbal score indicates that the student performed better in language abilities and therefore may learn better through the auditory channel, whereas a higher performance score indicates that the student performed better in the use of perceptual motor abilities and thus may learn better through the perceptual modality (Bush & Waugh, 1971, pp. 125–136). The teacher should also analyze individual subtest scores to determine a student's specific strengths and/or weaknesses.

TABLE 2.4
WISC-R Classifications, Standard Scores, Population Distribution

| WISC-R Standard Scores | Range of Intelligence | Percent of Population |
|---|---|---|
| 44 to 69 | Mental Defective | 2.2 |
| 70 to 79 | Borderline | 6.7 |
| 80 to 89 | Dull Normal | 16.1 |
| 90 to 109 | Average | 50.0 |
| 110 to 119 | Bright Normal | 16.1 |
| 120 to 129 | Superior | 6.7 |
| 130 to 156 | Very Superior | 2.2 |

*Note.* Reproduced by permission. Wechsler Intelligence Scale for Children—Revised. Copyright © 1974 by The Psychological Corporation. All rights reserved.

## ACHIEVEMENT

"In contrast to aptitude tests, which are intended to assess a pupil's potential in specific areas, achievement tests are intended to directly assess the pupil's skill development in specific academic areas" (Salvia & Ysseldyke, 1978, p. 125). Achievement tests fall into distinct categories, including screening devices, used to assess the student's level of functioning and to compare that level to the level of other students the same age; diagnostic achievement tests, used to pinpoint strengths and weaknesses in skill development; group tests, used for groups of students, up to an entire class; individual tests, used only on a one-to-one basis; norm referenced tests, standardized on national samples and thought to reflect national curricular trends; and criterion referenced tests, designed to reflect the objectives of specific academic content areas and to assess the extent to which students have attained very specific skills. (Salvia & Ysseldyke, 1978, p. 125)

Table 2.5 identifies a number of the most frequently used achievement tests by category. Perhaps one of the most well-known instruments is the Wide

Range Achievement Test (WRAT) (Jastak & Jastak, 1965). Available in two levels—level one for students 12 and younger and level two for students over the age of 12—the WRAT assesses achievement in three areas: reading, spelling, and math (Salvia & Ysseldyke). Scores on the WRAT are reported in grade equivalents, percentile ranks, and standard scores, which the teacher can easily compare to WISC-R standard scores. Limitations of the WRAT include its "questionable normative population and its limited behavior sampling," leading Salvia and Ysseldyle to recommend it for "global" assessment only (p. 161). Teachers should also note that the reading test on the WRAT does not measure reading comprehension.

A second widely used screening test is the Peabody Individual Achievement Test (PIAT) (Dunn & Markwardt, 1970). Areas assessed by the PIAT include mathematics, reading recognition, reading comprehension, spelling, and general information. Scores, reported in age equivalents, grade equivalents, per-

TABLE 2.5
Categories of Individually Administered Achievement Tests

| Screening Tests: Norm Referenced | Diagnostic Tests: Norm Referenced | Diagnostic Tests: Criterion Referenced |
|---|---|---|
| Peabody Individual Achievement Test (PIAT) (Dunn & Markwardt, 1970) | Woodcock Reading Mastery Tests (Woodcock, 1973) | The Fountain Valley Teacher Support System in Reading (Zweig Associates, 1971) |
| Wide Range Achievement Test (WRAT) (Jastak & Jastak, 1965) | Gilmore Oral Reading Test (Gilmore & Gilmore 1968) | Key Math Diagnostic Arithmetic Test (Connolly, Nachtman, &, Pritchett, 1971) |
| | Durrell Analysis of Reading Difficulty (Durrell, 1955) | Stanford Diagnostic Mathematics Test (Beatty, Madden, Gardner, & Karlsen, 1976) |
| | Gates-McKillop Reading Diagnostic Tests (Gates & McKillop, 1962) | Diagnosis: An Instructional Aid (Mathematics) (Guzaitis, Carlin, & Juda, 1972)) |
| | Diagnostic Reading Scales (Spache, 1963) | |

centile ranks, and standard scores, can be compared to WISC-R standard scores. Limitations of the PIAT include "inadequate subtest specificity . . . and grade equivalent scores at some levels which do not correlate well with WRAT scores" (Swanson & Watson, 1982, p. 271).

Among the diagnostic norm referenced tests listed in Table 2.5 the Woodcock Reading Mastery Test (Woodcock, 1973) is one of the most used. Divided into five separate tests—letter identification, word identification, word attack, word comprehension, and passage comprehension—the reading test is designed for students in grades K through 12. Because scores on the Woodcock Tests are reported in a number of ways—raw scores, mastery scores, grade scores, an easy reading level score, a failure reading level score, percentile ranks, standard scores, and stamines—Swanson and Watson call it "a comprehensive measure of reading performance" (p. 280). The classroom teacher can use the derived scores to group students for instruction. The main limitation of the Woodcock Reading Mastery Test lies in the difficulty a teacher may have in interpreting the Word Attack Test.

Criterion referenced diagnostic tests, tests that break down skills into specific steps, are especially helpful to the regular and special education teacher since they report on achievement of specific skills. With data from these tests, the teacher can easily identify specific problem areas and thus know where to begin when planning classroom instructional activities. Teachers frequently use the criterion referenced Key Math Diagnostic Arithmetic Test (Connolly, Nachtman, & Pritchett, 1971) which includes 14 subtests grouped into broad categories of content, operations, and applications. Scores are reported only in terms of grade equivalent. Swanson and Watson say "the Key Math is a very useful tool for identifying specific mathematical difficulties in . . . handicapped children" (p. 276).

## PERCEPTUAL MOTOR DEVELOPMENT

Tests of perceptual motor development attempt to assess visual and auditory skills. Since studies demonstrate the "significant relationship between visual perception and achievement in reading, arithmetic, and spelling, evaluation of visual processing" becomes important in a comprehensive evaluation (Swanson & Watson, p. 236). Before teachers can assess visual motor perception, they must evaluate a student's actual vision. To do so, teachers frequently use the Snellen Wall Chart, the Keystone Telebinocular, and the Titmus Vision Tester. When assessing student progress, teachers should also consider auditory perceptual abilities. And again, before assessing auditory functions, teachers must evaluate hearing acuity. Usually a school nurse, an audiologist, or a speech therapist conducts such hearing evaluations.

Perceptual tests are important because they help teachers identify problem areas or modality preferences in students. For example, if teachers discover

TABLE 2.6
Perceptual Motor Tests

| Visual-Perception Motor Tests | Auditory-Perceptual Motor Tests |
| --- | --- |
| Bender Visual Motor Gestalt Test (Bender, 1938) | Auditory Discrimination Test (Wepman, 1973) |
| Frostig Developmental Test of Visual Perception (Frostig, Lefever, & Whittlesey, 1966) | Goldman-Fristoe-Woodcock Auditory Skills Test Battery (Woodcock, 1976) |
| Developmental Test of Visual Motor Integration (Beery & Buktenica, 1967) | |
| Motor-Free Visual Perception Test (Colarusso & Hammill, 1972) | |
| Memory For Designs Test (Graham & Kendall, 1960) | |
| Revised Visual Retention Test (Benton, 1974) | |

that a student has difficulty processing information visually, they can try audi-tory instructional methods to improve achievement. Swanson and Watson warn teachers not to use these tests as "definitive diagnostic measures" because they do not usually meet "rigorous standards of reliability and validity," but they say the tests are "useful for clinical purposes" (p. 265). Table 2.6 identifies a number of these perceptual tests.

## LANGUAGE DEVELOPMENT

Educators typically define language as "vocabulary, grammar, and phonation," all of which can be assessed at three levels: "imitation, comprehension, and pro-duction" (Salvia & Ysseldyke, 1978, p. 342). Language is "one of the most com-plex systems of rules a child ever learns," and as Swanson and Watson point out, failure to master language "has far-reaching educational and social implica-tions" (p. 172). Because many children experience difficulty in language develop-ment, psychologists have developed numerous tests to help identify specific prob-lem areas. Indeed, so many language tests are available, they cannot be listed here. Teachers, then, should be alert to students' language and/or speech dif-ficulties and refer all such students for appropriate evaluation.

Students may have problems in either oral or written language. When stu-dents understand what teachers say to them but cannot formulate correct ver-bal responses, they have difficulties in oral language development. Similarly, students capable of oral verbal communication may get confused when they try to transfer thoughts into written language. Teachers should watch for incoherent combinations of words and for sentences that do not communicate the thought appropriately. Teachers can use the numerous tests available to screen students for either oral or written expression deficits.

As a rule, students with speech and/or language problems receive specialized services from a speech therapist; however, the teacher can assist the therapist by reinforcing certain activities in the regular classroom. Therefore, when a student receives speech therapy, the teacher should contact the therapist if at all possible.

## BEHAVIORAL ASSESSMENT

Psychologists use behavioral assessment to obtain "information that can be used to plan a treatment program" (Swanson & Watson, p. 285). Since treatment programs can be designed to include regular classroom teachers and parents as well as counselors and therapists, teachers should note any recommendations suited for the classroom. Teachers will find especially useful the information identifying behaviors that should be reinforced or eliminated, along with suggested methods for doing so.

Teachers should also familiarize themselves with available behavioral rating scales so that they can identify both students needing immediate referral and students with potential behavior problems. Some available rating scales are the Glueck Prediction Scale (Kvaraceus, 1966); Burks Behavior Rating Scale (Burks, 1969); Cassell Child Behavior Rating Scale (Cassell, 1972); Quay and Peterson Behavior Rating Scale (Quay & Peterson, 1967); and Walker Problem Behavior Identification (Walker, 1970). Public schools also frequently use the American Association of Mental Deficiency (AAMD) Adaptive Behavior Scale (Nihira, Foster, Shellhaas, & Leland, 1969) and the Vineland Social Maturity Scale (Doll, 1965). These two instruments are necessary when a student is being evaluated to determine mental retardation because by definition a retarded student must show deficits in both intellectual ability and adaptive behavior.

The AAMD Adaptive Behavior Scale is divided into two parts. Part I tests independent functioning, economic activity, physical development, language development, number and time concept, occupation-domestic, occupation-general, self-direction, responsibilities, and socialization. Part II tests violent and destructive behavior and hyperactive tendencies and maladaptive behavior related to personality and behavior disorders.

The Vineland Social Maturity Scale assesses students in the areas of self-help, self-direction, locomotion, occupation, communication, and social relations. In general, the scale identifies the skills an individual needs to acquire and/or develop to become an independently functioning adult.

## IMPLICATIONS FOR THE REGULAR TEACHER

During the 1960s and 1970s, groups inside and outside of education accused testing instruments and procedures of being biased and discriminatory. As a result, educators re-normed many well-known aptitude and achievement tests and developed new, more culturally unbiased, testing instruments. Realistically, tests never measure all they attempt to measure, but educators need them to make appropriate placement decisions, to develop effective instruction, and recently, to certify a student's competence before promotion and graduation. Since test data on students continues to be available, educators should learn to use the information more effectively. Teachers should consider test data as much a teaching tool as they do books, audio visual materials, blackboards, or laboratories. To meet the changing and continually demanding needs of a diverse population of students, educators need to use *all* available resources, including test data.

## SUMMARY

An understanding of the assessment process better prepares the classroom teacher for working with the handicapped student in the mainstream. The regular classroom teacher has an ongoing role during the entire assessment process, and assessment data can be of great value to the regular classroom teacher in preparing to teach the handicapped student. Chapter 3 presents detailed ideas for the next step in the instructional model, adapting the learning environment for the mainstreamed student.

## REFERENCES

Beatty, L. S., Madden, R., Gardner, E. F., & Karlsen, B. *Stanford diagnostic mathematics test.* New York: Harcourt Brace Jovanovich, 1976.

Beery, K. E., & Buktenica, N. *Developmental test of visual motor integration.* Chicago: Follett, 1967.

Bender, L. A visual motor gestalt test and its clinical use. *American Orthopsychiatric Association Research Monograph,* 1938, No. 3.

Benton, A. L. *The revised visual retention test (4th ed.).* New York: Psychological Corporation, 1974.

Burks, H. *Burks' behavior rating scales.* El Monte, Calif.: Arden Press, 1969.

Bush, W. J., & Waugh, K. W. *Diagnostic learning disabilities.* Columbus, Ohio: Charles E. Merrill, 1971.

Cassell, R. *The child behavior rate scale.* Bevely Hills, Calif.: Western Psychological Services, 1972.

Colarusso, R., & Hammill, D. *The motor-free test of visual perception.* San Rafael, Calif.: Academic Therapy Publications, 1972.

Connolly, A., Nachtman, W., & Pritchett, E. *Manual for the key math diagnostic arithmetic test.* Circle Pines, Minn.: American Guidance Service, 1971.

Doll, E. *Vineland social maturity scale.* Circle Pines, Minn.: American Guidance Service, 1965.

Dunn, L. M., & Markwardt, F. C. *Peabody individual achievement test.* Circle Pines, Minn.: American Guidance Service, 1970.

Durrell, D. D. *Durrell analysis of reading difficulty.* New York: Harcourt Brace Jovanovich, 1955.

Frostig, M., Lefever, W., & Whittlesey, J. R. *Administration and scoring manual for the Marianne Frostig Developmental Test of Visual Perception.* Palo Alto, Calif.: Consulting Psychologists Press, 1966.

Gates, A. I., & McKillop, A. S. *Gates-McKillop reading diagnostic tests.* New York: Teachers College Press, 1962.

Gilmore, J. V., & Gilmore, E. C. *Gilmore oral reading test.* New York: Harcourt Brace Jovanovich, 1968.

Graham, F., & Kendall, B. *Memory for designs test: Revised general manual* (Monograph supplement 2-UII), 1960, *11*, 147–188.

Grant, W. V. The demographics of education. *The Education Digest,* 1982, 47(5), 6–8.

Grossman, H. J. (Ed.). *Manual on terminology and classifications in mental retardation.* Washington, D.C.: American Association of Mental Deficiency, 1977.

Guzaitis, J., Carlin, J. A., & Juda, S. *Diagnosis: An instructional aid (mathematics).* Chicago: Science Research Associates, 1972.

Jastak, J. F., & Jastak, S. R. *Manual: The wide range achievement test.* Wilmington, Del.: Guidance Associates, 1965.

Kirk, S. A. *Educating exceptional children.* Boston: Houghton Mifflin, 1972.

Kvaraceus, W. *Anxious youth: Dynamics of delinquency.* Columbus, Ohio: Charles E. Merrill, 1966.

Lerner, J. W. *Children with learning disabilities.* Boston: Houghton Mifflin, 1976.

Nihira, K., Foster, R., Shellhaas, M., & Leland, H. *Adaptive behavior scales.* Washington, D.C.: American Association of Mental Deficiency, 1962.

Quay, H. C., & Peterson, D. R. *Manual for the behavior problem checklist.* Urbana, Ill.: University of Illinois Press, 1967.

The rude reality of educating the handicapped kids. *The American School Board Journal,* 1980, *167*(1), 29.

Salvia, J., & Ysseldyke, J. E. *Assessment in special and remedial education.* Boston: Houghton Mifflin, 1978.

Spache, G. D. *Diagnostic reading scales.* Monterey, Calif.: California Test Bureau/McGraw-Hill, 1963.

*State of Mississippi referral to placement guidelines.* Jackson, Miss.: State Department of Education, 1982.

Swanson, H. L., & Watson, B. L. *Educational and psychological assessment of exceptional children.* St. Louis, Mo.: C. V. Mosby, 1982.

Vergason, G. A. Assessment. In E. L. Meyen, G. A. Vergason, & R. J. Whelan (Eds.), *Instructional planning for exceptional children—Essays from Focus on Exceptional Children.* Denver, Colo.: Love Publishing Company, 1979.

Walker, H. *Walker problem behavior identification checklist.* Los Angeles: Western Psychological Services, 1970.

Wechsler, D. *Manual for the Wechsler adult intelligence scale.* New York: Psychological Corporation, 1955.

Wechsler, D. *Manual for the Wechsler intelligence scale for children.* New York: Psychological Corporation, 1949.

Wechsler, D. *Manual for the Wechsler intelligence scale for children—revised.* New York: Psychological Corporation, 1974.

Wechsler, D. *Manual for the Wechsler preschool and primary scale of intelligence.* New York: Psychological Corporation, 1967.

Wepman, J. W. *Manual of administration, scoring, and interpretation: Auditory discrimination test.* Chicago: Author, 1973.

Woodcock, R. W. *Goldman-Fristoe-Woodcock auditory skills test battery, technical manual.* Circle Pines, Minn.: American Guidance Service, 1976.

Woodcock, R. W. *Woodcock reading mastery tests.* Circle Pines, Minn.: American Guidance Service, 1973.

Zweig, R. L. & Associates. *Fountain Valley teacher support system in reading.* Huntington Beach, Calif.: Richard L. Zweig Associates, 1971.

# Chapter Three

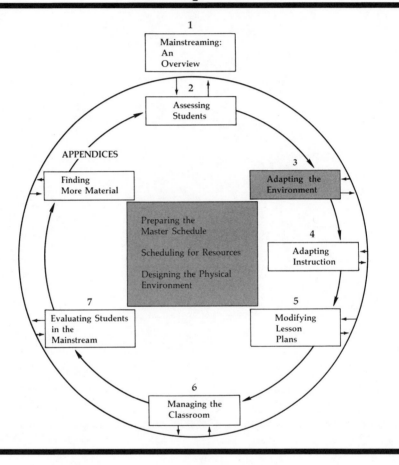

1 Mainstreaming: An Overview

2 Assessing Students

APPENDICES

Finding More Material

3 Adapting the Environment

Preparing the Master Schedule

Scheduling for Resources

Designing the Physical Environment

4 Adapting Instruction

5 Modifying Lesson Plans

7 Evaluating Students in the Mainstream

6 Managing the Classroom

# Adapting the
# Environment

Teachers instruct students within the tightly woven framework of the school day. For harmonious and structured management, schools design the school day around various types of schedules and physical arrangements. This framework affects students and teachers because it affects types of subjects, class size, resources, students' choice of subjects, and the educational program's philosophy. Schedules and physical environments vary in different schools, districts, and states. Regardless of the framework used, however, educators want to be able to adapt it to make instruction easier and more productive. This chapter presents strategies for doing so.

After teachers assess the needs of mildly handicapped students (actually, of all students), they prepare to teach. However, before adapting instruction, they must consider students' total learning environment. Figure 3.1 presents a model for adapting the learning environment before beginning instruction. Teachers should note the three major elements of adapting the total learning environment: preparing the master schedule, scheduling for resource, and designing the physical environment. Although not inclusive, the ideas presented here show teachers how necessary it is to prepare the learning environment before teaching.

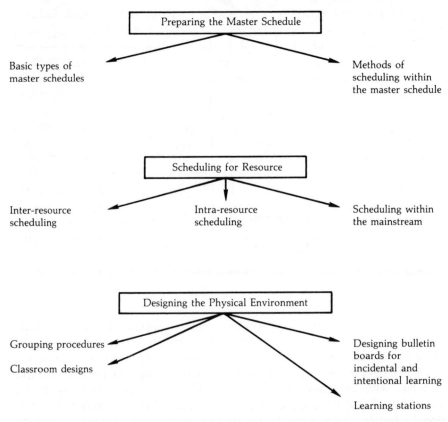

FIGURE 3.1. Adapting the Learning Environment

# PREPARING THE MASTER SCHEDULE

Schools organize the parts of a school day according to a master schedule. The soundness of this schedule determines the effectiveness of administrative detail, plant facilities, instruction, and overall school organization.

Both regular and special educators need a working knowledge of the school's master schedule. Special teachers need to understand the administrative framework of the school's schedule to place the mainstreamed student appropriately; regular classroom teachers need input into selecting the types and degrees of disabilities they will need to prepare for; and both can suggest minor changes that will prevent major mainstreaming problems.

An elementary school master schedule is less complex than a secondary master schedule because elementary schools have self-contained grade units with only occasional class changes for specific academic subjects such as reading or math. Many elementary schools function with heterogeneous grouping within each class, while some use the homogeneous grouping methods (having classes within one grade level grouped around students of similar ability and achievement). Elementary schools usually schedule art, music, and other nonacademic subjects on a weekly revolving basis.

Many elementary schools schedule the language arts and math blocks in the morning. Allowing the mildly handicapped student to float in and out of the block provides appropriate instruction and allows more time for other subjects. For example, a language arts block running for two and one-half hours may contain reading, spelling, and grammar skills sections. The handicapped student should be able to attend the spelling and the grammar skills sections in the regular classroom, for example, and attend reading in the resource room. Planning these blocks of time with the resource teacher before designing the elementary master schedule helps keep the daily schedule running smoothly.

At the secondary level, planning the master schedule becomes more difficult and placing the mildly handicapped student appropriately presents greater problems. The principal usually has the ultimate responsibility of making the master schedule; however, the guidance counselor or other individuals may do much of the actual planning. Whoever schedules mildly handicapped students should consult the special education teacher and the mainstreaming regular teacher before the master schedule is finished.

## BASIC TYPES OF MASTER SCHEDULES

Master schedules can be classified into two basic types, conventional (traditional) and flexible. Most American secondary schools use the conventional approach to master schedule planning. This type of schedule arranges the school day into five to seven instructional periods, each lasting from forty to fifty-five minutes, with allotments for lunch period and special arrangements for assemblies. The flexible approach to scheduling is slowly replacing this traditional schedule. Philosophically, the flexible approach permits the educator to exercise more control over the day's events. The flexible schedule moves away from the straight five to seven blocks of time and provides more creative ways of using the school day (i.e., extended first periods, rotating class days, a schedule change each week, etc.). See the Additional Reading list for sources on flexible scheduling.

## METHODS OF SCHEDULING WITHIN THE MASTER SCHEDULE

Once a school decides on a master schedule, it must place students within it. Schools usually use one of three types: computer scheduling, self-scheduling, or hand scheduling. No matter what kind of schedule administrators choose, the special and regular mainstreaming educator should provide input into class selection for the mildly handicapped student.

COMPUTER SCHEDULING   Because computers can carry the work load of many staff members, numerous schools have changed to computerized master scheduling. With the ability to store a large number of parameters in its memory, the computer assists administrators by rapidly printing individual student schedules.

Even though the computer efficiently schedules the day for large school populations, it presents several problems in scheduling mainstreamed students. For example, computerized scheduling prohibits the school from selecting particular regular teachers to work with mainstreamed students. It also makes grouping mildly handicapped students into particular resource classes or regular classes virtually impossible. Finally, the computer makes it especially difficult to meet the individual needs of mildly handicapped students. It is not flexible enough, for example, to schedule the student into morning sections rather than afternoon sections, to alternate required courses with electives, or to provide resource for academic relief.

SELF-SCHEDULING   A number of schools let students self-schedule all classes within the master schedule. Even though numerous schools succeed using the self-scheduling method, problems do occur. Kelly (1979) surveyed approximately 700 students to determine the variables that influenced them the most during scheduling. The students named parents, friends, counselors, teachers, and written information, with parents ranking as the most influential variable on self-scheduling. Kelly recommended that schools change pre-registration advising so that it coincides with parental and peer advice; change written materials; make self-scheduling procedures more rigid; and consider self-scheduling for juniors and computer scheduling for freshmen and sophomores.

Kelly failed, however, to identify other problems inherent in self-scheduling (e.g., class overcrowding, popularity contests among teachers, and the actual percentage of students selecting inappropriate classes). Most important,

Kelly omitted the self-scheduling of the mildly handicapped from his survey. If a school uses self-scheduling, teachers must consider the placement of the mildly handicapped student carefully and use the following suggestions to make the process go more smoothly. First, a resource teacher should be familiar with the overall master plan and the scheduling of all classes. In addition, each mildly handicapped student should be assigned to a resource teacher during the self-scheduling process. The school might impose some limitations on mildly handicapped students. For example, the school might designate the resource period or choose specific regular teachers to teach such students, leaving the students with only the option of period selection. Finally, the school should give mildly handicapped students a checklist of required courses before registration.

HAND SCHEDULING   Most of America's schools design the master schedule by having an administrator place the components of the school's day into the master plan by hand. Even though hand scheduling is a frustrating, tedious, and time-consuming job, it is the most efficient way to schedule the mainstreamed student. Whatever scheduling method a school uses, it should hand schedule all mildly handicapped students into the master plan.

Handicapped students need a great deal of individual attention, much of which is mandated by the IEP. Selecting appropriate classes for the mildly handicapped students involves paying such attention. Whoever schedules the handicapped student, for example, must consider the personality of the student, the personality of the teacher, and existing conflicts between students. Potential problems can be avoided through hand scheduling.

Hand scheduling also allows the resource teacher to place students in the same grade with common teachers; for example, the same English, math, or history teacher could have all the ninth grade mainstreamed students. Such an arrangement allows the regular classroom teacher and the special class teacher more time together to prepare instruction. At the same time, hand scheduling allows the scheduler to select those teachers who understand that students learn through different modes, at different rates, and with different strategies. On the other hand, hand scheduling allows regular classroom teachers to say which types of handicapped students they feel more adequate teaching. By carefully selecting a common core of teachers to serve all mainstreamed students, the scheduler reduces the number of teachers with whom a resource teacher has to communicate. Also, when a common core of regular teachers serves one grade level of mainstreamed students, the scheduler can plan common off-periods to allow for greater collaboration among the regular teachers. Finally, hand scheduling can also reduce the number of resource teachers with whom the regular teacher must communicate and thus reduce the regular teacher's paperwork.

Even though the advantages of hand scheduling the mainstreamed student outweigh the disadvantages, disadvantages do exist. For example, hand scheduling costs more time, money, and staff effort. Secretaries have to type the student schedules and class rolls for the teachers, and both the scheduling and the typing must be done in the summer. Also, staff members should complete the hand scheduling of mainstreamed students before they schedule regular students.

SPECIFIC CONSIDERATIONS IN SCHEDULING   After a school decides which type of master schedule to use for adapting the mainstreamed student's learning environment, it must try to avoid specific scheduling problems. Table 3.1 provides a checklist for avoiding such problems. Teachers and administrators should note that most planning problems can be avoided if all groups keep the lines of communication open.

Some school districts have also addressed more specific scheduling concerns. Although all of the following suggestions will not be appropriate for every school's situation, they give schools and teachers an idea of what they might aim for in scheduling. These districts recommend:

1. Having small classes—4 to 5 students per resource class
2. Allowing students in each resource class to have the same mainstream teachers when taking the same courses

TABLE 3.1
Checklist: Avoiding Problems in Planning Master Schedule for Mildly Handicapped

|  | Yes | No |
|---|---|---|
| 1. Include resource classes on the master schedule as a regular class offering. | _____ | _____ |
| 2. Obtain input from resource teacher about: student groupings desired (ability and personality); | _____ | _____ |
| selection of regular teachers, especially teachers to be avoided; and | _____ | _____ |
| other individual needs of mildly handicapped students. | _____ | _____ |
| 3. Obtain input from regular teachers about categories of students desired. | _____ | _____ |
| 4. Obtain input from counselors or teachers about peers to be separated from each other because of discipline problems. | _____ | _____ |
| 5. Obtain input from counselors or teachers about peers to be scheduled together for purpose of tutoring or assistance. | _____ | _____ |
| 6. Obtain input from resource teacher about possible conflicts between student's request and IEP. | _____ | _____ |

3. Grouping students in each resource class by grade or ability level—for example, four students who read poorly and need extra help, but are scattered among three eighth grade classes, should be in the same resource class
4. Including special education teachers in preparation of the school's master schedule so that they can prevent future scheduling problems and represent special student's needs
5. Scheduling special education teachers' off-periods around special students' resource schedules
6. Not scheduling the school's one-period elective offerings concurrently
7. Using special education teachers to select effective mainstream teachers for the students
8. Notifying the mainstream teacher when schedules are complete so that the teacher has time to select materials and prepare individual assignments
9. Balancing sections throughout the day (If courses are taught on different levels, sections should be available in the morning as well as in the afternoon.)
10. Planning morning sections for vocational students, co-op students, and athletes
11. Alternating academic courses with basic and college preparatory sections

Finally, in the process of preparing a master schedule, planners need to consider the needs of mainstreaming teachers. If at all possible, schools should offer such teachers some incentives for serving mildly handicapped students in the mainstream.

Once administrators, curriculum supervisors, and directors of special education identify the potentially good mainstreaming teachers by their ability, positive attitude toward the handicapped, enthusiasm, and concern for the self-concepts of students, they should praise and reinforce those teachers serving the handicapped by including mainstreaming teachers on committees to develop future changes and making them a part of the decision-making process; lightening mainstreaming teachers' class loads and exempting them from other duty assignments; selecting mainstreaming teachers to attend conferences or workshops at the expense of the school district; and asking mainstreaming teachers to serve as ongoing inservice trainers who assist other teachers in the school in deciding what help to give the mainstreamed student.

No matter what type of master schedule a school chooses, it must build some flexibility into that schedule for the benefit of its mildly handicapped students and the teachers who work with them.

# SCHEDULING FOR RESOURCE

The resource room has become a viable alternative to self-contained placements for educating the mildly handicapped student in the least restrictive environment. Presently, schools use numerous variations on the resource room model.

D'Alonzo, D'Alonzo, and Mauser (1979) describe the five basic types of resource rooms typically found in schools:

1. The *categorical*, which focuses on one primary type of handicap.
2. The *cross-categorical*, where clusters of two or more categories of children are grouped.
3. The *noncategorical*, where students with mild or severe learning and behavior handicaps are serviced with the possible inclusion of nonhandicapped students.
4. The *specific skills* resource room, where a specific curriculum area or deficit (i.e., reading, mathematics, etc.) is targeted.
5. The *itinerant resource room*, which is a mobile nonstationary resource environment that travels to the geographic area when and where the specialized education services are needed. (pp. 91–92)

Resource rooms provide mildly handicapped students with distinct advantages. Resource rooms expose mainstreamed students to more teachers, a broader knowledge base, and a wider range of role models. Assuming that the teachers have a positive attitude toward the mainstreamed student, they will enhance the student's self-worth. Resource rooms also make it possible for mainstreamed students to build and to maintain relationships with nonhandicapped peers and to have some nonhandicapped role and age models. The resource room gives mainstreamed students the opportunity for more intentional learning and more provisions for incidental learning (i.e., media, field trips, guest speakers, and group interaction), and the resource teacher can reinforce their regular class work. In fact, the resource room model is designed around constant and positive reinforcement and feedback. Finally, the resource room provides the mainstreamed student with additional time for completing class work, homework, or tests, with an environment free of anxiety, with alternative materials, learning stations, and equipment not available in the regular classroom, and with an environment more easily adaptable to special behaviors such as distractibility, short attention spans, hyperactivity, and so on.

Because schools have widely accepted the resource room as a teaching tool, they have had to focus on scheduling the mainstreamed student inter-resource, intra-resource, and within the mainstream classroom.

## INTER-RESOURCE SCHEDULING

Lieberman (1982) lists eight problems associated with scheduling mildly handicapped students inter-resource (i.e., scheduling between resource room and regular classroom). According to Lieberman, children spend too much time traveling between rooms; children moving in and out of classrooms cause confusion; teachers cannot keep track of individual children; the consistency of approach is jeopardized; the proliferation of specialists results in splintered services and greater scheduling difficulties; holding children accountable for what they missed while receiving services elsewhere is detrimental; but not holding children accountable for what they missed while receiving services elsewhere is controversial; and there is conflict between grouping in resource and individualizing to meet unique needs (p. 57). Also, sending special students to resource during regular class embarrasses students as they leave or enter the regular classroom, and taking special students out of subjects they often enjoy (i.e., art, music, physical education, assembly, etc.) to go to resource can create frustration. Table 3.2 suggests some solutions for these problems.

TABLE 3.2
Inter-Resource Scheduling: Problems and Solutions

| Scheduling Problem | Suggested Solutions |
| --- | --- |
| Too much time traveling to room assignments | Provide core of teachers in one area of building to cut traveling to a minimum. |
| | Block resource students by grade levels so that only one grade group at a time moves to a new room. |
| | Assign resource teacher to a certain number of grades and locate the resource class within that grade cluster. |
| Movement of children during classes | Students go to resource or mainstreamed class during class change at secondary level and during subject changes at elementary level. |
| | Assign seats for special students entering mainstreamed class, thus eliminating confusion about where to sit. |
| | Make seating chart for each class period and quickly check for missing students. |
| Teachers cannot keep track of individual students | Use seating charts to check for missing students. |
| | Provide mainstreaming teachers with charts of classes and mainstreamed students in each class. |
| | Provide all regular teachers with a short check form: teacher checks period, lists absent students, and dates form. |

TABLE 3.2 (continued)

| Scheduling Problem | Suggested Solutions |
| --- | --- |
| Consistency of approach jeopardized | Provide mainstreamed students with individual weekly schedules of services they will receive and location of services.<br><br>Make younger children's schedule in picture form.<br><br>For younger children use small alarm clocks set for service times. Aides may reset clocks for students receiving numerous services. For example: |

| | 1st | 2nd | 3rd | 4th |
| --- | --- | --- | --- | --- |
| | Reading | | Math | |
| | | Speech | | PT |

| Scheduling Problem | Suggested Solutions |
| --- | --- |
| Proliferation of specialists, resulting in splintered services and greater scheduling difficulties | Group students by IEP objectives. Deliver services in groups.<br><br>Carefully plan schedules with children in mind. Assign specialists by age groups and/or IEP objectives.<br><br>Collaborate with other schools, when necessary, to secure specialist services. |
| Holding children accountable for what they missed while receiving services elsewhere | Do not remove children from subjects that they will be responsible for later.<br><br>Plan with mainstreamed teacher so that students are not behind when they return to classroom. |
| Not holding children accountable for what they missed while receiving services | Students should receive same content in resource so that they will not be behind when they return to regular classroom.<br><br>Alternative grading, promotion, and/or graduation requirements may be necessary for students who continue to function below grade level. |

TABLE 3.2 (continued)

| Scheduling Problem | Suggested Solutions |
| --- | --- |
| Conflict between grouping in resource and individualizing to meet unique needs | Inform mainstreaming teachers how to meet handicapped student's needs individually and in groups. |
| | Assign projects to groups, making sure certain parts meet the special needs of handicapped students. |
| | Provide peer tutor for special student. Have peer tutor record the lesson. Then mainstreamed student can work independently at learning station. |
| | Individualizing for mainstreamed students does not differ from individualizing for regular students. |
| Sending special students to resource during class embarrasses them when they leave or return | Change classes when bell signals change for periods. |
| | Never announce "It is time for you to go to resource." |
| | Consider resource just another class period. |
| | At the elementary level, send student to resource when other students are putting books away for next class. |
| Taking special students out of subjects they enjoy, such as art, music, physical education, assembly, etc., to go to resource. | Allow special student to attend special subject areas. On days when special subjects are offered, arrange resource for different period. |

# INTRA RESOURCE SCHEDULING

According to Hart (1981), scheduling within the resource room, intra-resource scheduling, requires close attention to structure. Children who have limited attention spans, who perseverate in their activities, and who have difficulty transferring learning from one activity to another, can all benefit from a carefully developed schedule. Hart lists three major things a teacher should consider when developing the resource room schedule.

First, the teacher should present the most difficult subject while the students are fresh. For example, elementary schools commonly schedule reading and language arts during the first time blocks. Secondary schools should also consider placing subjects requiring the most concentration during the morning periods. Second, teachers need to make schedules for resource students consistent so that they become familiar with the day's events. Teachers should discuss schedule changes, such as a field trip or a guest speaker, with the students before they occur. Finally, after students become thoroughly comfortable with the schedule, teachers should deliberately alter it once in awhile. In this way, teachers can make their students more comfortable with change, too. (pp. 130–31)

These considerations apply primarily to those students who spend a large percentage of the school day in the resource room. But structure in the resource room is also important for those students who attend only one or two periods of resource and spend the remainder of their day in regular academic courses or electives. Such students also need an established routine. For example, a teacher might require them to check their assignment box for the day's activities when they enter the classroom rather than wait for the resource teacher to tell them what to do. Also, the student needs to keep materials and books in a definite place and maintain separate notebooks for each subject. In addition, students should follow set procedures when completing homework, studying for tests, and/or taking tests within the resource room. Following a daily routine helps the student, who often feels anxious and frustrated, to develop good work habits and a sense of stability and security. Figure 3.2 offers two examples of mildly handicapped students' schedules within the resource room setting.

## SCHEDULING WITHIN THE MAINSTREAM

As resource students move into regular classes, teachers must make numerous adjustments in their teaching, and they must adapt the learning environment for those students. A little preparation—the suggestions discussed in inter- and intra-resource scheduling and the additional hints below—will make scheduling within the mainstream flow smoothly:

1. Before beginning a new task, give the mainstreamed student a warning: simply announce to the class or to the mainstreamed student in private that in five minutes, the old assignment will end and a new task will begin.
2. Give instructions in short, direct sentences.
3. List the instructions sequentially on the board.
4. Give a short handout to students so that they will know the expectations for the period.
5. Hand out written assignments, with expected date of completion, at the end of the period.
6. Be sure that the student understands all assignments.

7. Give a copy of the day's schedule and assignment to the resource teacher for reinforcement.

Once teachers have adapted the learning environment through appropriate scheduling, they can turn their attention to the physical environment. Slowly, teachers accommodate the entire instructional process to the mainstreamed student.

# DESIGNING THE PHYSICAL ENVIRONMENT

When a school system has completed the master schedule and has placed all children into classes, teachers can design the physical environment for instruction: grouping the children, designing the classroom, setting up learning stations, and presenting bulletin boards for incidental and intentional learning.

## GROUPING PROCEDURES

Grouping procedures vary from school to school and from teacher to teacher. Many teachers feel that grouping within the classroom creates an even heavier work load. However, children do learn at different rates and therefore do not always learn best in one large group. According to Affleck, Lowenbraun, and

Student A—Second Period Resource

| | |
|---|---|
| 9:00 to 9:10 | Teacher reviews spelling words. |
| 9:10 to 9:20 | Student studies words. |
| 9:20 to 9:30 | Teacher calls out words. |
| 9:30 to 9:50 | Student defines words and writes sentence with each word. |
| 9:50 to 9:55 | Teacher reviews assignments for the next period and homework assignments with student. |

Student B—Third Period Resource

| | |
|---|---|
| 10:00 to 10:15 | Teacher explains English homework. |
| 10:15 to 10:40 | Student works in group with other students on English homework and assignment. |
| 10:40 to 10:55 | Student works independently at computer station on English exercise. |

FIGURE 3.2. Examples of Mildly Handicapped Students Scheduled Intra-Resource

Archer (1980), because of "the diversity of academic skills found within any regular classroom, small-group instruction is more appropriate than whole-group instruction for basic academic subjects" (p. 152).

Labeling groups can be a problem, because no matter what the teacher calls the groups, all children know which ones are bright, average, and slow. Because creative grouping allows for a diversity of academic skills, it eliminates labels and give students the freedom to move among groups.

CREATIVE GROUPING   Creative grouping may be used at the secondary or elementary level. Teachers set up the groups by academic subjects and then break the subjects into specific objectives or skills. Teachers assign a student to a creative group based on the specific skill that the student needs to work on. No student is locked into a group, because once the student masters the skill, he or she moves into another group. Figure 3.3 presents a creative group in which a student completes a skill, keeps a personal record, and then moves on.

|  | Jason | Julia | Scott | Valerie | Matt |
|---|---|---|---|---|---|
| Identifies penny, nickel, and dime by name. |  |  |  |  |  |
| Identifies penny, nickel, and dime by value. |  |  |  |  |  |
| Identifies quarter, half dollar, and dollar by name. |  |  |  |  |  |
| Identifies quarter, half dollar, and dollar by value. |  |  |  |  |  |

FIGURE 3.3. Creative Groups

VARIATIONS ON CREATIVE GROUPING   Creative grouping may include at least three variations, all working simultaneously: a learning station, a seat work station, and a small group instructional station. When class begins, the teacher color codes or numbers the stations and gives each student a direction card or uses a list on the board to indicate the station the student should use first. Remember, a student who masters a given skill can enter a new creative group.

PEER TUTORS FOR CREATIVE GROUPS   Teachers should not overlook one of a school's most valuable resources—its students. Within creative groups, teachers can assign peer tutors to assist those students having difficulty with the content of a lesson. Peer tutors may be glad to record assignments for the mildly handicapped student to listen to for extra reinforcement. Peers also work well one-on-one: using a flannel board, manipulating real or paper money, or assisting a mildly handicapped student start a brief instructional period at the computer terminal. At the secondary level peers often succeed when they help small groups of handicapped students look up their study questions at the end of chapters, work on classwork or homework assignments, and participate in study or review sessions. A peer can also call out words to handicapped students during group spelling tests. Because teachers often give handicapped students alternative spelling words that correspond better to their individual needs, administering their tests in this manner eliminates embarrassment. In addition, handicapped students often need to have their words called out more slowly, and using peers and grouping for spelling tests makes such an adaptation possible.

## DESIGNS FOR THE CLASSROOM

Whether at the secondary or elementary level, classroom designs are important because they dictate whether a teacher uses small group instruction, one-on-one group instruction (one student per group), or total group instruction. Once teachers decide which type of instructional design to use during a lesson, they can alter room arrangements to meet instructional need. No one design works best for every student. Teachers need to change from time to time. Students can often help to choose a viable design for the day's lesson. Figure 3.4 suggests different designs for small group instruction, one-on-one group instruction, and total class design.

## DESIGNING LEARNING STATIONS

A learning station is a selected space in the classroom where students may go to work on a new assignment or on a skill or concept previously taught. The learning station approach to teaching or reinforcing skills saves the classroom teacher's time and energy. At the same time, the learning station allows the mainstreamed student freedom of choice in activities, successful completion of tasks, and immediate feedback for correct or incorrect responses. The learning station also gives the teacher a way to individualize instruction and to work with specific educational objectives. Commonplace in elementary schools, learning stations are used infrequently in secondary classrooms. Yet learning stations can provide the secondary teacher with a desirable instructional alternative, too.

SETTING UP THE LEARNING STATION    If a teacher has never used the learning station approach to learning or has used only commercial learning stations, a review of the criteria for establishing a good station may be helpful. Voight (1973) lists six criteria to consider in establishing such centers:

Small Group Instruction

One-on-One Instruction

Total Group Instruction

FIGURE 3.4. Designs for Group Instruction

1. Each learning center should contribute to the achievement of the individual's purposes. Each child should confront basic skills, facts, concepts, and large ideas.
2. The learning center should deal with a significant area of study that the student finds interesting. It should be open-ended to foster individual creativity. It should provide opportunities to develop problem solving, critical thinking, and creative thinking. It should challenge an individual to strive toward higher levels of learning.
3. Learning experiences at the center should be related to past personal

experiences and should lead to broader and deeper new experiences.

4. Learning center activities should have practical time limits related to the child's developmental level so that the child can complete tasks.

5. Directions at each learning center should help the student quickly gain an overview of the task. Directions need to be clearly stated so that the student understands where to begin and when he has completed the task successfully.

6. The design of learning centers should depend on the subject matter presented to the student. (pp. 2–3)

With the criteria for learning stations established, the teacher must decide what subject to emphasize within a station. There are many different types of stations: reading stations, math stations, just-for-fun stations, social studies stations, vocational interest stations, things-to-make stations, and so on. The creative teacher can think of many more possibilities. Kaplan, Kaplan, Madsen, and Taylor (1973) suggest that teachers seriously consider the reasons for student and teacher use. They say that the learning station can serve the student as a self-selected activity for independent study; a follow-up of a lesson; an activity in place of a regular assignment; or an enrichment activity. (p. 21) For the teacher the learning station can become a place for the follow-up of lessons; a place for small group instruction; and an excellent resource for individualized activities. (p. 21) But a learning station should never be a place for busy work or for getting students out of the way for a few minutes.

After teachers establish standards for the learning center and decide on subject areas, they must locate resources. Piechowiak and Cook (1976) suggest teachers begin by going through the enrichment materials that have probably been stored away. Also, teachers should notify other teachers about items needed in the center. Supplies will multiply rapidly. Other suggestions from Piechowiak and Cook include the following:

1. Break language arts material into short lessons and write them on individual task cards.

2. Group math sheets into skill areas, and combine then in a box with plastic overlays and grease pencils, thus making programmed learning kits.

3. Gather good art projects, divide them into step-by-step procedures, and write the directions on cards for independent use at the make-it table.

4. Cross index the basal science and social studies texts. Make them available for student research.

5. Accumulate odds and ends of everything—valuable materials for the art center, the make-it table, or experimentation.

6. Record some of your favorite children's stories for the listening center. Devise follow-up activities to check comprehension.

7. Make some blank books for creative writing. Gather pictures for writing and thinking exercises.

8. Use old basal readers and workbooks; they may supply a wealth of material for activity cards. Cut them apart and make books of individual stories.

Rip up pages to use for word study activities. Cut pictures to use for phonic task cards or sequential development exercises.

9. Do the same thing with old math texts. Turn the supplemental exercises in the back into math games.

10. Spend allotted school funds for a variety of materials. Instead of buying 30 copies of the same reading text, buy five different series in groups of six. When teachers use learning stations, they no longer need to place large group orders for texts.

11. Collect the tables, chairs, boards, and other items that other teachers discard—they may be just the thing one needs later.

12. Haunt the media center. Most directors are delighted to have someone interested in audiovisual aids, and when they know the type of material teachers are looking for, they will do all they can to locate it.

13. Rediscover the school building. Some valuable resources may be hiding in the back of the storage closet. (Piechowiak & Cook, 1976, pp. 20–21)

DESIGNING LEARNING STATIONS BASED UPON GENERAL PRINCIPLES OF LEARNING   If teaching is the interaction between teacher and learner, effective teaching is planning that interaction between teacher and learner and basing it upon learning principles. Teachers should use three general principles of learning—acquisition, retention, and transfer—when designing learning stations. Table 3.3 list these three general principles of learning with definitions and corresponding strategies for teaching each principle.

As teachers construct their learning stations, they should divide their material into the three different teaching strategies. They can even set up three different kinds of stations: the acquisition station, the retention station, and the transfer station. At each station, base the activities offered on particular strategies for teaching. Refer to Table 3.3 for specific strategies to use with each activity.

## LEARNING STATION FOR ACQUISITION

As seen in Table 3.3, acquisition means the learning of a new skill, or original learning. The teacher may or may not build within the learning station all ten of the teaching strategies for acquisition, but all of them can help the teacher teach a new skill.

INSTRUCTION AND INTENT   To teach a student a new skill, the teacher must first get the student's attention on the task. Making the acquisition station colorful and attractive gets the student's attention, and then the teacher can give instructions. For example, a teacher can provide step-by-step directions, one step per three-by-five-inch index card, for each task. Younger children's directions can be in picture form. Teachers can also use tape recorders to give directions. So that students can move efficiently from step to step without omis-

TABLE 3.3
General Principles of Learning and Strategies for Teaching Each Principle

| Principle of Learning | Definition | Strategies for Teaching |
|---|---|---|
| Acquistion | Original learning; the learning of a new skill | • Instruction and intent<br>• Whole and parts methods<br>• Distribution of practice<br>• Amount of material<br>• Recitation<br>• Knowledge of results<br>• Amount of practice<br>• Oral and visual presentations<br>• Orientation and attention<br>• Structure |
| Retention | Remembering over an extended period of time | • Overlearning<br>• Type of retention measure<br>• Instructions to recall<br>• Reminiscence |
| Transfer | Taking what is learned in one situation and using in a second situation | • Intertask similarity<br>• Instructions to transfer<br>• Overlearning |

Note. From *Program Development in Special Education* by P. Wehman and P.J. McLaughlin, 77-101. Copyright 1981 by McGraw-Hill Book Company. Adapted by permission.

sions, teachers should hand out checklists or tape them to the learning station. Wall charts with picture and word clues are excellent instructional tools. Since students themselves can effectively present information, why not assign student assistants to each learning station on a rotating basis to give verbal directions and demonstrations?

WHOLE AND PARTS METHODS   Whole methods present a task as a whole, while parts methods present a task in parts. Some children learn better using the whole method: the teacher presents the whole—for example, the word *dog*—then breaks the word down into parts or sounds.

Other children learn better by using the parts method. The teacher, then, must break the skill down into the steps required to complete or learn it and place the steps in sequential order so that the child can work from the simplest step to the most difficult. This technique, called shaping, means teaching each step in a sequence before moving to the next. In an acquisition center, the teacher can put each step on a separate sheet of paper or checklist. If the student completes a step correctly, the teacher checks it off and tells the student to go to the next step. For older students who learn best by the parts method, the teacher can select a literary work, for example, and record it on tape so that students can listen to it in sections. Periodically, the tape pauses and requires the students to complete a short exercise. This activity makes the student write statements about the story in sequential order.

DISTRIBUTION OF PRACTICE    The amount of distribution of practice depends on the attention span of the student. On the back of an activity card, the teacher can list the student's name and type of practice needed. Students with short attention spans should practice for a given period of time, such as 10, 15, or 20 minutes, and then move to a different activity. Students with longer attention spans, on the other hand, should practice until they achieve a set number of correct responses.

AMOUNT OF MATERIAL    Material amount refers to the size of the task and the number of items in the task. This amount should vary. For example, though several worksheets in math may have the same content, the teacher should make sure each sheet has a different number of items. The teacher should then number the sheets and assign them to students according to their needs at the time.

RECITATION    Recitation means practicing a new task after the teacher has removed the original lesson. For example, after reviewing a new list of vocabulary words, the student uses the words without having the list. The teacher might introduce the new word *car*, have the student find as many pictures of cars as possible, and then ask the student to use the word *car* in three simple sentences. Or, the teacher might use a tape recorder to present new words orally, and then have the student repeat sentences into the recorder.

KNOWLEDGE OF RESULTS    Instant feedback is necessary for students to know whether their responses are correct or incorrect. Computers can give immediate feedback, and self-correcting materials also provide students with a quick response to answers. Teachers may want to adapt the following suggestions for their own learning stations.

1. Provide a math problem in puzzle format so that only the correct answer completes the puzzle.
2. Put the correct response on the reverse side of activity cards.
3. Develop overlays for tests, such as fill-in-the-blank, multiple choice, or true-false.
4. Develop overlays for activities so that correct answers appear either beside the answer given by the student or on top of the student's answer.

AMOUNT OF PRACTICE    "Amount of practice is the total number of practice sessions (the time) students spend to learn a task" (Wehman & McLaughlin, 1981, p. 85). The teacher should vary materials and practice by providing a variety of activities based on the teaching of the same concept. For example, in a math acquisition station, provide many different types of activities to teach the same multiplication concept.

ORAL AND VISUAL PRESENTATIONS Teachers should present materials both orally and visually so that students grasp concepts better. Visual presentations include bulletin boards, transparencies, flashcards, TV, filmstrips, games, and pictures. Oral presentations include tape recorders, TV, radio, and recorders with earphones.

ORIENTATION AND ATTENTION "Orientation means surveying information and getting ready to respond to it. Attention is the selective scanning of information to focus on particular instances" (Wehman & McLaughlin, 1981, p. 85). Within the acquisition station, the teacher can use this principle by outlining stories, color coding important events, or underlining particular concepts or facts.

STRUCTURE Finally, teachers should organize material so that the student understands the task at hand. Before sending the student to the acquisition station to select a task, outline the activities to be used. Perhaps the teacher could prepare a brief flow chart for each activity, showing how to begin, what to do, and what to do when finished.

## LEARNING STATION FOR RETENTION

Retention is remembering over an extended period of time what has been previously taught. Basically, there are four strategies for teaching retention: overlearning, type of retention measure, instructions to recall, and reminiscence.

OVERLEARNING Overlearning means practicing beyond the point of learning a new skill, beyond acquisition. The teacher should stock the learning station for retention with numerous activities designed to reinforce the newly acquired skill.

TYPE OF RETENTION MEASURE A teacher can use different retention measures to help a student remember material. According to Blake (1974), these measures are as follows:

> *Recognition* is the selection of previously learned items from unlearned or false items, for example, a multiple-choice test.
> *Structured recall* is supplying items within a specific context, for example, essay tests and items starting with the verbs, name, list, etc.
> *Relearning* is the time or effort required to relearn previously learned material. (Blake, 1974, p. 254)

Teachers should design retention stations, then, with a specific type of retention in mind. For example, if the teacher plans to give a multiple-choice test over activities studied in the station, he or she should direct the student to recognize items and facts for an objective test.

INSTRUCTIONS TO RECALL   "Instructions to recall refers to directing the student to learn with the specific idea of recalling the material at a later time" (Wehman & McLaughlin, 1981, p. 91). Within the station, the teacher should specifically label activities and color code or underline important information that the student will need to know at a later date.

REMINISCENCE   After a long practice session and rest, the student should have an increase in performance. To plan for reminiscence, the teacher can design short check-up tests for the student to complete after rest and extended practice.

## LEARNING STATION FOR TRANSFER

Transferring means that the student takes what is learned in one situation and uses it in a second situation. Strategies for teaching transfer include intertask similarity, instructions to transfer, and overlearning.

INTERTASK SIMILARITY   This strategy shows the student the similarity between two different tasks. For example, a teacher could show the student working on manuscript writing how to move to cursive writing. Or, the teacher might show the student that multiplication is an extension of addition.

INSTRUCTIONS TO TRANSFER   Here, the teacher shows the student how learning in situation one will be useful in situation two: learning basic math facts will help the student keep a checkbook; learning certain words will transfer into pattern reading; and filling out forms directly relates to applying for a job, a driver's license, or a social security card.

OVERLEARNING   Overlearning means practice beyond the point of mastery. Care must be taken to present the same concepts within different activities or techniques. Boredom does not aid overlearning.

Figure 3.5 presents three learning stations designed for acquisition, retention, and transfer. By applying these general principles of learning to the design of learning centers, the teacher prepares a more effective physical environment for the student.

## ADVANTAGES OF LEARNING STATIONS FOR THE MAINSTREAMED STUDENT

Learning stations serve multiple purposes in instructing students. For one thing, the teacher saves time during the day because a group or an individual can work alone at the station. In addition, learning stations in mainstream classrooms have the following specific advantages:

FIGURE 3.5. Learning Stations

☐ Many students prefer to work alone, and the learning station gives them this option;

☐ Self-correcting learning stations provide immediate feedback on correct or incorrect response without embarrassment;

☐ Mainstreamed students can work at their own rates without pressure;

☐ With a variety of activities presented, students can select the most appropriate;

☐ Because students in the mainstream may work below the level of other students in the regular classroom, learning stations provide them with appropriate activities at their levels;

☐ Activities at the learning station can reinforce the objectives specified on the mainstreamed student's IEP;

☐ And finally, learning centers reinforce the modality strength of the mildly handicapped student.

For example, if the student learns better visually, the teacher can present more activities in a visual manner, but if the student learns better auditorially, the teacher can put activities on tape recorders.

## DESIGNING BULLETIN BOARDS FOR INCIDENTAL AND INTENTIONAL LEARNING

Most classrooms have at least one bulletin board. Teachers usually design bulletin boards as seasonal decoration or as special places to display work, but bulletin boards can also reflect a specific learning purpose. Bulletin boards designed for incidental learning are simply placed around the room in hope that students will pick up a little extra learning. For example, in one school the halls are painted to look like highways, street signs hang over classroom doors, and the ABC's run around the walls. It is even hard to get a drink without learning a little multiplication. As children line the halls, incidental learning takes place in every direction. Many books have ideas that teachers can use to design bulletin boards. See Figure 3.6 for examples from various academic subjects.

On the other hand, intentional learning is planned learning. Teachers can base bulletin boards on a lesson or current events. One school has a "good morning news" bulletin board for the class. The teacher broadcasts the news and each student brings an item for the bulletin board or announcements. This method uses intentional learning in a first-class form.

Teachers must adapt the learning environment before adapting instruction. But once they have prepared the master schedule, planned scheduling for resource with the best interest of the child in mind, and designed the actual physical environment of the room, they can take a close look at how to teach.

## SUMMARY

This chapter focuses on adapting the learning environment for the mildly handicapped student in the mainstream. Preparing the school environment for the

A.

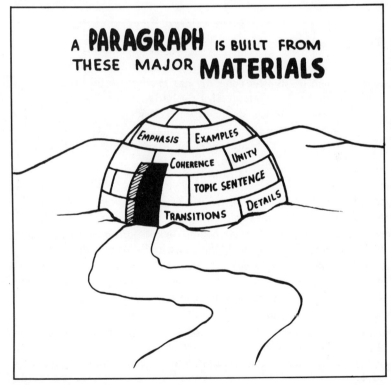

B.

FIGURE 3.6. Bulletin Board Ideas (*Note. A.* From *Science Bulletin Boards* by M. Vessel and H. Wong, 41. Copyright 1962 by Pitman Learning, Inc. Reprinted by permission. *B.* From *Language Arts Bulletin Boards* by C.G. Thompson, 42. Copyright 1967 by Pitman Learning, Inc. Reprinted by permission. *C.* From *Mathematics Bulletin Boards* by B.S. Swabb and M. Thompson, 12. Copyright 1971 by Pitman Learning, Inc. Reprinted by permission.)

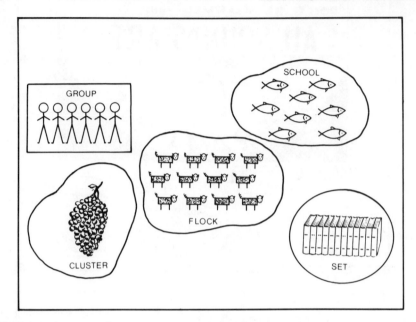

C.

FIGURE 3.6. (continued)

handicapped student's maximum learning builds a framework for presenting instruction. When the master schedule has been carefully planned, when the resource schedule has been adapted for the handicapped student, and when the physical environment has been designed with consideration for the mainstreamed student, the teacher can begin the instructional process. Chapter 4 presents an overview of learning and a triad model for adapting instruction for the handicapped student in the mainstream.

## REFERENCES

Affleck, J. Q., Lowenbraun, S., & Archer, A. *Teaching the mildly handicapped in the regular classroom.* Columbus, Ohio: Charles E. Merrill, 1980.

Blake, K. A. *Teaching the retarded.* Englewood Cliffs, N.J.: Prentice-Hall, 1974.

D'Alonzo, B. J., D'Alonzo, R. L., & Mauser, A. J. Developing resource rooms for the handicapped. *Teaching Exceptional Children,* 1979, *11*(3), 91–96.

Hart, V. *Mainstreaming children with special needs.* New York: Longman, 1981.

Kaplan, S. W., Kaplan, J. A. B., Madsen, S. K., & Taylor, B. K. *Change for children.* Pacific Palisades, Calif.: Goodyear, 1973.

Kelly, L. K. Student self-scheduling—Is it worth the risks? *NAASP Bulletin,* 1979, *63* (424), 84–91.

Lieberman, L. M. The nightmare of scheduling. *Journal of Learning* Disabilities, 1982, *15*(1). 57–58.

Piechowiak, A. B., & Cook, M. B. *Complete guide to the elementary learning center.* West Nyack, N. Y.: Parker, 1976.

Swabb, B. S., & Thompson M. *Mathematics bulletin boards*. Belmont, Calif.: Fearon Publishers, 1972.

Thompson, C. G. *Language arts bulletin boards*. Belmont, Calif.: Fearon Publishers, 1968.

Vessel, M., & Wong, H. *Science bulletin boards*. Belmont, Calif.: Fearon Publishers, 1962.

Voight, B. C. *Invitation to learning*. Washington, D.C.: Acropolis Books, 1973.

Wehman, P., & McLaughlin, P. J. *Program development in special education*. New York: McGraw-Hill, 1981.

## ADDITIONAL READING

Austin, D. B. *The high school principal and staff develop the master schedule*. New York: Bureau of Publications, 1960.

Bishop, L. K. *Individualized educational systems*. New York: Harper and Row, 1971.

Bush, R. N., & Allen, D. W. *A new design for high school education: Assuming a flexible schedule*. New York: McGraw-Hill, 1964.

Davis, H., & Bechard, J. *Flexible scheduling*. Cleveland: Educational Research Council of America, 1968.

Holzman, A. G., & Turkes, W. R. *Optimal scheduling in educational institutions*. Pittsburgh: University of Pittsburgh, 1964.

Manlove, D. C., & Beggs, D. W. III. *Flexible scheduling*. Bloomington: Indiana University Press, 1965.

Murphy, J. *School scheduling by computer—The story of GASP*. New York: Educational Facilities Laboratories, 1964.

Petrequin, G. *Individualizing learning through modular-flexible programming*. New York: McGraw-Hill, 1968.

Saville, A. *Instructional programming—Issues and innovations in school scheduling*. Columbus, Ohio: Charles E. Merrill, 1973.

Swenson, G., & Keyo, D. *Providing for flexibility in scheduling and instruction*. Englewood Cliffs, N. J.: Prentice-Hall, 1966.

Trump, L. J., & Baynham, D. *Guide to better schools: Focus on change*. Chicago: Rand McNally, 1961.

Wiley, D. W., & Bishop, L. K. *The flexibly scheduled high school*. West Nyack, N. Y.: Parker, 1968.

*Year-round school*. Washington, D.C.: American Association of School Administrators, 1960.

# Chapter Four

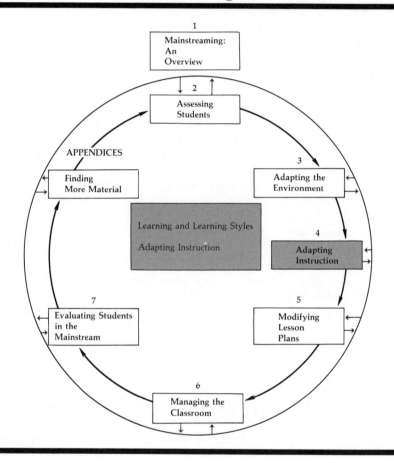

# Adapting Instruction

The teacher's major responsibility to the school, to children, and to the total community lies in instruction. Good instructional planning paves the way for an organized school day and for the smooth delivery of information vital to the academic development of children. But instead of defining instruction as only the imparting of specific content, teachers should see instruction as an ongoing process: the teacher delivers information to children who receive and assimilate it. When teachers adapt instruction to meet the needs of all children, especially mildly handicapped students in the mainsteam, they discover that they deliver information more effectively and students learn it more easily. Instruction becomes a continuous process of presenting information, adapting information, representing information, and testing for concept mastery. Making adapting a natural component of this continuum of instruction helps the mildly handicapped student succeed in the regular classroom.

This chapter presents a model for adapting instruction for mildly handicapped students in the mainstream. The first section of the chapter covers learning, learning styles, domains of learning, and task analysis for more efficient learning. This introductory section provides the background for the second section, which presents a triad model for adapting instruction at either the elementary or the secondary level. Teachers can apply the model's general ideas and suggestions to their particular classes and adapt instruction by adapting their teaching techniques, media, and presentation of academic content.

# LEARNING AND LEARNING STYLES

Students ultimately want to learn to acquire knowledge or skills. Designing and implementing effective instruction so that students learn to their fullest capacity challenges us all. If learning means the acquiring of knowledge or skills and the teacher wants to help the student acquire that learning, then the teacher needs to understand the process of learning in general. The following sections on learning styles, conditions affecting learning styles, learning domains, and task analysis will better acquaint teachers with that process.

## LEARNING STYLES

A student's individual approach to learning is his or her learning style. Knowledge of the different ways a student may approach a learning situation and awareness of the influences on these approaches pave the way for successful teaching. Charles (1980) suggests that students generally approach learning situations in one of three distinct ways: as adventurers, ponderers, or drifters. Adventurers respond quickly, are impulsive, show little concern with the way parts fit together to make a whole, and do not worry excessively about doing things the correct way or about producing incorrect answers. Ponderers are more reflective and analytic in nature and have the ability to synthesize information. A ponderer can work on a task for a long time without getting bored, but wants reassurance from authority sources about correct responses. The drifter is "more mechanical, plodding, and hesitant" (Charles, 1980, p. 68) and depends on others for motivation and initiative. Drifters work better in groups than in one-on-one situations and require reinforcement to keep working on a task.

Some mildly handicapped students may use one learning style or another, but many of them reflect a composite of the different styles. Thus, mildly handicapped students may reflect different learning styles or a composite of styles, showing once again that children learn in many different ways.

In addition to having a distinctive approach to a learning situation, the student has a cognitive style. According to Fuhrmann, "the cognitive components of learning styles are those intellectual characteristics, the functioning of which create learning. . . . Each of us develops a typical approach in our use of our cognitive characteristics to perceive, to think, and to remember. This approach constitutes our cognitive learning style" (Fuhrmann, 1980, p. 2).

Keefe (1979) places the many cognitive styles into two major categories: *"reception styles,* which deal primarily with perceiving and analyzing functions, and *concept formation and retention styles,* which deal primarily with generating hypotheses, solving problems, and remembering" (Fuhrmann, p. 6). According to Fuhrmann these two major cognitive categories "can be described by a series of continua, with an individual style being found at any point" (p. 2). See Table 4.1 for individual differences in reception and in concept formation and retention styles.

TABLE 4.1
Continua of Styles

---

| Reception |
| --- |

Field dependent ◄─────────────────────────────────► Field independent

Witkin, Goodenough, and Oltman (1977) have conducted extensive study into the degree of influence the surrounding environment has on an individual's perception. Field dependent persons are heavily influenced by the background or context in which an item is embedded. Field independent persons perceive items discretely, without being influenced by the background.

Acceptance of incongruity ◄─────────────────────► Preference for
or unreality                                       conventional ideas
                                                   and reality

Klein and his associates (1962) studied readiness to accept perceptions that differ from the conventional. People tolerant of incongruity more willingly accept the unusual, while those less tolerant resist acceptance until they have extensive data.

Receptive ◄───────────────────────────────────────► Preceptive

McKenney and Keen (1974) label *receptive* those who tend to take in raw data as it is, while *preceptives* assimilate data into preformed concepts.

Systematic ◄──────────────────────────────────────► Intuitive

McKenney and Keen also differentiate the tendency to develop ordered plans (systematic) from the tendency to develop spontaneous ideas and understandings (intuitive).

TABLE 4.1 (continued)

| Concept Formation and Retention |

Impulsive ◄─────────────────────────────────► Reflective

    Kagan (1966) labeled quick responders impulsive, slow responders reflective. Reflective thinkers tend to accomplish less than impulsives, but they are more accurate in their responses.

Focusing ◄─────────────────────────────────► Scanning

    Schlesinger (1954) describes the different ways people attend to detail in their attempts to solve problems. Focusers approach problems by narrowing their perception to intensify a solution, while scanners approach problems by broadening their perception to get a broad view. Scanners see the forest; focusers see the trees.

Broad Categorizing ◄─────────────────────────► Narrow Categorizing

    Brunner and Tajfel (1961) differentiate people by their preference for either including many items in a category to insure not leaving something out or including few items to insure excluding irrelevant items.

Abstract ◄─────────────────────────────────► Concrete

Cognitive ◄────────────────────────────────► Cognitive Simplicity

    Individual preference for complexity and abstraction vs. simplicity and concreteness has been studied by Harvey, Hunt, and Schroder (1961) and Kelly (1955). The abstractor effectively processes highly divergent, even conflicting information, while the concretizer prefers consonant information.

Leveling ◄─────────────────────────────────► Sharpening

    Gardner (1959) studied memory processing. Leveling is roughly equivalent to generalizing, the process of merging new concepts with previously assimilated ideas. Sharpening is roughly equivalent to discrimination, in which the differences of new information from old are emphasized.

*Note.* From *Models and Methods of Assessing Learning Styles* by B. S. Fuhrmann, paper prepared for the Virginia Educational Research Association, 1980. Copyright 1980 by B. S. Fuhrmann. Reprinted by permisson.

# CONDITIONS AFFECTING LEARNING STYLES

In addition to an awareness of the learning styles outlined by Charles and Fuhrmann, teachers should understand the many other conditions affecting the way children learn. The interaction between teaching and learning styles, students' perceptual styles, time, sound, seating arrangements and place, class procedures, group size, and students' attention spans—all these factors influence the learning process.

INTERACTION BETWEEN TEACHING AND LEARNING STYLES   How students respond, how well they respond, or why they do not respond at all often depends on the interaction between teaching and learning styles. Johnson (1976) describes two student learning styles, the "dependent prone" and the "independent prone," and the Fuhrmann-Jacobs model of social interaction (1980) adds a third, the "collaborative prone." A student may learn in all three styles but prefer a certain style in a certain situation. Thus, if a student prefers the dependent style for learning new information, but the teacher presents the material in the independent style, the student may not learn as quickly or as well as he or she could. Teachers should try to match their teaching styles to their students' learning styles as often as possible or to vary their teaching styles so that in any given situation, different students can use the learning style they prefer. See Table 4.2 for a description of the three learning styles and the learner needs, teacher roles, and teacher behaviors that correspond to those styles.

Usually, mildly handicapped students in a mainsteamed classroom prefer the dependent learner style. But when mainstreamed students have some information about the subject, they tend to use the collaborative style. Teachers can use the table to match their teaching styles to their students' styles, thus improving the students' chances of learning.

PERCEPTUAL STYLES   A student's perceptual style refers to the sense through which the student best receives information: visual (sight); auditory (hearing); or kinesthetic (touching). Most children tend to use one perceptual style more than the others. For example, 80 to 85 percent of all people are visual learners and so learn best when they can see the information presented, such as with lessons on the blackboard, overhead projectors, filmstrips, etc. Auditory learners, however, learn best when they can hear the information presented. Thus, a classroom teacher using the lecture method can help the visual learner by recording the lecture for the student to play back later. Kinesthetic learning means learning through touch and some students need kinesthetic feedback to learn. For example, the teacher can provide sandboxes so that students draw or trace the letters of the alphabet in the sand and get kinesthetic feedback. Teachers need to plan instruction so that it addresses the student's dominant perceptual mode or covers all the learning modes. Table 4.3 presents information about the three perceptual learning modes, the observable behaviors connected to each, and useful teaching techniques for each mode. Teachers should use this table solely as a model and expand upon the guidelines as appropriate.

TIME   Children learn better at different times of the day. For this reason teachers try to schedule academic subjects during students' most alert times. For example, most teachers would not schedule math after strenuous physical education class because students would be too tired to concentrate. And, reading instruction during the last period of the day does not benefit many children. In the secondary setting, however, teachers usually do not have the option of scheduling subjects at their most appropriate time. They can, however, be aware of time within the school day and try to adapt lesson plans accordingly.

TABLE 4.2
Learner and Teacher Descriptors

| Learner Style | Learner Needs | Teacher Role | Teacher Behavior |
|---|---|---|---|
| Dependent style may occur in introductory courses, languages, some sciences when learners have little or no information upon entering course. | Structure<br>Direction<br>External reinforcement<br>Encouragement<br>Esteem from authority | Expert<br><br>Authority | Lecturing<br>Demonstrating<br>Assigning<br>Checking<br>Encouraging<br>Testing<br>Reinforcing<br>Content transmitter<br>Grading<br>Materials designer |
| Collaborative style may occur when learners have knowledge, information, ideas and would like to share them or try them out. | Interaction<br>Practice<br>Probe myself and others<br>Observation<br>Participation<br>Peer challenge<br>Peer esteem<br>Experimentation | Co-learner<br><br>Environment setter | Interacting<br>Questioning<br>Providing resources<br>Modeling<br>Providing feedback<br>Coordinating<br>Evaluator<br>Manager<br>Process observer<br>Grader |
| Independent style may occur when learners have much more knowledge or skill upon entering the course and want to continue to search on own. May feel instructor cannot offer as much as they would like. | Internal awareness<br>Experimentation<br>Time<br>Nonjudgmental support | Facilitator | Allowing<br>Providing requested feedback<br>Consultant<br>Listener<br>Negotiator<br>Evaluator |

*Note.* From *A Practical Handbook for College Teachers* by B. S. Fuhrmann and A. F. Grasha (Boston: Little, Brown & Co., 1983), 115. Copyright 1980 by B. S. Fuhrmann and B. Jacobs. Slight modifications under "Teacher Behavior." Reprinted by permission.

TABLE 4.3
Learning Processes in the Perceptual Modes

| Pupil Strengths | Pupil Weaknesses | Teacher Formal Assessment Techniques | Teacher Informal Assessment Techniques | Instructional Techniques |
|---|---|---|---|---|
| | | Auditory Modality | | |
| Follow oral instructions very easily. | Lose place in visual activities. | Present statement verbally; ask pupil to repeat. | Observe pupil reading with the use of finger or pencil as a marker. | Reading: Stress phonetic analysis; avoid emphasis on sight vocabulary or fast reading. Allow pupils to use fingers, etc., to keep places. |
| Do well in tasks requiring phonetic analysis. | Read word by word. | Tap auditory pattern beyond pupil's point of vision. Ask pupil to repeat pattern. | Observe whether pupil whispers or barely produces sounds to correspond to reading task. | |
| Appear brighter than tests show. | Reverse words when reading. | | | Arithmetic: Provide audio tapes of story problems. Verbally explain arithmetic processes as well as demonstrate. |
| | Make visual discrimination errors. | Provide pupil with several words in a rhyming family. Ask pupil to add more. | Observe pupil who has difficulty following purely visual directions. | |
| Sequence speech sounds with facility. | Have difficulty with written work; poor motor skill. | Present pupil with sounds produced out of field of vision. Ask if they are the same or different. | | Spelling: Build on syllabication skills, use sound clues. |
| Perform well verbally. | Have difficulty copying from the blackboard. | | | Generally: Use work-sheets with large unhampered areas. Use lined widespaced paper. Allow for verbal rather than written response. |

TABLE 4.3 (continued)

| Pupil Strengths | Pupil Weaknesses | Teacher Formal Assessment Techniques | Teacher Informal Assessment Techniques | Instructional Techniques |
|---|---|---|---|---|
| | | Visual Modality | | |
| Possess good sight vocabulary. | Have difficulty with oral directions. | Give lists of words which sound alike. Ask pupil to indicate if they are the same or different. | Observe pupil in task requiring sound discrimination, i.e., rhyming, sound blending. | Reading: Avoid phonetic emphasis; stress sight vocabulary, configuration clues, context clues. |
| Demonstrate rapid reading skills. | Ask "what are we supposed to do?" immediately after oral instructions are given. | Ask pupil to follow specific instructions. Begin with one direction and continue with multiple instructions. | Observe pupil's sight vocabulary skills. Pupil should exhibit good sight vocabulary skills. | Arithmetic: Show examples of arithmetic function. |
| Skim reading material. | Appear confused with great deal of auditory stimuli. | Show visually similar pictures. Ask pupil to indicate whether they are the same or different. | Observe to determine if pupil performs better when able to see stimulus. | Spelling: Avoid phonetic analysis; stress structural clues configuration clues. |
| Read well from picture clues. | Have difficulty discriminating between words with similar sounds. | Show pupil a visual pattern, i.e., block design or pegboard design. Ask pupil to duplicate. | | Generally: Allow a pupil with strong auditory skills to act as visual child's partner. Allow for written rather than verbal response. |
| Follow visual diagrams and other visual instructions well. | | | | |
| Score well on group tests. | | | | |
| Perform nonverbal tasks well. | | | | |

## Tactilekinesthetic Modality

| Characteristics | | Assessment | | Teaching Suggestions |
|---|---|---|---|---|
| Exhibit good fine and gross motor balance. | Since tactilekinesthetic is usually a secondary modality, pupil depends on the guiding or preferred modality. | Ask pupil to walk balance beam or along a painted line. | Observe pupil in athletic tasks. | Reading: Stress the shape and structure of a word; use configuration clues, sandpaper letters, and/or words. |
| Exhibit good rhythmic movements. | | Set up obstacle course involving gross motor manipulation. | Observe pupil maneuvering in classroom space. | |
| Demonstrate neat handwriting skills. | Weakness may be in either the visual or auditory mode. | Have pupil cut along straight, angled, and curved lines. | Observe pupil's spacing of written work on a paper. | Arithmetic: Use objects in performing the arithmetic functions, provide buttons, packages of sticks, etc. |
| Demonstrate good cutting skills. | | Ask child to color fine areas. | Observe pupil's selection of activities during free play—does pupil select puzzles or blocks as opposed to records or picture books? | Spelling: Have pupil write word in large movements, i.e., in air, on chalkboard, on newsprint; use manipulative letters to spell the word. Call pupil's attention to feel of the word. Have pupil write word in cursive to get feel of the word by flowing motion. |
| Manipulate puzzles and other materials well. | | | | |
| Identify and match objects easily. | | | | |

*Note.* From *Teaching Children with Special Needs: Elementary Level* (Owings Mills, Md.: Maryland State Department of Education, Division of Instructional Television). Copyright by Maryland State Department of Education, Division of Instructional Television. Reprinted by permission.

SOUND   The amount and intensity of sound also affect students' learning styles. Many students prefer quiet surroundings, and background or classroom noises interfere with their learning. Teachers may need to place children easily distracted by sounds, as many mildly handicapped children are, in quiet places, such as learning centers, and give them earphones that filter noise. Smaller classes lower noise levels, and study carrels also provide a quiet area for learning. Teachers can make carrels from various types of materials; wooden dividers, fabric tightly stretched between frames, or egg cartons stapled together all provide functional and attractive carrels.

SEATING ARRANGEMENTS   When students first come into class, where do they sit? Do they return to the same places the next day? Teachers attending a class or meeting prefer certain places—by the window, next to the door, on the front row, in the back of the room, etc.—and children also have such seating preferences. Teachers should try to provide students with a seating arrangement flexible enough for variety but structured enough for consistency. Some students lose interest in assigned tasks when they sit in the same seats day after day. Some possible variations are: sitting on small mats on the floor, taking students to the library for class, or going outside for the lecture. One secondary school, for example, provides learning stations under the trees and uses logs for seating. Teachers then register for outside stations at the times they want.

When adapting classroom seating arrangements for mildly handicapped students, the teacher must consider any special needs the children may have. Also, many mildly handicapped students are easily distracted and need to be placed close to the teacher.

CLASS PROCEDURES   Class procedures based on the teacher's awareness of students' various learning styles are more effective. Matching assignments to learning styles, such as assigning students to projects, library work, reports, seat work, or learning centers, is important, especially since the average class assignment is usually too difficult for the mildly handicapped student. The teacher can divide the same assignment into several short segments and use a variety of techniques for presenting the information. Class evaluation procedures also should vary according to learning styles. A teacher can evaluate a mildly handicapped student's work, for example, by simply observing, collecting work samples, or using formative evaluation procedures. Matching the evaluation procedure to the student's learning style helps the teacher evaluate instructional objectives as well as appropriately evaluate the student.

Class procedures must also take into account the emotional aspects of learning styles. Fuhrmann (1980) eloquently summarizes Dunn, Dunn, and Price's (1979) work on these emotional elements: motivation, persistence, responsibility, and structure.

A teacher need only give requirements and resources to highly motivated students, but poorly motivated students need special attention to bring out their interest and desire to learn. For example, a student poorly motivated by a traditional lecture class may be highly motivated by a programmed text or small discussion group.

The same length and type of assignment is probably not appropriate for all students, because both attention span and persistence vary so greatly. Furthermore, persistence is related to motivation: the more motivated a student is to achieve in a particular learning experience, the more persistent he or she is likely to be in completing the task. Sequenced learning tasks, with clearly defined steps and a final goal, offer the teacher some flexibility in meeting the needs of students with differing degrees of persistence.

Like motivated students, responsible students need only clear assignments and resources. Irresponsible students, however, often experience failure and discouragement in such an environment. Usually students lacking responsibility have historically failed to achieve in school and therefore lack the confidence to assume responsibility. Teachers must attend first to their lack of confidence by assuring them small successes: individualizing assignments, breaking objectives into smaller components, trying experimental assignments, and using all types of learning aids and resources may encourage such students.

Students also differ in their response to structure, to the specific rules and directions they must follow to achieve certain objectives. The more creative often like a wide variety of options from which to choose, while the less creative may respond better to a single, well-defined method. Again, the emotional elements are related to one another, since the more motivated, persistent, and responsible students require less structure than do the less motivated, less persistent, and less responsible. (p. 17)

Teachers, therefore, need to make assignments, instruct, evaluate students, and carry out various other class procedures on the basis of what they can determine about their students' learning styles and the emotional factors contributing to those styles.

GROUP SIZE    The group size most effective for instruction varies according to the different learning styles of students and the content and purpose of the instruction. Some students learn better in small groups, some in large groups, whereas others learn best on a one-to-one basis. Careful analysis of student performance helps the teacher select the most appropriate method, but most mildly handicapped students do not function well in large groups, very small groups and one-to-one instruction usually work more effectively with them.

ATTENTION SPAN    Although every student has a different attention span, many mildly handicapped students have short ones. Thus, teachers in the mainstream should vary teaching techniques and activities accordingly. In fact, teachers who match task to attention span find that students master tasks at a faster rate.

For example, a teacher can divide a math lesson for a student with a short attention span into working problems at the desk, completing additional problems at the board, and going to the learning center to continue with the same math skill but in a different setting. Teachers should first evaluate tasks according to the type of attention span required to complete them and then adapt the tasks and the delivery of them to the variations of attention spans within the classroom.

## DOMAINS OF LEARNING

After teachers understand students' various learning styles and how certain conditions affect those styles, they need to know about the three domains or taxonomies of learning: cognitive, affective, and psychomotor. Instruction falls into one of these three domains and then into one of several levels within each domain. Teachers, to know their instructional domain and level, should consult Table 4.4, which presents the major levels of the three taxonomies as constructed by Bloom (1956), Krathwohl, Bloom, and Masia (1964), and Dave (1970).

A teacher's instructional objectives fall into a specific level of one of the taxonomy structures. Usually, teachers teach in the cognitive domain. Teachers should determine the student's present level within the cognitive domain and begin teaching at that level. For example, if an English teacher presents a unit

TABLE 4.4
Major Levels of Cognitive, Affective, and Psychomotor Domains

| Level | Objective | Description |
|---|---|---|
| | | Cognitive |
| Basic (low) | Knowledge | The learner can recall information (i.e., bring to mind the appropriate material). |
| | Comprehension | The learner understands what is being communicated by making use of the communication. |
| | Application | The learner uses abstractions (e.g., ideas) in particular and concrete situations. |
| | Analysis | The learner can break down a communication into its constituent elements or parts. |
| | Synthesis | The learner puts together elements or parts to form a whole. |
| Advanced (high) | Evaluation | The learner makes judgments about the value of material or methods for a given purpose. |

TABLE 4.4 (continued)

| Level | Objective | Description |
|---|---|---|
| **Affective** | | |
| Basic (low) | Receiving (or Attending) | The learner is sensitized to the existence of certain phenomena or stimuli. |
| | Responding | The learner does something with or about the phenomenon beyond merely perceiving it. |
| | Valuing | The learner believes that a thing, behavior, or phenomenon has worth. |
| | Organization | The learner arranges internalized value into a system of priorities. |
| Advanced (high) | Characterization (or Value complex) | The learner organizes the value hierarchy into an internally consistent system. |
| **Psychomotor** | | |
| Basic (low) | Imitation | The learner begins to make an imitation (i.e., copy) when exposed to a behavior. |
| | Manipulation | The learner performs an act according to instructions. |
| | Precision | The learner performs an act independent of a model or instructions. |
| | Articulation | The learner coordinates a series of acts by establishing appropriate sequences and harmony. |
| Advanced (high) | Naturalization | The learner acts automatically and spontaneously with the least amount of energy. |

Note. From *Disturbed Students: Characteristics and Educational Strategies* by H.L. Rich (Baltimore: University Park Press, 1982), 229-230. Copyright 1982. Reprinted by permission. Original material adapted from *Taxonomy of Educational Objectives: The Classification of Educational Goals, Handbook I: Cognitive Domain* edited by B.S. Bloom et al. (New York: Longman, Inc., 1956), Copyright © 1956 by Longman, Inc.; *Taxonomy of Educational Objectives: The Classification of Educational Goals, Handbook II: Affective Domain* edited by D.R. Krathwohl et al. (New York: Longman, Inc., 1964), Copyright © 1964 by Longman, Inc.; and *Taxonomy of Educational Objectives: Psychomotor Domain* by R.H. Dave (New Delhi, India: National Institute of Education, 1970), Copyright © 1970 by the National Institute of Education. Reprinted by permission of the publishers.

on sentence writing (synthesis) and a mildly handicapped student learning the parts of speech (knowledge) is mainstreamed into the class, the teacher must switch to the knowledge level for that student. The student's present level determines where the teacher should begin teaching. Table 4.5 presents the cognitive domain's levels and explains how each level relates to the mildly handicapped student.

TABLE 4.5
Cognitive Domain and the Mildly Handicapped Student

| Level | Considerations for the Mildly Handicapped Student |
|---|---|
| Knowledge | If the teacher uses a variety of teaching methods and adapts content, mildly handicapped students can succeed at this level. Long-term retention may be difficult. |
| Comprehension | Most mildly handicapped students can comprehend information. Repetition may be necessary. Concrete rather than abstract information is easier to comprehend. Children with comprehension problems need special assistance. |
| Application | Applying concrete information rather than abstract is easier for students. Hands-on teaching and functional uses of information makes application easier for students. |
| Analysis | Use whole-part-whole teaching method. Make analysis concrete by letting mildly handicapped students see or touch the division of whole into parts. |
| Synthesis | Use whole-part-whole teaching method. Make synthesis concrete by letting mildly handicapped students see or touch the combining of parts into a whole. |
| Evaluation | Most difficult level for many mildly handicapped students. Evaluation in life situations is a natural teaching approach here. |

## TASK ANALYSIS

Special education teachers use a model similar to Bloom's domains of learning, a model referred to as task analysis. According to Wehman and McLaughlin (1981), task analysis "provides an instructional sequence and allows for the presentation of materials in small chunks" (p. 60). Educators break a concept or skill down into small steps and place the steps in sequential order. In applying the task analysis model, the regular classroom teacher uses the same principle underlying Bloom's domain of cognitive learning: the teacher identifies the specific skill being taught and breaks the skill down into steps, from the easiest to the most difficult. Table 4.6 shows how a task analysis works: learning how to use the dictionary has been broken down into 14 steps.

A mildly handicapped student with no dictionary skills would have difficulty beginning with step 10 in the task analysis sequence, but because the task has been broken down into such small steps, the teacher can begin where the student presently functions, be it step one or higher. When teaching a concept

TABLE 4.6
Task Analysis of Dictionary Skill

| | |
|---|---|
| TA-1 | Given five books, including a dictionary, the student will point to and state the function of the dictionary. |
| TA-2 | Given directions to say the alphabet, the student will recite it in proper sequence. |
| TA-3 | Given a random selection of ten letters, the student will arrange them in alphabetical order. |
| TA-4 | Given a list of not more than ten words, beginning with different letters, the students will write the words in alphabetical order. |
| TA-5 | Given a list of not more than ten words, beginning with the same first letter, the student will write the words in alphabetical order. |
| TA-6 | Given a list of not more than ten words beginning with the same first two letters, the student will write the words in alphabetical order. |
| TA-7 | Shown a dictionary page, the student will point to and state the function of the guide words. |
| TA-8 | Shown a dictionary page, the student will point to and state the function of the entry words. |
| TA-9 | Given oral directions to state the meaning of the word "definition," the student will do so. |
| TA-10 | Given a list of two guide words and a list of entry words, the student will write those entry words that come between the two guide words. |
| TA-11 | Given a list of entry words and a dictionary, the student will write the page number on which the entry word is found. |
| TA-12 | Shown an entry word in a dictionary, the student will state the number of definitions listed for that word. |
| TA-13 | Given a list of entry words and a dictionary, the student will find the words and write definitions for each word. |
| TA-14 | Given a sentence containing a specific word, the student will write the definitions of the word as used in that sentence. |

Note. From "Reading Competency #6a–Gets Information From Resource Material: Dictionary" in *Basic Skills Sequence in English* (Montpelier, Vt.: Vermont State Department of Education, Division of Special Education and Pupil Personnel Services), 10. Copyright by Vermont State Department of Education, Division of Special Education and Pupil Personnel Services. Reprinted by permission.

or skill in a specific academic area, teachers need to analyze the skill and decide whether or not the student has the prerequisite skills for learning it. If teachers think the student is ready to learn the new skill, then they need to examine the skill further to see if they can organize it into sequential steps. Breaking a new task into small, sequential steps makes learning easier for the mildly handicapped student.

However, if teachers see that a student does not complete or understand the task assigned, they must review the way they present the material. Perhaps they are still at a level above the student's ability range, or perhaps the skill should be broken down into even smaller parts. Once teachers understand students' learning styles and learning levels, have decided on what skill to teach, and have broken that skill down into small steps, they can teach the skill using the triad model for adapting instruction.

## ADAPTING INSTRUCTION

Teaching involves showing a learner how to do something or providing the learner with knowledge. However, one can also think of the teaching process as a three-part model: the teaching technique, the media used, and the presentation of specific academic content. Each of these parts can be adapted for the mildly handicapped student in the mainstream.

## ADAPTING TEACHING TECHNIQUE

A teaching technique or strategy is a method of imparting knowledge, skills, or concepts to a learner. A history of education shows that colleges and universities have recommended various teaching techniques to educators, who in turn have used those techniques in public and private schools. How teachers teach and what type or types of strategies they employ depend greatly on previous training, models observed, areas of interest, value judgments, and common sense. According to Jarolimek and Foster (1981), "there is a great deal of disagreement, even among well-informed persons, about what constitutes good

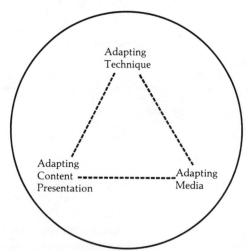

FIGURE 4.1. Triad Model for Adapting Instruction

teaching and how teaching should take place" (p. 109). The following section, then, does not try to teach teachers how to teach, but simply presents a variety of teaching techniques that teachers can use in different situations. Teachers will find that they can modify many of these techniques for the mildly handicapped. More specifically, this section covers adapting instruction within three major teaching techniques: mastery learning, teaching modes, and Bloom's taxonomy.

MASTERY LEARNING    Mastery learning, a term first used by Bloom (1968), provides the learner with immediate feedback from the teacher and a process for making corrections when necessary. According to Guskey (1981), the mandates of Public Law 94-142 emphasize individualizing instruction for the handicapped student. The move to individualize, however, can increase managerial problems within the classroom. The diversity of students' abilities, demands placed on teachers for learner outcomes, increased class sizes due to economic constraints, and demands for new instructional skills, are all pressures that can be eased by using one instructional strategy—mastery learning.

Bloom says that the teaching and evaluation process needs "some sort of 'feedback and corrective' procedure," a way of monitoring student progress so that teachers can "certify competent learners," "diagnose individual learning difficulties (feedback)," and "prescribe specfic remediation procedures (correctives) . . . . When the student does not understand a concept or makes an error, the ideal tutor first identifies the error, then re-explains the concept from a different perspective or in a different manner, and finally checks the student again before moving on" (Guskey, p. 12).

According to Guskey, mastery teaching has three major steps. First, the teacher divides a year's or semester's material into small segments or units. Pacing of the units is left up to the teacher. Second, instruction begins and an evaluation is conducted. And third, test questions are carefully designed to test only the units taught. If the student answers any questions incorrectly, he or she consults the key: alternative sources for further instruction and for finding the correct answer accompany each test question.

Through this systematic correction of missed questions, students master more of the material. Mastery learning works well with mildly handicapped students because it allows the teacher to individualize instruction within the group setting of the regular classroom. Table 4.7 presents the three steps of mastery learning and suggests ways to adapt or apply each step in the mainstreamed classroom.

ADAPTING TECHNIQUES CORRELATED WITH SPECIFIC MODES    Jarolimek and Foster (1981) say that there are four major teaching modes: the expository mode, the inquiry mode, the demonstration mode, and the activity mode (Table 4.8). Each mode has specific teaching techniques common to it, and teachers can adapt or modify all these techniques for their mainstreamed students.

TABLE 4.7
Adapting Mastery Learning for the Mainstream

| Steps in Mastery Learning | Possible Adaptations for the Regular Classroom Teacher |
|---|---|
| Step 1—Divide material into units or objectives for teaching. | Select teaching objectives on instructional level of student. |
| | Select units on student's interest level. |
| | Consult with special education teacher about units or objectives the handicapped students may be unable to complete. |
| Step 2—Begin instruction. Conduct evaluation. | Determine prerequisite skills needed before teaching objective. |
| | Use task analysis to break down objectives. |
| | Consider different teaching techniques for objectives. |
| | Note student's learning style. |
| | Assign tutors to assist student in learning objectives. |
| | Use alternative grouping procedures. (See Chapter 3.) |
| | Adapt evaluation process. (See Chapter 7.) |
| Step 3—Students check test questions missed and go to key to find additional resources for relearning missed items. | Be sure students were able to answer test questions: could they read the test, did they understand the directions, did the test questions need modification? |
| | Assist students in finding supplementary resources for missed test questions. |
| | Before student begins remedial work, assess material: is it on student's instructional level? |
| | Be sure student understands what to do. |
| | Assign peer tutor to mainstreamed student for reading material, answering questions, etc. |

Teaching in the expository mode centers around the "concept *exposition*, which means most simply to provide an explanation" (Jarolimek and Foster, 1981, p. 110). This mode, probably the most popular among educators, requires extensive directive teaching. The class focuses on the teacher, who explains or disseminates the information, and students are involved only minimally. See Table 4.9.

TABLE 4.8
Specific Techniques Used in Various Teaching Modes

| Expository Mode | Inquiry Mode | Demonstration Mode | Activity Mode |
| --- | --- | --- | --- |
| Lecture | Asking questions | Experiments | Role playing |
| Telling | Stating hypotheses | Exhibits | Construction |
| Sound filmstrip | Coming to | Simulation | Preparing exhibits |
| Explanation | conclusions | and games | Dramatizing |
| Panels | Interpreting | Modeling | Processing |
| Recitation | Classifying | Field trips | Group work |
| Audio recording | Self-directed study | | |
| Motion pictures | Testing hypotheses | | |
| Discussion | Observing | | |
| | Synthesizing | | |

Note. Adapted from "Specific Methods Associated with Various Modes of Teaching" in *Teaching and Learning in the Elementary School*, 2nd ed., by J. Jarolimek and C. D. Foster (New York: Macmillan Publishing Co., Inc., 1981), 131–132. Copyright © 1981, by Macmillan Publishing Co., Inc. Reprinted by permission.

The inquiry mode involves "asking questions, seeking information, and carrying on an investigation" (Jarolimek and Foster, 1981, p. 116). Basically, the inquiry mode of teaching follows five steps: "1) defining a problem, 2) proposing hypotheses, 3) collecting data, 4) evaluating evidence, and 5) making a conclusion" (p. 116). The teacher's guidance is still important, but the inquiry mode allows for more teacher-pupil interaction and encourages a team approach to teaching (Table 4.10). For mildly handicapped students, however, the teacher often needs to provide some additional structure.

Essential components of the demonstration mode are "showing, doing and telling" (Jarolimek and Foster, p. 120). The demonstration mode, like the expository mode, depends on directive teaching and is discussed in Table 4.11. Because this method presents information in a concrete way, it is essential that teachers use it in instructing mainstreamed students.

The activity mode of teaching "can best be described as a set of strategies that involve pupils in learning by doing things that are, for the pupils, meaningfully related to the topic under study" (Jarolimek and Foster, p. 127). This method of teaching is best described by an old Indian proverb "I hear and I forget, I see and I remember, I do and I understand." Teachers using the activity mode provide students with actual experience and thus a clearer understanding of concepts (Table 4.12).

BLOOM'S TAXONOMIES OF LEARNING   As teachers teach, they basically deliver information, require students to learn the information, and ask questions from one of the six levels of Bloom's cognitive taxonomy to see if students have retained the information. See Table 4.13 for a review of these levels.

Teachers often use various teaching methods without realizing that specific techniques may dictate taxonomy levels and that a particular taxonomy level

TABLE 4.9
Alternative Teaching Techniques for Expository Mode

| Teaching Techniques | Alterations or Modifications for Mainstreamed Students |
|---|---|
| Lecture | • Provide lecture outlines<br>• Provide copy of lecture notes<br>• Use transparencies to provide visual presentation simultaneously with lecture |
| Telling | • Be specific in information given<br>• Be sure you have student's attention<br>• For students with short attention spans, give information in small segments |
| Sound filmstrip | • Provide visuals when possible<br>• Give earphones to students easily distracted by sounds |
| Explanation | • Keep simple and direct<br>• Give in simple declarative sentences<br>• Provide outline of explanation |
| Audio recording | • Present with visuals<br>• Give earphones to students easily distracted by sounds |
| Motion pictures | • Orient to movie before showing<br>• Be sure length is appropriate<br>• Place students with auditory problems close to sound<br>• Review main points of film<br>• Provide brief outline of main points |
| Discussion | • Ask questions you know students can answer<br>• Keep discussions short<br>• As points are made, list on board or transparency<br>• Divide class into groups for brief discussions |

may be too difficult for the mildly handicapped student. Teachers need to understand that some techniques can be used only at certain taxonomy levels, whereas other techniques can be adapted so that they reach various levels. Table 4.14 presents the six taxonomy levels with corresponding teaching techniques for each level. Possible modifications are sometimes suggested.

A natural part of instruction is asking questions. Teachers ask questions to assess student attention and comprehension, but they need to realize that questions also reflect taxonomy levels. Adapting instruction for students in the mainstream involves knowing the level of one's questions and changing that level if necessary. Questions directed to mainstreamed students should relate to their specific levels of learning. For example, if the teacher asks a main-

TABLE 4.10
Alternative Teaching Techniques for Inquiry Mode

| Teaching Techniques | Alterations or Modifications for Mainstreamed Students |
|---|---|
| Asking questions | • Ask questions on appropriate level of taxonomy scale; vary questions to meet different taxonomy levels of students<br>• Call student's name before directing a question to him or her<br>• Do not embarrass students by asking questions they cannot answer |
| Stating hypotheses | • Have students choose from two of three hypotheses instead of having to formulate their own |
| Coming to conclusions | • Present alternative conclusions |
| Interpreting | • Assign peer tutor to help<br>• Present alternative interpretations |
| Classifying | • Use concrete instead of abstract concepts |
| Self-directed study | • Give specific directions about what to do<br>• Make directions short, simple, and few<br>• Collect and place resources for study in one area |
| Testing hypotheses | • Assign peer tutor to help |
| Observing | • Give explicit directions about how to and what to observe<br>• Provide sequential check list of what will happen so student sees steps<br>• Have student check off each step observed |
| Synthesizing | • Assign peer tutor to help<br>• Provide model of whole |

streamed student whether a particular story may produce negative feelings toward a certain cultural group (evaluation level), the student may be confused and unable to respond. See Table 4.15 for sample questions from the six taxonomy levels.

## ADAPTING MEDIA

As teachers adapt their teaching techniques to meet their students' various learning styles, they can enhance their teaching even further by using media or adapting the media they already use. The following section on adapting media presents information on using computers in the mainstream and suggests adaptations of other selected media.

TABLE 4.11
Alternative Teaching Techniques for Demonstration Mode

| Teaching Techniques | Alterations or Modifications for Mainstreamed Students |
|---|---|
| Experiments | • Provide sequential directions<br>• Have student check off each completed step<br>• If teacher demonstrates, let student assist<br>• Be sure student fully understands purpose, procedures, and expected outcome of experiment<br>• Set up incidental learning experience |
| Exhibits | • Assign projects according to students' instructional level<br>• Have student select project topic from a short list<br>• Provide directions and list of materials needed<br>• Be sure project *does not* require skills student lacks<br>• Have students display their exhibits |
| Simulations | • Do not embarrass students by requiring them to do something they cannot do<br>• Make sure student understands directions, terms used, and expected outcome |
| Games | • Design games in which acquisition of skills, not winning, is the priority<br>• Make directions simple<br>• Highlight important directions with color codes<br>• With peer tutor, let student prepare own game<br>• Design games, emphasize skills needed by student |
| Modeling | • Model only one step at a time<br>• Use task analysis on steps<br>• Use visual models when possible |
| Field trips | • Prepare students by explaining destination, purpose, expected behavior, and schedule. |

TABLE 4.12
Alternative Teaching Techniques for Activity Mode

| Teaching Techniques | Alterations or Modifications for Mainstreamed Students |
|---|---|
| Role playing | • Be sure student understands role<br>• Short lines or no lines at all may be best<br>• Respect privacy of student who does not want role<br>• Let such a student assist another role player |
| Constructing | • Select project for students or have them select from a short list<br>• Try to use projects that include special education objectives<br>• Provide sequential checklist |

TABLE 4.12 (continued)

| Teaching Techniques | Alterations or Modifications for Mainstreamed Students |
|---|---|
| Preparing exhibits | • Assign peer tutor to help<br>• Use alterations suggested under Constructing |
| Dramatizing | • Respect privacy of those who do not want parts<br>• Let such students help others prepare sets, etc. |
| Processing | • Clearly state steps<br>• Make steps sequential and short |
| Group work | • Assign peer tutor<br>• Select activity student can succeed in<br>• Use variety of grouping procedures (See Chapter 3) |

TABLE 4.13
Bloom's Cognitive Taxonomy

| Knowledge | Requires memory only, repeating information exactly as memorized (define, recall, recognize, remember, who, what, where, when). |
|---|---|
| Comprehension | Requires rephrasing, rewording, and comparing information (describe, compare, contrast, rephrase, put in your own words, explain the main idea). |
| Application | Requires application of knowledge to determine a single correct answer (apply, classify, choose, employ, write an example, solve, how many, which, what is). |
| Analysis | • Identify motives or causes<br>• Draw conclusions<br>• Determine evidence (support, analyze, conclude, why) |
| Synthesis | • Make predictions<br>• Produce original communications<br>• Solve problems (with more than one possible answer) (predict, produce, write, design, develop, synthesize, construct, how can we improve, what happens if, how can we solve, can you devise) |
| Evaluation | • Make judgments<br>• Offer opinions (judge, argue, validate, decide, evaluate, assess, give your opinion, which is better, do you agree, would it be better) |

Note. From "Review of the Taxonomy" in *Classroom Teaching Skills: A Workbook* by J. M. Cooper, J. Hansen, P. H. Martorella, G. Morine-Dershimer, D. Sadker, M. Sadker, S. Sokolve, R. Shostak, T. Ten Brink, and W. A. Weber (Lexington, Mass.: D. C. Heath and Co., 1977), 118. Copyright 1977 by D.C. Heath and Co. Reprinted by permission. Original material adapted from *Taxonomy of Educational Objectives: The Classification of Educational Goals, Handbook I: Cognitive Domain* edited by B.S. Bloom et al. (New York: Longman, Inc.), Copyright © 1956 by Longman, Inc. Reprinted by permission of the publisher.

TABLE 4.14
Teaching Techniques and Their Taxonomy Levels°

| Teaching Technique | Knowledge | Comprehension | Application | Analysis | Synthesis | Evaluation |
|---|---|---|---|---|---|---|
| Unit teaching<br>  Excellent technique for including all<br>  levels of students. | X | * | * | * | * | * |
| Spelling bees<br>  Can be adapted for mildly handicapped<br>  students.<br>  Use mainstreamed student as<br>  scorekeeper or to provide feedback<br>  on responses. | X | | | | | |
| Language experience approach<br>  Good technique for nonreaders or<br>  those students below reading levels.<br>  Assists in group instruction allowing<br>  for individualization.<br>  Teaches language by having students<br>  relate events that teacher records, in<br>  writing, and then students read. | X | X | * | * | * | * |
| Projects<br>  May be adapted to interest and<br>  instructional level of student. Good<br>  for pairing students with peer<br>  helpers. | X | X | X | * | * | * |

Kinesthetic learning
: An excellent technique for mainstreamed students. Involves touch. Examples: use sand, salt, sugar for tracing letters of the alphabet. Paste yarn on letters or letter combinations for tracing with finger as student says sound.

Learning centers
: Learning centers are specific areas set aside in room for enhancing instruction of a skill or concept. Activities can range from a low taxonomy level to a high level. Be sure to identify activities appropriate for mainstreamed student's instructional level.

Rote learning
: May be modified for interest purposes. Use transparencies, flash cards, word games, etc. to vary approach to rote learning.

Discovery learning
: Student is allowed freedom in finding expected outcomes to a problem.

Lectures
: Lectures can be modified by providing visual and auditory presentations simultaneously with lecture.

| Method | | | | | | |
|---|---|---|---|---|---|---|
| Kinesthetic learning | X | X | * | * | * | * |
| Learning centers | X | * | * | * | * | * |
| Rote learning | X | | | | | |
| Discovery learning | X | X | X | X | X | X |
| Lectures | X | X | * | * | * | * |

TABLE 4.14 (continued)

| Teaching Technique | Knowledge | Comprehension | Application | Analysis | Synthesis | Evaluation |
|---|---|---|---|---|---|---|
| Brainstorming<br>A technique that allows students to present as many ideas on a topic as they can think of. | X | X | * | * | * | * |
| Modeling or demonstrations<br>An excellent technique for mildly handicapped students.<br>May be used in group work with different learning objectives for different levels of students. | X | * | * | * | * | * |
| Seat work<br>May be individualized for each student within classroom. | X | * | * | * | * | * |

[a]X—required level of learning.
*—may be extended to these levels.

TABLE 4.15
Sample Questions by Taxonomy Levels

| Taxonomy Level | Sample Questions |
|---|---|
| Knowledge | 1. What is the largest city in America?<br>2. Who is the secretary of state?<br>3. Who wrote *Macbeth*?<br>4. From what country does the United States import most of its tin? |
| Comprehension | 1. What is the main idea of this short story?<br>2. Compare socialism and capitalism.<br>3. What is the meaning of this cartoon?<br>4. In your own words, explain what your textbook suggests were the main causes of the Civil War. |
| Application | 1. According to our definition of imagery, which of the following passages contains an example of imagery?<br>2. You have been given an algebraic equation to solve. Which of the following answers is correct?<br>3. We have studied the rule concerning the placement of a comma after an introductory adverbial clause. Write and punctuate a sentence that illustrates this rule.<br>4. Give an example of the rule of supply and demand. |
| Analysis | 1. Why do many school children indicate they have lost respect for the office of the presidency?<br>2. What evidence can you find to support the statement that Oedipus is a tragic hero?<br>3. Analyze Abraham Lincoln's delivery of the Gettysburg Address, and indicate what you think are the key elements in his oratory style.<br>4. After considering the following evidence, what is your conclusion about the case? |
| Synthesis | 1. Write a short story that has war as its central theme.<br>2. What ways can you think of by which we might prevent a war from ever occurring again?<br>3. If there were never another war, how do you think human beings might change?<br>4. Create a picture that expresses your feelings about war. |
| Evaluation | 1. Do you think your textbooks express prejudice against any minority group?<br>2. Which of these two books do you consider to be the better one?<br>3. What is your opinion of the judge's ruling in this court case?<br>4. How would you evaluate this teacher? |

*Note:* From *Classroom Teaching Skills: A Workbook,* James M. Cooper, gen. ed. (Lexington, Mass.: D. C. Heath and Co., 1977), 118–119. Copyright © 1977 by D. C. Heath and Co. Used by permission of the publisher.

COMPUTER INSTRUCTION FOR MAINSTREAMED STUDENTS    A 1981 survey conducted by the U.S. Department of Education determined that approximately one-half of our nation's school districts provide students with access to at least one microcomputer or computer terminal (Coburn, Kelman, Roberts, Snyder, Watt, & Weiner, 1982). Thus, computers are rapidly becoming an integral part of American education. Melmed (1982) predicts that by the year 1990, elementary and secondary students will have access to a computer on the average of thirty minutes each day. Melmed also points out that such technology allows educators to provide more appropriately designed instruction to meet the backgrounds and needs of individuals. Computer technology may enable regular educators to actually meet the part of Public Law 94-142 that says all children with learning problems should receive an education that meets their individual needs. No matter what the children's category or disability, they should receive efficiently delivered and effectively coordinated multi- and interdisciplinary instruction.

J. S. Bruner's theory of instruction points out the need for individualized educational programming for mildly handicapped students. Bruner (1968) believes that mental growth is not a gradual accumulation. Rather, he compares such growth to a staircase with landings—periods of "spurts" in mental growth followed by "rests" (p. 27). He further explains that the spurts depend on the student's development of various capacities, which themselves must often be nurtured by others. For Bruner, the "steps are not clearly linked to age: some environments can slow the sequence down or bring it to a halt, others move it along faster" (p. 27).

Thus, for Bruner, students do not generally hinder their own mental development. Instead, problems occur when students encounter a "set curriculum" that "confines [them] to a fixed pathway" (p. 127). Bruner therefore advocates a curriculum that acknowledges students' individual differences in problem-solving ability; degree of interest; previously acquired skills; preferred learning style; rate of learning; and need for extrinsic motivation (p. 71). For Bruner, an effective curriculum contains different ways of activating children, presenting sequences, pacing children, and putting things. A curriculum, in short, must contain many tracks leading to the same goal (p. 71). Using computers would help schools design such flexible curricula.

Schiffman, Tobin, and Cassidy-Bronson (1982) also believe that computer-assisted instruction may prove ideally suited for handicapped students. They write

> There is great support for computer effectiveness in the field of special education. Nowhere are the benefits of learning with personal computers more dramatic than with the handicapped whose physical, cognitive, and learning limitations have been a barrier to an education and to a productive life. (p. 422)

Also advocating computers for use in special education, Hannaford and Sloane (1981) say that the microcomputer will become an invaluable tool because it will "allow highly interactive learning" (p. 54). They identify many advantages of computerized instruction for handicapped students, but chief among them are the following. The computer makes a multisensory approach to learning possible; can be used to teach a wide range of subject matter; can be used with diverse populations; remembers student responses; provides instant feedback; gives a variety of reinforcements; and provides diagnostic and prescriptive information. (pp. 54–57)

To effectively implement computer technology in elementary and secondary schools, teachers and administrators must learn about the educational applications currently available. Aiken and Brown (1980) identify several, such as computer-assisted instruction (CAI), experimental learning, programming and algorithmic formulation, problem-solving, word processing, and computer literacy or awareness.

Perhaps the most widely recognized application to date, especially for mildly handicapped students, is computer-assisted instruction. Definitions vary slightly from authority to authority, but generally computer-assisted instruction can be subdivided into four or five major categories (Coburn et al., 1982; Watkins & Webb, 1981), including:

1. Drill and Practice—designed to give students feedback and supplement regular instruction
2. Tutorial—designed to instruct students by using a programmed format instead of regular instruction
3. Demonstration—designed to assist teachers in demonstrating concepts, relationships, and processes
4. Simulations—designed to enable students to experiment with various solutions to real problems, such as the nuclear arms race
5. Instructional Games—designed to develop students' problem-solving abilities, reinforce previously learned concepts, and maintain high interest and motivation, such as with the spelling game, Hangman

Computers and computer-assisted instruction will soon be commonplace in the mainstream and in the resource room because they help teachers to acknowledge individual differences among students.[1]

ADAPTING AV FOR MAINSTREAMED STUDENTS   Since many mainstreamed students learn in different perceptual styles, that is, in visual, auditory, and

[1] Parts of this section on computer instruction for the mainstream are used with permission from B. Englebert, *A study of the effectiveness of microcomputer-assisted math instruction on the achievement of selected secondary learning disabled students*, dissertation in progress at the University of Southern Mississippi, Hattiesburg, Mississippi, Ch. 1, pp. 8–10, 12–13; Ch. 2, pp. 10–12, 23–24, 27–28.

tactile ways, teachers should use visual aid materials addressing a variety of perceptual styles in their instruction. See Table 4.16 for the perceptual styles that some standard AV equipment addresses. Possible adaptations of standard AV equipment to use in instructing mildly handicapped students follow.

Teachers can use the **overhead projector** to: make visuals of main points in lectures; make a visual outline of a lecture; encourage students to write down the main points of stories or chapters on their own transparencies; encourage student participation in math by presenting math problems on a transparency—student can write answer on transparency (or on blackboard, if teacher uses blackboard instead of screen to reflect projector's image); orient students to new material by using colored grease pencils to underline, circle, etc., the main points of a lecture written on transparencies; encourage class discussions or stimulate interest by placing objects (flowers, shapes, etc.) on a transparency; and reinforce directions by writing directions on transparency (visual) as one repeats those directions (oral).

Fuhrmann and Grasha (1983) suggest the following ways to make **transparencies** more effective. Orient transparencies horizontally rather than vertically so that they won't become distorted when projected and lower portions won't fall below eye level. Use fine-tipped, water-based felt pens or wax-based AV pencils (grease pencils). Place a clear plastic sheet on top of frequently used transparencies and use this plastic sheet to highlight or emphasize parts of the more permanent transparency. Use several transparencies in an overlay fashion to build an idea or concept. Use a variety of colors to highlight related concepts. Use only boldface or primary type when typing on transparencies. Include only a few points or items per transparency, because too much information on a transparency inhibits its impact. Reveal only one item on a trans-

TABLE 4.16
Selected Media and the Perceptual Learning Styles They Address

| Media | Visual | Auditory | Tactile |
|---|---|---|---|
| 16 mm film | X | X | |
| Filmstrips | X | X | |
| Overhead projector | X | | X |
| Video tapes | X | X | |
| Language master | X | X | X |
| Tape recorder | | X | |
| Opaque projector | X | | |
| Computers | X | X | X |
| Graphic materials | X | | X |
| Slides | X | | |
| Slides with audio | X | X | |
| Bulletin boards | X | | X |

parency at a time. Onion skin paper makes an especially good screen because the teacher can see through it to the transparency underneath. Use colored plastic for permanent shapes—arrows, brackets, geometric shapes—used repeatedly. Use a thermofax copier to transfer original printed materials to transparencies. Use the media center to learn about other, more complex, methods for making transparencies. Mount your permanent transparencies on cardboard for easy handling and filing. (Fuhrmann & Grasha, 1983, pp. 234–235)

**Videotapes** allow teachers to tape and play back class activities, reinforce important lectures for students needing extra help, and cover portions of classes that resource students miss. Teachers can use 16 mm **films** to reinforce lectures, or they can let students make their own 8 mm films as a group project.

**Tape recorders** are invaluable sources for supplementing visual work. Teachers can use them to: reinforce the correct pronunciation of words; record the correct pronunciation of sounds the speech therapist is working on; help those students easily distracted (give them earphones); reward students by letting them record for pleasure; help students evaluate themselves in reading by having them record stories; reinforce lectures by recording them; give students immediate feedback by recording study questions at ends of chapters, pausing for student response, and then recording correct response; encourage student participation in class by having students record their own experiences to use in language experience exercises. In addition, the teacher can record every other page of a text for slow readers; this technique reduces the reader's frustration level. Finally, mainstreamed students in social studies and science classses can often learn the concepts but cannot read the texts. The teacher can record social studies and science chapters for these students to listen to as they follow along in the text. Peer tutors can help with this recording.

Teachers should use **graphic materials** to help students identify subjects visually and to display students' progress.

And finally, teachers can make abstract lectures more concrete, turn incidental learning into intentional learning, and encourage students to participate in their lessons by using **bulletin boards.** Teachers and students can design bulletin boards to complement units, lectures, or concepts.

Using AV materials enables teachers to meet the differing styles of their students. As a result, AV materials enhance instruction for the mildly handicapped student in the mainstream.

## ADAPTING PRESENTATION OF ACADEMIC CONTENT

After teachers select the teaching technique and media necessary to deliver the lesson, they should also consider alternative ways of presenting the academic content. For example, teachers usually teach reading from a basal reader, being careful to follow the teacher's manual, standardized worksheets, etc. But mildly handicapped students may not be able to reach objectives or finish assignments when such standard procedures are followed. Their success may depend on the teacher's being able to modify the presentation of content. The regular class teacher can often help mildly handicapped students solve their various problems with assignments by adapting academic content in some way. A discussion of those problems follows, with some ideas for ways to adapt presentation of content.

CANNOT COMPLETE REGULAR CLASS ASSIGNMENT   Regular class teachers often become concerned when mildly handicapped students cannot complete in-class or homework assignments. Of course, if mildly handicapped students could do all of the work just like everyone else, they probably would not be receiving special education services. Thus, the regular class teacher should ask the following questions about the mainstreamed student:

1. Does the student have the skills to complete the required task?
2. If not, does the student have the prerequisite skills for *beginning* the required task?
3. Does instruction begin at the student's functioning level?
4. Has the student's learning style been determined?

If the above questions have been answered in the affirmative, and the student still has trouble completing the assignment, the teacher should adapt the content's presentation. To modify the presentation of content for more effective class instruction, teachers might try the following suggestions.

Activity:       Completing worksheet assignment
Adaptation:     Teachers use dittoed worksheets often. Suggestions for preparing teacher-made worksheets and/or adapting commercially produced worksheets follow:

1. Type all items on the worksheet, if possible. Handwritten worksheets are hard to read and do not duplicate as well as typed worksheets.
2. Prepare worksheets so that only a few items or problems will be presented per page. Visually distracted students find it difficult to read a crowded worksheet.
3. For worksheets commercially prepared, cut the sheet into halves or circle certain items to be answered in bold colors.
4. Do not give mainstreamed students a stack of worksheets to be completed at one time. This procedure frustrates students, and often they will not attend to the task.
5. Rewrite commercial worksheets to meet the reading level of individual students.

Activity:          Sentence writing
Adaptation:        Prepare substitution tables (Anderson, Greer, & Odle, 1978)
                   for teaching sentence structure. Begin with a simple sentence
                   substitution table using the subject—predicate pattern.

| 1 | 2 |
|---|---|
| Girls | play. |
| Boys | run. |
| Children | sing. |

This activity can be extended from teaching simple agreement
between subjects and predicates to more complicated sentences.

| 1 | 2 | 3 |
|---|---|---|
| I'm | | to White Haven. |
| You're | | home. |
| He's | | to school. |
| She's | going | to Frayser. |
| It's | | to Dixiemart. |
| We're | | to the grocery. |
| You're | | downtown. |
| They're | | to the Post Office. |

*Note.* From *Individualizing Educational Materials
for Special Children in the Mainstream* edited by
R. M. Anderson, J. G. Greer, and S. J. Odle (Baltimore:
University Park Press, 1978), 177. Copyright 1978 by University Park Press. Reprinted by permission.

Activity:          Punctuation
Adaptation 1:      Record sentences on a tape recorder. Provide a worksheet with
                   the same sentences clearly written and punctuation marks
                   omitted. As students listen to each sentence, they follow along
                   on the worksheet and add the correct punctuation. The teacher
                   may want to include two or three choices of punctuation marks
                   at the end of each sentence so students can circle correct re-
                   sponses.
                   Is your house on fire   ( . ! ? )
Adaptation 2:      Use cartoon characters and put sentences to be punctuated in
                   speech bubbles. Again, providing a selection of punctuation
                   marks may be helpful.

Adaptation 3:   Give students a punctuation key to use when punctuating sentences. The key consists of four cards, each containing a punctuation mark and sample key words or sentences.

| What    When | WOW | Today is | Wash your |
|---|---|---|---|
| ? | ! | Monday | hands |
| Who     How | OH | I am Sue | |

Adaptation 4:   In preparing worksheets or listing sentences on the board, group sentences by punctuation types. For example, list all sentences requiring question marks, periods, etc. together. After students have the skill, begin to mix the sentences, first using only two types of punctuation marks, and then adding a third.

Activity:        Compound words
Adaptation:      Give students a work list with three columns. Tell students to select the first word from Columns 1 and 2 and place in Column 3. After students have acquired the concept, mix the words in Column 1 and 2, have students select the appropriate word from Column 1, and match with a word from Column 2 to make a compound word in Column 3.

| Column 1 | Column 2 | Column 3 |
|---|---|---|
| After | Noon | Afternoon |
| Some | One | Someone |
| With | Out | Without |
| Any | Body | Anybody |

Activity:           Spelling

Adaptation 1:   Divide the spelling list into halves or fourths, if necessary, for mildly handicapped students. Many times, the mainstreamed students can learn how to spell the words, but not as quickly.

Adaptation 2:   Provide "structure spellers" for students who have trouble remembering all of the words on the spelling list.

                    interesting   i __ t __ __ e __ __ __ __ g

                    America    __ me __ i __ __.

Activity:           Reading signs

Adaptation:      Students learning math skills will often answer incorrectly because they do not attend to signs. Color code the signs or circle the signs in bold colors to call attention to them or arrange math problems on the page by signs. For example, all addition on the first two rows, subtraction on the next two rows, etc. Mixed math signs on the page make solving problems too difficult for students who have problems concentrating or reading signs.

Activity:           Money

Adaptation:      Make the concept of money meaningful to mildly handicapped students by using paper money. Begin by using several paper one dollar bills. To show that two half dollars constitute one dollar, cut one paper dollar in half; then place the two halves on the whole paper dollar and ask the student to put the cut paper dollar together. This activity functions just like putting parts of a puzzle together. The activity may be extended to fourths of a dollar, tenths of a dollar, etc.

Activity:           Addition and subtraction

Adaptation:      Mainstreamed students often find it difficult to keep math aligned as they perform computations. Block off each column of numbers so that students don't get distracted visually.

```
 ---------------      ----------------------      ---------------
      7 | 2           (1) |     |                      3 | 6
   +  3 | 4              4 |  8  | 6                 -  1 | 5
   ---------           + 3 |  5  | 1                 ---------
                          |     |                       2 | 1
                        8 |  3  | 7                  ---------------
                       ----------------------
```

Activity:           Division

Adaptation:      Use a model to teach division. Fade the model as the student begins to understand where each number belongs.

$$\overline{8\,|\,32} \qquad \overline{8\,|\,32} \qquad \overline{8\,|\,32}$$

Activity:          Lab assignments
Adaptation:        A major assignment in science classes is the lab. Many schools
                   ask students to complete part of a lab assignment sheet be-
                   fore the teacher's demonstration, and upon completion of the
                   demonstration, to finish the remainder of the lab assignment
                   sheet. Table 4.17 presents a standard lab assignment sheet and
                   how to adapt the assignment for the mainstreamed student.

TABLE 4.17
Adaptation of Lab Assignment

| Lab Assignment Outline | Standard Student Response | Adaptations for Mainstreamed Students |
|---|---|---|
| Title of Lab | Student completes. | Fill in for student. |
| Materials | Students completes from observing teacher or from reading text. | Complete for student or let peer tutor assist. |
| Purpose of Lab | Student completes from text or lecture. | Complete for student. |
| Lab Procedures | As teacher demonstrates, students record the procedures. | List procedures on the board so student can follow each step. Provide a check sheet and have student check off each step. |
| Observations | Student records the observed experiment. | Let student record the observed demonstration into a tape recorder. |
| Conclusion | Student records. | This step requires evaluation level of Bloom's taxonomy, so teacher may choose to omit it for mainstreamed student. |
| Analysis Questions | Students respond. | Provide answers for mainstreamed student. |

CANNOT READ CLASS ASSIGNMENT   A common problem for the mildly handi-capped student in the regular class is reading—too often the mildly handicapped student simply cannot read the regular assignment. The reading levels of the assignment and the student are incompatible. Below are suggestions the regu-lar class teacher can try in adapting and/or modifying material too difficult for students to read.

Activity:         Following directions
Adaptation:       Frequently, mainstreamed students will be at grade level in math, but below grade level in reading skills. For these stu-dents, record directions in the text on a tape recorder. Label the tape with the text page numbers. Students can then play the tape, listen to the directions, follow along in the text, and usually complete the assignment.

Activity:         Reading from the required text
Adaptation 1:     Record each section/chapter of the text on tape. Put one chapter on each tape and record each page number (i.e., page one, page two). This method provides easy access to each chapter and to each page.

Adaptation 2:     Rewrite chapters in text using simple language, low vocabu-lary, etc. The student can have access to revised text in re-source or at home but use original text in class. That way, student does not feel out of place in class.

Activity:         Studying the review questions at the end of the chapter
Adaptation:       Mainstreamed students often find it difficult to locate answers to review questions at the end of each chapter. Either provide the page number in the chapter where answer to review ques-tion can be found or supply answers to the questions for students. (For mainstreamed students, *learning* the correct answer is more important than spending hours *searching* for the correct answer.)

Activity:         Social studies/science fact finding
Adaptation:       For the mainstreamed student, provide the essential facts to be learned. Either give the students the facts to learn, provide a peer tutor to help the student "fact find," or give the page numbers where the facts can be found.

CANNOT COMPLETE WHOLE ASSIGNMENT   Frequently, mildly handicapped students can complete only part of the assignment. As Anderson, Greer, and Odle (1978) point out, "at any point in the learning process, the child may have

TABLE 4.18
Task Analysis of Mathematics Textbook's Content

| Major tasks and subtasks | Instructional examples on page: | Test examples on page: |
|---|---|---|
| **Addition** | | |
| Addition combinations | 5–7 | 9–13, 462 |
| Tens in addition | 14 | 14–15 |
| Hundreds in addition | 14 | 16 |
| Column addition | 16–17 | 17–27, 56, 454, 458 |
| Regrouping in addition | 28 | 28–29 |
| Estimating sums | 30 | 31–34, 37, 55–56 |
| Mental addition | 35 | 35–36 |
| **Subtraction** | | |
| Subtraction combinations | 7–9 | 9–13, 463 |
| Tens in subtraction | 14 | 15, 38 |
| Hundreds in subtraction | 14 | 15–16, 38 |
| Regrouping in subtraction | 40–41 | 42–47, 56, 455, 459 |
| Expanded notation | 42 | 42 |
| Subtraction of fractions | 48–49 | 49–51 |
| Estimating differences | 51 | 51–52, 53–56 |
| Mental subtraction | 53 | 53–55 |
| **Multiplication** | | |
| Multiplication combinations | 57–59, 60, 62–63 | 59, 61, 464 |
| Properties of multiplication | 66 | 67 |
| Number pairs and graphs | 70–71 | 71 |
| Multiplying, using tens | 72, 74–75 | 72–73, 76–77 456, 460 |
| Multiplying, using a machine | 78–81 | 81 |
| Mental multiplication | 82, 86 | 82–83, 86–88 |
| Estimating products | 84 | 84–85, 88 |
| **Division** | | |
| Division combinations | 65 | 65, 465 |
| Properties of division | 66 | 67 |
| Division involving remainders | 67 | 68–69, 92, 457, 461 |
| Dividing number by single digit | 69, 92–93 | 68, 93, 103, 457, 461 |
| Dividing, using tens | 72, 92 | 78, 89, 94–95, 103, 457, 461 |
| Trial quotients | 95–97 | 97–98 |
| Estimating quotients | 96–99 | 99–100, 102–103 |
| Mental division | 101 | 101–102 |

*Note.* From *Individualizing Educational Materials for Special Children in the Mainstream* edited by R. M. Anderson, J. G. Greer, and S. J. Odle (Baltimore: University Park Press, 1978), 169. Copyright 1978 by University Park Press. Reprinted by permission.

failed to acquire mastery of any skill or concept necessary for success at subsequent levels" (p. 168). Such gaps in acquiring a skill then make it difficult for mildly handicapped students to go beyond a certain point in an assignment. Anderson, Greer, and Odle suggest that teachers can help prevent such gaps from occurring by using task analysis on textbooks: divide the text into smaller sections and rearrange those sections in sequential order. The teacher needs to assess the text, break it down into skills, and reorganize those skills for easier teaching *and* learning. Anderson, Greer, and Odle suggest three steps for teachers to follow in rearranging textbooks. First, teachers should study the table of contents and identify the skills covered by the book. Second, divide those skills into major tasks and subtasks and arrange subtasks seqentially, in order of planned instruction. And third, tabulate page numbers for examples of all the subtasks. These examples can then be used in class as exercises, as practice assignments, or as test examples or questions. (p. 168) See Table 4.18 for an example of using task analysis to reorganize the content of a mathematics textbook.

Using task analysis to break down textbooks for mainstreamed students offers them more opportunities for success. They can acquire major skills more easily when the instructional material is organized for quick access to specific and smaller skills.

Teachers can also reorganize language arts texts so that they can sequentially teach the skills required at a specific level. Many times the major subjects in a basal language arts text, as listed in the table of contents, are not in sequential order. For example, the table of contents may list these areas: writing sentences, writing letters, parts of speech, writing paragraphs, and using correct punctuation. But learning the parts of speech is a prerequisite skill for writing sentences, just as knowing how to write a paragraph is necessary before one can write letters correctly. To reorganize the table of contents, the teacher must first decide what the prerequisite skills are for each major area. Table 4.19 presents excerpts from a basal language arts text and a sequential reorganization of the table of contents. The teacher does not deviate from the basic topics to be taught, but simply redesigns the order of the material. By rearranging texts into small, sequential skills, the teacher makes it possible for mainstreamed students to complete assignments.

TABLE 4.19
Reorganizing a Table of Contents

| Original Table of Contents | Sequentially Reorganized Table of Contents |
| --- | --- |
| Writing sentences | Parts of speech |
| Writing letters | Writing sentences |
| Parts of speech | Using correct punctuation |
| Writing paragraphs | Writing paragraphs |
| Using correct punctuation | Writing letters |

When teachers remain versatile in the ways they present subjects, they help mainstreamed students learn, but they also help keep *all* students motivated and persistent. Adapting presentation of academic content for students in the mainstream helps those students master objectives and material that, under normal conditions, would go unlearned.

## SUMMARY

The discussion in Chapter 4 has centered around learning—learning styles, domains of learning, and task analysis—and teaching—adapting technique, media, and presentation of content. Both elementary and secondary teachers can apply this information about learning and the model for adapting instruction to their own instructional processes. If specific examples presented here do not apply to a teacher's given situation, they can be adapted still further. Chapter 5 will cover how teachers can adapt their lesson plans for mildly handicapped students in the mainstream.

## REFERENCES

Aiken, R. M., & Brown, L. Into the 80s with microcomputer-based learning. *Computer*, 1980, *13*(7), 11–16.

Anderson, R. M., Greer, J. G., & Odle, S. J. (Eds.). *Individualizing educational materials for special children in the mainstream*. Baltimore: University Park Press, 1978.

*Basic skills sequence in English.* Montpelier, Vt.: Vermont State Department of Education, Division of Special Education and Pupil Personnel Services.

Bloom, B. S. Learning for mastery. (UCLA-CSEIP) *Evaluation Comment*, 1968, *1*(2).

Bloom, B. S. (Ed.). *Taxonomy of educational objectives: The Classification of Educational Goals. Handbook I: Cognitive domain.* New York: Longman, 1956.

Bruner, J. S. *Toward a theory of instruction.* New York: Norton, 1968.

Bruner, J. S., & Tajfel, H. Cognitive risks and environmental change. *Journal of Abnormal Psychology*, 1961, *62*, 231–241.

Charles, C. M. *Individualizing instruction* (2nd ed.). St. Louis, Mo.: C. V. Mosby, 1980.

Coburn, P., Kelman, P., Roberts, N., Snyder, T. F., Watt, D. H., & Weiner, C. *Practical guide to computers in education.* Reading, Mass.: Addison-Wesley, 1982.

Cooper, J. M., Hansen, J., Martorella, P. H., Morine-Dershimer, G., Sadker, D., Sadker, M., Sokolve, S., Shostak, R., Ten Brink, T., & Weber, W. A. *Classroom teaching skills: A workbook.* Lexington, Mass.: D. C. Heath, 1977.

Dave, R. H. *Taxonomy of educational objectives: Psychomotor domain.* New Delhi, India: National Institute of Education, 1970.

Dunn, R., Dunn, K., & Price, G. E. *Learning styles inventory manual.* Lawrence, Kan.: Price Systems, 1979.

Englebert, B. *A study of the effectiveness of microcomputer-assisted math instruction on the achievement of selected secondary learning disabled students.* Dissertation in progress, University of Southern Mississippi, Hattiesburg, Mississippi.

Fuhrmann, B. S. *Models and Methods of Assessing Learning Styles.* Paper presented at Virginia Educational Research Association, August, 1980.

Fuhrmann, B. S. & Grasha, A. F. *A practical handbook for college teachers.* Boston: Little, Brown, 1983.

Gardner, R. W. Cognitive control: A study of individual consistencies in cognitive behavior. *Psychological Issues,* 1959, *1.*

Guskey, T. R. Individualizing instruction in the mainstream classroom: A mastery learning approach. *Educational Unlimited,* 1981, *3*(1), 12–15.

Hannaford, A., & Sloane, E. Microcomputers: Powerful learning tools with proper programming. *Teaching Exceptional Children,* 1981, *14*(2), 54–57.

Harvey, O. J., Hunt, D. E., & Schroder, H. M. *Conceptual systems and personality organization.* New York: John Wiley, 1961.

Jarolimek, J., & Foster, C. D. *Teaching and learning in the elementary school* (2nd ed.). New York: Macmillan, 1981.

Johnson, G. R. *Analyzing college teaching.* Manchaca, Tex.: Sterling Swift, 1976.

Kagan, Jerome. Reflection-impulsivity: The generality and dynamics of conceptual tempo. *Journal of Abnormal Psychology,* 1966, *71,* 17–24.

Keefe, J. W. *Student learning styles: Diagnosing and prescribing programs.* Reston, Va.: National Association of Secondary School Principals, 1979.

Kelly, G. A. *The psychology of personal constructs.* New York: Norton, 1955.

Klein, G. S., Gardner, R. W., Schlesinger, H. J. Tolerance for unrealistic experience: A study of the generality of cognitive control. *British Journal of Psychology,* 1962, *54,* 41–45.

Krathwohl, D. R., (Ed.). *Taxonomy of educational objectives: The Classification of Educational Goals. Handbook II: Affective domain.* New York: Longman, 1964.

McKenney, J., & Keen, P. How managers' minds work. *Harvard Business Review,* 1974, *53*(3), 79–90.

Melmed, A. S. Information technology for U. S. schools. *Phi Delta Kappa,* 1982, *63*(5), 308–311.

Rich, H. L. *Disturbed students: Characteristics and educational strategies.* Baltimore: University Park Press, 1982.

Schiffman, G., Tobin, D., & Cassidy-Bronson, S. Personal computers for the learning disabled. *Journal of Learning Disabilities,* 1982, *15*(7), 422–425.

Schlesinger, H. J. Cognitive attitudes in relation to susceptibility to interference. *Journal of Personality.* 1954, *22,* 354–374.

*Teaching children with special needs (elementary level).* Owings Mills, Md.: Maryland State Department of Education, Division of Instructional Television.

Watkins, M. W., & Webb, C. Computer assisted instruction with learning disabled students. *Educational Computer,* 1981, *1*(3), 24–27.

Wehman, P., & McLaughlin, P. J. *Program development in special education.* New York: McGraw-Hill, 1981.

Witkin, H. A., Moore, C. A., Oltman, P. K., Goodenough, D. R., Friedman, F., Owen, D. R., & Raskin, E. Role of field-dependent and field-independent cognitive styles in academic evolution. A longitudinal study. *Journal of Educational Psychology,* 1977, *69*(3), 197–211.

# Chapter Five

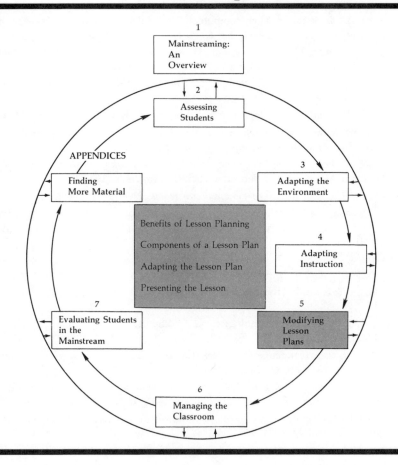

1
Mainstreaming:
An
Overview

2
Assessing
Students

APPENDICES

Finding
More Material

3
Adapting the
Environment

Benefits of Lesson Planning

Components of a Lesson Plan

Adapting the Lesson Plan

Presenting the Lesson

4
Adapting
Instruction

7
Evaluating Students
in the
Mainstream

5
Modifying
Lesson
Plans

6
Managing the
Classroom

# Modifying Lesson Plans

MODIFIED LESSON PLAN

Lesson plans are blueprints of the day's events that dictate student-teacher inter-actions and instructional outcomes. Jarolimek and Foster (1981) say the daily lesson plan contains "specific provisions for teaching and learning" that make possible "the successful interaction of instruction and management" (p. 189). Lesson plans may be general, outlining plans for the year or semester, some-what more specific, scheduling activities for a week, or very specific, organiz-ing teaching on a daily basis.

This chapter presents the benefits of effective lesson planning, the basic parts all lesson plans should contain, models teachers can use to adapt regular lesson plans to meet the needs of mildly handicapped students, and techniques for presenting the lessons themselves. For students in the mainstream, adapta-tions in lesson planning sometimes mean the difference between failure and suc-cess in acquiring skills or concepts.

## BENEFITS OF LESSON PLANNING

Lesson plan formats and ways of presenting lessons vary from teacher to teacher. But effective teaching usually springs from a well-planned, well-organized, and well-presented lesson plan. Hoover and Hollingsworth (1975) suggest that lesson planning has several benefits. For example, plans serve the teacher as "useful guidelines or blueprints." They must, however, remain flexible enough to allow the teacher to adapt to whatever situation may arise. In fact, if the prepared teacher has set up "general goals, some definite activities, and some specific sources of materials," then students can play a part in planning. Planning also allows the teacher to direct attention to the "important problems of motivation and individual differences." Indeed, planning often increases the teacher's under-standing of the problems students have with learning. Planning lessons can help a teacher both focus and balance "goals, subject matters, activities, and eval-uation." The teacher can even use the lesson plan as a "reference to important statistics, illustrations, difficult words, special procedures," etc. Teachers who make notes on their plans after lessons are done can then use their plans to improve their teaching in later years. Finally, since every teacher plans lessons in a different way, planning allows a teacher to put a personal stamp on the lesson and the classroom. (pp. 159–160)

## COMPONENTS OF A LESSON PLAN

All lesson plans have several essential parts, although different authors may name these parts differently. Jarolimek & Foster (1981), for example, provide a simple and useful description of major lesson plan parts. The *purpose* states instructional objectives, including what students should learn from the lesson. The *learning process* lists learning materials or media needed to teach the lesson.

The *sequence of lesson* describes the work-study activities that will occur during the lesson. And finally, the *evaluation* describes the activities designed to close the lesson. (p. 190)

Certain components—objectives, teaching techniques (procedures), media, presentation of content (activities), and evaluation—always appear in a well-constructed lesson plan, no matter what names or formats are used. The Division of Teacher Education at Virginia Commonwealth University has developed a lesson plan guide containing three major parts: the procedure, resources, and evaluation.[1] Since this guide provides the foundation for some of the discussion on lesson plans in this chapter, a detailed description follows.

The *procedure*, covering what happens during the lesson, consists of an introduction to the lesson, the lesson's development, and its summary. In the lesson plan's introduction, the Virginia Commonwealth University guide suggests the teacher state and/or demonstrate what students should learn, use a provocative question, artifact, or hands-on activity to stimulate student interest in the lesson, or link the present lesson to past lessons or student experiences. In the development section, the teacher selects activities to achieve the lesson's purpose, describes those activities, and chooses an instructional model around which to organize the lesson. Then, in the summary part of the procedures, the teacher chooses how to conclude the lesson: students describe what they have learned by performing one of several activities, such as question/discussion, demonstration, presentation of project, etc.

In the lesson plan's *resources* section, the teacher identifies any materials and/or media that will be used to achieve the lesson's purpose. Such resources may include pages or chapters in a pamphlet, text, or workbook, filmstrips or films, guest experts, field experience, special settings, art supplies, cooking supplies, AV equipment, etc.

The lesson plan also includes an *evaluation* section, in which the teacher notes ways to assess student learning and/or the success of the lesson. Teachers can assess students by checking behavioral objectives, using informal questions, or administering formal pre- and posttests. Or a teacher may choose to have students check their own work by providing them with feedback, a model of a completed activity, or an illustration of the lesson's concept or process. Teachers can also plan to have students assess each other's work. To determine the lesson's degree of success, a teacher may analyze students' reactions during the lesson, the value of the lesson as a learning experience, and/or one's own teaching performance.

---

[1]The Division of Teacher Education uses this lesson plan guide for all instructional programs in the School of Education at Virginia Commonwealth University. The following discussion is adapted from: *Student Teaching Handbook,* pp. 21–22. Copyright 1982 by the Division of Teacher Education, School of Education, Virginia Commonwealth University. Adapted with permission.

# ADAPTING THE LESSON PLAN

The regular class teacher may use one of two models for adapting a regular class lesson plan for mildly handicapped students in the mainstream. Teachers wishing to adapt the Virginia Commonwealth University lesson plan guidelines may use the first model. Teachers with a different lesson plan format may use the second model, which is based upon the three steps in adapting instruction: adapting the teaching technique, adapting the media, and adapting the presentation of content. Each model applies ideas from Chapters 3 and 4 to the process of adapting the lesson plan.

## MODEL I: ADAPTING COMPONENTS OF A REGULAR CLASS LESSON PLAN

Organized instruction has its basis in the well-prepared lesson plan. Model I suggests ways teachers can adapt or modify the components of the Virginia Commonwealth University format.

PROCEDURE  In this major section of the lesson plan, the teacher must determine the instructional makeup of the lesson as well as the sequence the lesson should follow. See Table 5.1 for ways to adapt each component according to the suggestions for mildly handicapped students made in Chapters 3 and 4.

The introduction to the lesson plan should contain a major instructional objective and a list of all subobjectives. The teacher thinks in terms of preparing the student for the lesson itself and wants to make sure that instructional objectives are on the student's level and in sequential order. Additionally, the teacher should include an assessment of the students' prerequisite skills in the plan's introduction.

Next, the teacher plans how to develop the plan's instructional activities. Here, the teacher must consider several things in relationship to mainstreamed students: adapting the learning environment; teaching for acquisition, retention, and transfer; using task analysis to break down the activities into smaller parts; organizing activities according to taxonomy level; and adapting the presentation of each activity's content and one's teaching techniques. Then, the teacher must plan the lesson's closing activities and how to encourage student participation in describing what they have learned.

RESOURCES  The teacher also needs to plan what materials and/or media to use in the lesson and how to adapt those resources for mainstreamed students. Assessing the instructional level of materials, matching perceptual learning styles to media, using a variety of materials and/or media, and adapting the learning environment—all are part of developing resources.

TABLE 5.1
Model I: Adapting Components of Regular Class Lesson Plan

| Lesson Plan Components | Application of Chapters 3 and 4 |
| --- | --- |
| | PROCEDURE |

Introduction

| | |
| --- | --- |
| State what student should learn: | Select instructional objective for lesson. List subobjectives. Use task analysis to break down all subobjectives. State objectives for mildly handicapped students in the appropriate taxonomy levels. |
| Demonstrate what student should learn: | Provide model of completed assignment (whole-part-whole method). Provide sequential directions. Check Table 4.11 for alternative teaching techniques in demonstration mode. |
| Use mind-capturer or activator: | Use manipulative or hands-on activity to boost interest. Note whether or not students have prerequisite skills for mastering objective. Alter objective at this point, if necessary. |
| Link to past lessons or students' experiences: | Ask questions (on students' taxonomy levels) about past lessons. Provide example from own experience and relate to lesson (the modeling technique). Ask students to share similar experiences; relate student comments to present lesson. |

Development

| | |
| --- | --- |
| Select and describe activities designed for lesson's instructional objective: | Assign peer tutors to mildly handicapped students. Organize creative groups for instruction. Select grouping arrangements. |
| Select activities designed for acquisition, retention, and transfer: | Teach for acquisition by selecting appropriate instructional activities and implementing each activity with appropriate instructional strategy (See Table 3.3). Use task analysis to break down all activities for teaching for acquisition. Teach for retention by selecting appropriate instructional activities and implementing each activity with appropriate instructional strategy (See Table 3.3). |

TABLE 5.1  (continued)

| Lesson Plan Components | Application of Chapters 3 and 4 |
|---|---|
| | Use task analysis to break down activities for teaching for retention. |
| | Teach for transfer by selecting appropriate instructional activities and implementing each activity with appropriate instructional strategy (See Table 3.3). |
| | Use task analysis to break down all activities for teaching for transfer. |
| Organize all activities according to taxonomy level: | List all activities. |
| | Organize all activities, from lowest level of difficulty to highest level of difficulty. |
| | Present activities on student's functioning level. |
| Identify and modify content of, and teaching technique for, each activity: | State *content* of each activity and use suggestions in Chapter 4 to adapt or modify presentation of that content. |
| | State *teaching technique* for each activity and use models in Chapter 4 to select alternate technique or adapt stated technique. |
| Summary | |
| Conclude lesson: | Select closing activities on instructional level of mainstreamed students. |
| | Assess student's mastery of concept(s). |
| Students describe what they have learned: | Assist mainstreamed students in selecting what to share. |
| | Students tell about what they have learned. |
| | Students draw pictures of what they have learned. |
| | Students present projects. |
| | RESOURCES |
| Compile materials for presenting lesson: | Assess instructional level of materials. |
| | Select variety of materials to address different perceptual learning styles. |
| Select appropriate media for lesson: | Use suggestions in Chapter 4 to adapt media. |
| | Select variety of media. |
| | Match media to perceptual learning styles. |
| Prepare resources for adapting learning environment: | Create bulletin boards for incidental and intentional learning. |

TABLE 5.1  (continued)

| Lesson Plan Components | Application of Chapters 3 and 4 |
|---|---|
| | Design learning centers to enhance instruction. |
| | **EVALUATION** |
| Teacher assesses student learning: | Use model in Chapter 7 to adapt regular classroom test for mildly handicapped students. |
| | Assess effectiveness of instructional objective. |
| | Assess instructional level of activities. |
| | Assess activities not mastered and consider further adaptations of plan. |
| Student assesses self: | Give student self-correcting materials for immediate reinforcement. |
| | Provide models to which students can compare their work. |
| Students assess each other: | Provide one-on-one peer tutor to give feedback. |
| | Oversee student assessment of peers (peer's criticism of mildly handi-capped student can harm handicapped student's self-concept). |
| Teacher assesses self: | Were all students included in lesson plan's activities? |
| | Did each student experience success? |
| | Was I aware of the instructional level of each student? |
| | Did each student reach expected learning outcome? |
| | Did I effectively manage student behaviors? |
| | Was the learning environment adapted to meet students' learning needs? |
| | What changes should I make the next time I present the lesson? |

EVALUATION   The teacher must also make evaluation part of the lesson plan. Such evaluation can include one or more of the following: the teacher's assessment of students, the student's assessment of self, the student's assessment of peers, and the teacher's assessment of self. Just as with procedures and resources, the teacher needs to adapt the evaluation process for mainstreamed students and include those adaptations in the lesson plan.

# MODEL II: ADAPTING AN INTACT LESSON PLAN USING THE TRIAD MODEL

Teachers who have already developed lesson plans and/or use a different lesson plan format from the one used in Model I should use Model II for adapting the regular class lesson plan. See Table 5.2 for the steps teachers should follow in adapting the already intact regular education lesson plan for mainstreamed students.

First, the teacher should record the grade level where the handicapped student presently functions and the subject being taught. Next, the teacher should identify the particular perceptual preference of the student, type of attention span, reading level, learning style, etc. and consider all such variables when adapting the regular class lesson plan. For example, if the student has a short attention span, the lesson can be divided into short segments so that the student stays on task without getting bored. Or if the reading level of the lesson is not on the instructional level of the student, teachers may need to modify the reading content. Then, using the triad model presented in Chapter 4, the teacher isolates the lesson plan's teaching techniques, media, and content and adapts them to meet the needs of mainstreamed students.

Teachers wishing to use Model II can see examples of how to adapt the teaching techniques, media, and content of a regular lesson plan in Table 5.3. This table represents suggestions, not completed lesson plans, for applying the triad model for adapting instruction to various lesson plan formats.

TABLE 5.2
Model II: Adapting Regular Education Lesson Plan for Mainstreamed Students

---

1. Identify population.
   a. Grade level
   b. Subject
   c. Type of handicap
2. Identify specific information about mildly handicapped students.
   a. Visual learner
   b. Auditory learner
   c. Hyperactive
   d. Easily distracted
   e. Short attention span
   f. Low reading level
   g. General instructional level for academic subject
   h. Other individual differences
3. Identify specific teaching techniques and/or strategies in present lesson plan of regular teacher.
4. Identify media being used in regular teacher's lesson plan.
5. Identify specific content and way it is presented in regular lesson plan (basic number facts, subject-verb agreement, etc.).
6. Modify steps, 3, 4, and 5 for mainstreamed students by using triad model.

---

# PRESENTING THE LESSON

While planning lessons, teachers should also think about how they will present those lessons to students. Cooper et al. (1977) suggest five stimulus variation techniques that teachers can use to more effectively deliver the lesson: the kinesic variation, focusing, shifting interaction, pausing, and shifting the senses.

The kinesic variation directly contrasts with the teacher's sitting behind the desk for an entire lesson and assumes a teacher will move from place to place within the room to improve communication. The movements should be smooth and natural, not distracting from the lesson or to the student. The kinesic variation includes one or a combination of the following: moving freely from right to left and then from left to right in front of the classroom; moving freely from front to back and then from back to front; and moving freely among and/or behind students. (p. 124)

Focusing is the "teacher's way of intentionally controlling the direction of student attention" (p. 136). Focusing can be verbal or behavioral or both. Teachers can focus students' attention by asking specific questions and by using accent words such as, for example, look, how, find, etc. Or, teachers can use body language—facial expressions, eye contact, pointing, other hand gestures, etc.—to attract attention.

Shifting interaction refers to the teacher's use of one or another interaction styles: teacher-group, teacher-student, student-student. The teacher-group interaction puts the teacher in control, lecturing and directing discussion as needed. The teacher-student interaction style is also teacher directed, but the teacher becomes more of a facilitator, asking questions to clarify a story or answering questions raised by students after completion of a lab assignment. The student-student interaction style centers around students, with the teacher "redirecting student questions to other students for comment or clarification" (p. 138). (See also Chapter 4, "Learning and Learning Styles.")

Teachers can also use pauses or moments of silence quite effectively during a lesson. For example, a teacher can completely regain students' attention by becoming silent. Cooper et al. (1977) list ten effective uses of pausing:

1. It can break informational segments into smaller pieces for better understanding. Reading oral problems or dictating material for transcription requires careful attention to the effective use of pausing.
2. It can capture attention by contrasting sound with silence (alternating two distinctly different stimuli). Remember that attention is maintained at a high level when stimuli are varied, not when one increases the intensity of a single stimulus.
3. It can be a signal for students to prepare for the next teacher action.
4. It can be used to emphasize or underscore an important point.
5. It can provide time for thinking about a question or formulating an answer.
6. It can prevent teachers from unconsciously dominating discussion.

TABLE 5.3
Adapting Excerpts of Lesson Plans Using the Triad Model

| | Regular Lesson Plan | Adapting Teaching Technique | Adapting Media | Adapting Presentation of Content |
|---|---|---|---|---|
| | | The Aztecs of Mexico | | |
| Teaching Technique | 1. Display map of Mexico. <br> 2. Discuss how Aztecs contributed to our society. <br> 3. Students *compare* Mexico during Aztecs' time and today. <br> 4. From blank map, fill in major cities in Mexico. <br> 5. Discuss similarities and differences of today's houses and Aztecs' huts. | 1. Show map of Mexico and relationship to America. <br> 2. Use task analysis to break down lesson. <br> 3. Before teacher lectures, students listen to lecture on tape. <br> 4. Use lecture outline for students to follow. <br> 5. Because comparing requires evaluation, only present information to mainstreamed students at this point. (Comparisons will be difficult.) <br> 6. Provide students with completed maps. Color code major cities. <br> 7. Discuss housing during another lesson. It is not appropriate for this day's lesson. | 1. Raised maps for tactile purposes are helpful. <br> 2. Use movie or film strip on Mexico for orientation before lesson. <br> 3. When students compare today's Mexico with the Aztecs' Mexico, use transparencies to list suggestions. <br> 4. Tape record music from Mexico to create interest. <br> 5. Get books (many levels) from library for students to read. <br> 6. Prepare bulletin board with as much "incidental" learning as possible. | 1. Tape record chapter or unit in text on Mexico for low level reading students. <br> 2. Maps should have cities marked. Or, give students blank and completed maps so they can copy cities' names. |
| Media Content | Handouts of maps <br> History of the Aztecs in Mexico | | | |

# Teaching ABC Order

**Teaching Technique**

*Day 1:* Activity with flash cards, placing cards in ABC order.
*Day 2:* Teacher writes 26 words on board for students to place in ABC order by first letter.
*Day 3:* Students place words in ABC order by first and second letters.
Techniques: Lecture, demonstration, student activity.

**Media** Flash cards
**Content** Teaching ABC order

1. Use task analysis to break down lesson.
   a. Students must know ABCs.
   b. Students must know sequential order of ABCs.
   c. Using spelling words from reading, begin putting in ABC order a *small* number of words.
2. Techniques: Prepare ABC learning centers, use task analysis, present in smaller segments or steps than suggested in original lesson, use peer tutors to assist student, present lesson with more teacher demonstration instead of emphasis on seat work.

1. Flash cards with letters.
2. Flash cards with words.
3. Tape record words to be listened to while they are also presented visually.
4. Let students use transparencies for alphabetizing words.
5. Place numerous hands-on activities in learning center.

1. Use sand for tracing letters in ABC order.
2. Delete number of words to be alphabetized to a number small enough to work with.
3. Provide prompting sheets: alphabet written down side. (Memory load is reduced when visual prompts are presented.)
4. Use self-correcting flash cards.

7. It encourages teachers to listen to individual student responses. (Remember, people do not listen well when they are talking.)
8. It can create suspense or expectation. The effective reader of all types of literature uses the pause to stir the emotions and heighten the anticipation of the listener.
9. It can help provide a model of listening behavior for other students.
10. It can be used to show disapproval of undesired student behavior. (p. 139)

Shifting senses means presenting information through more than one of the five senses—seeing, touching, hearing, smelling, and tasting. The importance of the teacher's shifting senses for mainstreamed students cannot be overestimated because assimilating information through various perceptual modalities helps those students learn the information in as many ways as possible. (See also Chapter 4, "Learning and Learning Styles.")

Teachers who use these stimulus variation techniques enhance their teaching. When teachers have planned the lesson carefully, adapted it, when necessary, for mainstreamed students, and included techniques for adding variety to the presentation, they have increased their chances of stimulating all their students to learn.

## SUMMARY

As teachers prepare their lesson plans, they should take a few moments to make simple adaptations that will allow mildly handicapped students in the mainstream to successfully complete the required lesson. Using either Model I or Model II, regular teachers can make such adaptations part of the ongoing process of lesson preparation. Teachers will discover that when they adapt their lesson plans and presentations to the needs of mildly handicapped students, those students *can* learn their lessons. Chapter 6 will provide the teacher with some practical techniques for managing the classroom.

## REFERENCES

Cooper, J. M., Hansen, J., Martorella, P. H., Morine-Dershimer, G., Sadker, D., Sadker, M., Sokolve, S., Shostak, R., Ten Brink, T., & Weber, W. A. *Classroom teaching skills: A workbook.* Lexington, Mass.: D. C. Heath, 1977.

Hoover, K. H., & Hollingsworth, P. M. *Learning and teaching in the elementary school.* Boston: Allyn and Bacon, 1975.

Jarolimek, J., & Foster, C. D. *Teaching and learning in the elementary school* (2nd ed.). New York: Macmillan, 1981.

*Student teaching handbook.* Richmond, Va.: Division of Teacher Education, School of Education, Virginia Commonwealth University, 1982.

# Chapter Six

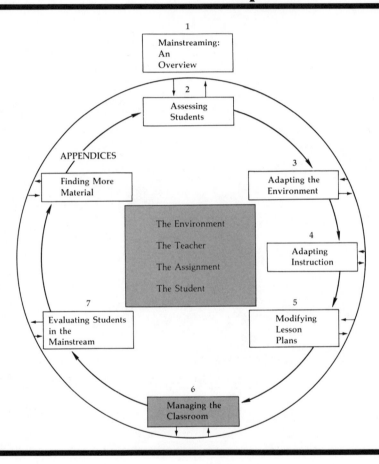

# Managing the Classroom

Managing the classroom is an ongoing process that occurs simultaneously with teaching. When teachers have assessed their students properly, when they have carefully adapted the learning environment, and when they have modified their lesson plans and instruction to fit student needs, most management problems will disappear. But no system is foolproof; sometimes problem behaviors detract from the positive instructional atmosphere teachers have so carefully built.

Classroom management, however, means more than merely discouraging inappropriate behaviors. It includes all the factors (events, circumstances, people) that affect student behavior. The environment, the teacher, the assignments, and the student all contribute to students' behavior in the classroom; teachers, if they are to successfully manage their classrooms, must understand all these contributing factors.

As more handicapped students enter the mainstream and regular classroom teachers face increasingly heterogeneous classes, those teachers increasingly need practical management techniques for both handicapped and nonhandicapped students.

## THE ENVIRONMENT

The term environment covers the physical organization of the classroom, grouping procedures, management systems, and peers within the environment. Looking constructively at the environment of the classroom and doing some preventive planning will often alleviate classroom management problems.

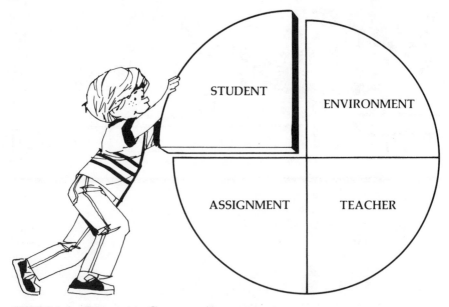

FIGURE 6.1. Elements in Classroom Management

# PHYSICAL ORGANIZATION OF THE CLASSROOM

The physical environment of a classroom should stimulate students if effective learning is to occur. See Table 6.1 for a checklist teachers can use to evaluate the effectiveness of the classroom's physical environment. Physical environment includes all physical aspects of the room: wall areas, lighting, floors, and room area. Being aware of the classroom's physical organization can help teachers prevent classroom problems.

TABLE 6.1
Checklist for Effective Classroom Environment

|  | Yes | No |
|---|---|---|
| Wall Area |  |  |
| Walls clean to prevent distractions | ____ | ____ |
| Bulletin boards neatly designed and seasonally up-to-date | ____ | ____ |
| Bulletin boards available for student use and display | ____ | ____ |
| Windows clean or neatly covered | ____ | ____ |
| Blackboards in view of all students, clean, and undamaged. | ____ | ____ |
| Lighting |  |  |
| Proper window lighting | ____ | ____ |
| Ceiling lighting sufficient | ____ | ____ |
| Floors |  |  |
| Clean | ____ | ____ |
| Obstructive objects removed | ____ | ____ |
| Barrier free for wheelchairs, etc. | ____ | ____ |
| Room Area |  |  |
| Appropriate chair sizes for age level | ____ | ____ |
| Arrangements for left- as well as right-handed students | ____ | ____ |
| Areas provided for small group instruction | ____ | ____ |
| Areas provided for independent instruction | ____ | ____ |
| Areas in room designated for specific behaviors, i.e., quiet time, reading in two's, game areas, motor areas, art areas. | ____ | ____ |
| Learning centers provided | ____ | ____ |
| Study carrels provided | ____ | ____ |
| Areas designated for listening to tapes, i.e., recording of lessons, chapters in books | ____ | ____ |

# GROUPING PROCEDURES

To prevent problem behaviors, teachers should also plan to use various grouping procedures: learning centers designed around general principles of learning, groups arranged by objectives, and small groups and seat work. Teachers may also group by mental age rather than chronological age in the mainstreamed classroom. In most regular classrooms, teachers automatically place students by chronological age (CA), the children's ages at the time. But mildly handicapped students function at levels lower than their CAs; that is, their mental ages (MA) are younger than their CAs. For example, a student 10 years old may function academically as a 7-year-old. Using mental age for grouping allows more homogeneity in academic grouping and thus helps the mildly handicapped student obtain instructional objectives more readily. When the teacher groups students where learning can occur, classroom problems diminish. However, teachers may still want to group mainstreamed students for subjects such as art, P.E., music, etc. on a CA basis, thus allowing them to interact with their age peer group as well.

# MANAGEMENT SYSTEMS

Teachers use various management systems in a well-organized classroom, such as rules, reinforcements, and teaching techniques. By effectively introducing structured rules, teachers can control the environment of the class and prevent inappropriate behaviors. For example, the teacher should let all students, and especially handicapped students, know what behaviors are permitted. Often much inappropriate behavior will disappear when students know their limits. For teachers, setting rules for behavior establishes a structure for managing the classroom environment, and for students, working within the boundaries of the rules establishes a structure for being responsible. Teachers may use the following guidelines when setting rules:

1. Involve students in formulating the rules.
2. Keep the list of rules short.
3. Keep the rules themselves short and to the point.
4. Phrase the rules, when possible, in a positive form.
5. Rather than mention the rules when someone has misbehaved, remind students about them at other times.
6. Post rules in a conspicuous place and review them regularly.
7. Record the number of times rules are reviewed with the class.
8. Make different sets of rules for different activities.
9. Let students know when those different rules apply.
10. Be careful to make rules that can be enforced.
11. When a student breaks a rule the first time, review the rule on a one-to-one basis. Tell the student that he or she must now be familiar with the rule

since it has just been reviewed, explain that the next infraction of the same rule will result in a consequence, and make clear exactly what that consequence will be.

## PEERS WITHIN THE ENVIRONMENT

A composite of different cultures, religions, home environments, and value systems exists in any classroom, and teachers need to be aware of the resulting multiplicity in personalities. For example, when teachers realize that some students work better with others and some work more efficiently alone, children will learn that everyone works differently. A teacher who encourages an open climate in which peers learn to work separately *and* together also prepares a viable framework for peer management.

Additionally, peers of mildly handicapped students get their behavioral cues from the teacher about accepting or not accepting the handicapped students. Teachers open to change and willing to help mainstreamed students will soon find that all children in the class reflect the same positive attitude. Regrettably, the reverse is also true.

## THE TEACHER

The teacher sets the tone in the classroom, the key controlling classroom variables. The teacher adjusts the lighting, controls the temperature, arranges the seating, decides on the method of lesson presentation, elects when to give a test, and chooses what type of test to administer. The teacher sets the affective atmosphere of the classroom and the stage for learning. According to Purkey (1978), the teacher alone has the power to invite or not invite each student to learn. The teacher's attentiveness, expectations, encouragement, attitudes, and evaluations strongly influence students' perceptions of themselves as learners. An impetus to learning as well as a controlling factor in the classroom management process, the teacher's behavior influences the students' behavior. To assess their potential influence on student behavior, teachers can ask themselves the following questions:

- ☐ Do I leave my personal problems at home?
- ☐ Am I in good physical as well as emotional health?
- ☐ Am I happy with my role in life?
- ☐ Does my voice convey confidence?
- ☐ Does my walk convey confidence?
- ☐ Do I have a positive self-concept?
- ☐ What is my attitude toward my peer group?
- ☐ What is my attitude toward children?
- ☐ Do I accept the responsibility of mainstreaming handicapped students?

☐ Do I feel comfortable admitting a mistake?
☐ Will I change my opinion when a valid reason for doing so is presented?
☐ Do I have a sense of humor?
☐ Can I laugh at myself?
☐ Am I an attentive listener?
☐ Do I teach subjects or children?

Weber, in Cooper et al. (1977), lists teacher behaviors that contribute to effective teaching.[1] From this list, teachers can select and develop the behaviors that will help them manage their own particular classroom situations more appropriately. According to Weber,

1. The teacher encourages students to communicate openly.
2. The teacher talks to the situation rather than to the character or personality of the student when handling a problem.
3. The teacher expresses his or her true feelings and attitudes to students.
4. The teacher makes his or her expectations clear and explicit to students.
5. The teacher reinforces appropriate student behaviors.
6. The teacher trains students to perform leadership functions and shares leadership with them.
7. The teacher listens attentively to students.
8. The teacher accepts students as persons of worth.
9. The teacher does not behave in a punitive or threatening manner.
10. The teacher displays an awareness of what is going on in the classroom.
11. The teacher praises the accomplishments of the group.
12. The teacher uses expressions indicating that the students constitute a group of which he or she is a member.
13. The teacher elicits and accepts student expressions of feelings.
14. The teacher clearly communicates appropriate standards for student behavior.
15. The teacher clarifies the norms of the group.
16. The teacher provides students with opportunities to work cooperatively.
17. The teacher ignores inappropriate student behavior to the extent possible.
18. The teacher encourages the establishment of productive group norms.
19. The teacher does not ridicule or belittle students.
20. The teacher does not encourage student competition.
21. The teacher communicates an awareness of how students feel.
22. The teacher respects the rights of students.
23. The teacher accepts all student contributions.
24. The teacher guides students in practicing productive group norms.
25. The teacher encourages and supports individual and group problem solving.

[1]From "Classroom Management" by Wilford A. Weber in *Classroom Teaching Skills: A Workbook*, James M. Cooper, gen. ed. (Lexington, Mass.: D. C. Heath and Co., 1977), 237–239. Copyright © 1977 by D. C. Heath and Co. Reprinted by permission of the publisher.

26. The teacher provides students with opportunities to succeed.
27. The teacher removes students from rewarding situations or removes rewards from students in the event of misbehavior under certain circumstances.
28. The teacher initiates, sustains, and terminates classroom activities with smoothness.
29. The teacher directs attention toward the group rather than toward the individual during the general classroom activities.
30. The teacher allows students to experience the logical consequences of their behavior when physically safe to do so.
31. The teacher praises the accomplishment of the student rather than the student himself or herself.
32. The teacher accepts students and encourages students to be accepting of one another.
33. The teacher promotes group morale by helping students engage in total class activities.
34. The teacher makes use of "time out" to extinguish inappropriate student behavior.
35. The teacher uses nonverbal communication that supports and is congruent with his or her verbal communication.
36. The teacher promotes group unity.
37. The teacher encourages students to use time wisely.
38. The teacher trains students to behave appropriately in the teacher's absence.
39. The teacher displays the ability to attend to more than one issue at a time.
40. The teacher discusses issues with students rather than arguing with them.
41. The teacher accepts a productive level of noise in the classroom.
42. The teacher is nonjudgmental in discussing problem situations.
43. The teacher anticipates certain types of problems and works to prevent them.
44. The teacher respects student privacy.
45. The teacher treats students as persons capable of dealing with their own problems.

When trouble occurs in the classroom, teachers should first assess the environment and then themselves. Often, teachers can manage the classroom more effectively by changing their own behavior. When teachers have evaluated both the environment and themselves but still have difficulty managing student behaviors, they should look at assignments next.

# THE ASSIGNMENT

Frequently, the source of students' behavior problems lies within classroom assignments. Various aspects of an assignment can influence a student's behavior.

## DIRECTION FOR INSTRUCTION

When a mildly handicapped student does not attend to the lesson, consider the way directions were given. Mildly handicapped students will often put their heads on their desks, begin to "act out," or scribble on their papers when they do not understand instructions. Frequently, the teacher has not clearly stated the directions or has not delivered them in a mode the student can understand. Teachers can never assume that a student hears or sees the directions and must observe the student's behavior to see if the student begins the task correctly. When giving instructions to the mildly handicapped, the teacher should try to make directions clear and simple; present directions orally as well as visually; have a selected place on the board for directions; get the class's attention before presenting directions; give directions one at a time; have students repeat the directions without drawing attention to mainstreamed students; ask if there are any questions; give directions about what to do if students need help (i.e., raise hands); and encourage students to do a good job by using positive statements such as, "I can't wait to see all these good papers."

## DIFFICULTY OF ASSIGNMENTS

Most people have experienced being given a task to complete and finding it impossible to do no matter how hard they tried. Mildly handicapped students feel this way frequently. When the assignment seems too difficult for the student, the teacher should

1. Never assume that all handicapped students will complete the same quantido *all* of the regular class work just like everyone else. (If this were possible, the student probably would not be considered handicapped.)
2. Always assume that the assignment needs adapting so that the difficulty level will be reduced.
3. Never assume that all handicapped students will complete the same quantity of work as their peers do. They may have the skills but cannot do the masses of worksheets required of everyone else.
4. Always assume that the assignment needs to be broken down into small sequential steps.
5. Always assume that teaching must start at the first step in the sequence.
6. Never assume that a mildly handicapped student has copied the assignment from the board to the assignment booklet correctly.
7. Make copies of the assignments for a week and give both the student and the resource teacher a copy.

## ADAPTING THE ASSIGNMENTS

Teachers must continually adapt regular class assignments for mildly handicapped students, according to the unique needs of each. The basic instructional model of this book applies whether the teacher assigns group classwork, seat work, or homework. When teachers see instruction as a continuous process, with adapting and modifying as constants in that process, instruction begins to fit the child instead of the child fitting the instruction. Teachers can apply the following ongoing steps when adapting the assignment:

1. Always assess the assignment for the appropriate instructional level.
2. Use feedback from the assessment to dictate the amount and area of adaptations.
3. Use assignments as ongoing parts of class discussion, seat work, learning centers, and homework.
4. Consistently modify the teaching techniques and media used, as well as the content.
5. Relate all activities within an assignment directly to the objectives of the assignment.
6. Make all activities with an assignment sequential (that is, each activity builds on the previous activity).
7. Break assignments down into small increments.
8. Distribute practice within an assignment instead of massing it. That is, use short practice periods instead of long practices.
9. Begin all assignments with a planned opening, a purpose. Ask questions related to the assignment, make a statement to arouse interest, or provide activities to create interest.
10. Orient students to the major points of the assignment. For example, underline main ideas, list main ideas on the board, color code the topics to be studied, or give a lecture outline.
11. Announce when the assignment is *nearly* completed, thus giving prior warning to the handicapped student.
12. Assess the assignment's *length* and *difficulty* when the mildly handicapped student seems overwhelmed by the work or does not finish the assignment. Do not punish students by making them finish assignments during break time or after school. Tell students, after they have completed the assignment, where they should put their work and what they should do next.

## ADAPTING MATERIALS

Finally, in adapting the assignment, teachers should systematically observe the materials used. Because at least 75 percent, and as much as 99 percent, of a student's instructional time is arranged around the materials used in the classroom (Wilson, 1978), it is important that teachers spend enough time selecting or altering the materials used with assignments. Teachers should ask themselves the following questions as they select materials for assignments:

1. Does the level of the material match the student's instructional level?
2. Does the material follow a sequential format and require little special equipment?

3. Does the material insult the student's dignity?
4. Does the material have several evaluational steps?
5. Does the material adequately meet the instructional objectives for the student?
6. Is the material compatible with teaching methods, style, and approach?
7. Does the material suit the student's learning style?
8. Are supporting materials such as teachers' manuals, resources, etc., available?
9. Is the material on the student's interest level?

Often the teacher does not have the opportunity to select the materials to be used in the classroom. However, one can always analyze and perhaps adapt the available materials.

Adapting the assignment appropriately helps prevent potential classroom problems. When teachers create a stable environment, encourage positive attitudes, and choose appropriate assignments, classroom management problems usually do not occur. However, sometimes even these measures are not enough. Sometimes students misbehave even though teachers have prepared themselves, the classroom, and the assignments with the utmost care.

# THE STUDENT

Without students, the classroom would stand empty, the material go unused, the curriculum remain undeveloped, and teachers jobless. Since all efforts are expended for the student in the class, the teacher must look at the student as the source of a behavior problem after the environment, oneself, and the assignment have been ruled out. When deciding on what type of preventive measure or intervention technique to use, the teacher must be acutely aware of the characteristics each student brings to the classroom: social, emotional, physical, and academic. An aware teacher allows the shy student to participate successfully, the overactive child to run a filmstrip projector, and the physically handicapped child to keep score. Teachers can prevent problems by considering students' needs when planning student activities.

This section in classroom management covers preventive planning before mainstreaming, managing those behaviors Long and Newman (1980) call surface behaviors, managing behaviors not so easily prevented, and rewarding students within the classroom.

## PREVENTIVE PLANNING BEFORE MAINSTREAMING

Increasingly, handicapped students are moving into regular classes, some for the entire day, others for only short blocks of time. Preparing the mainstreamed student emotionally as well as academically has become a vital concern for regular teachers. The special educator should inform the regular teacher about the mildly handicapped students' unique needs. Then the special and regular teacher can plan the necessary modifications together. Salend and Viglianti (1982) have prepared an excellent instrument to use for preventive planning prior to main-streaming. This classroom variables analysis form may serve a dual purpose. First, the special teacher can send the analysis form to the regular class teacher before mainstreaming, and thus become aware of the regular class variables that will affect the special student. Second, the regular class teacher, seeing a mildly handicapped student in difficulty, can complete the form and return it to the special teacher for additional input. Then, the special teacher will know what to expect in the regular classroom and can plan preventive measures before the regular class periods begin. Note that this form assesses the environment and the materials as well as the demands on students of any classroom and teacher. See Table 6.2 for this form.

TABLE 6.2
Classroom Variable Analysis Form

Teacher: _____    Subject: _____

Grade: _____    Date: _____

Teacher Completing the Observation:_____

A.  INSTRUCTIONAL MATERIALS AND SUPPORT PERSONNEL
    1.  What textbooks are used in the class? What are the grade levels of the texts?



    2.  What supplementary materials are used in the class? What are the grade sup-plementary materials?



    3.  What types of media are frequently used in the classroom?
        _____ television       _____ slides             _____ record player
        _____ films            _____ overhead projector  _____ audio tapes
        _____ filmstrips
        _____ others (please list)_____
        _____

    4.  What type(s) of support personnel are available in the classroom? How often are they available?
        _____ aide             _____ volunteer           _____ peer tutor
        _____ others (please list)
        _____

TABLE 6.2 (continued)

---

B. PRESENTATION OF SUBJECT MATTER
1. How often does the teacher . . .                          *% of time*
   a. lecture?                                           _____
   b. use the blackboard?                                _____
   c. use indivualized instruction?                      _____
   d. use small group instruction?                       _____
   e. use large group instruction?                       _____
   f. use individual centers?                            _____
   g. others (please list)                               _____
      _____                  _____
   _____                 _____

2. What is the language and vocabulary level used by the teacher?

C. LEARNER RESPONSE VARIABLES
1. How often is the student required to . . .
                                                              *% of time*
   a. take notes?                                        _____
   b. copy from the board?                               _____
   c. read aloud in class?                               _____
   d. do independent work?                               _____
   e. participate in class?                              _____
   f. others (please list)                               _____
      _____                  _____
   _____                 _____

2. In what ways can a student request assistance in the classroom?

3. How are directions given to students? How many directions are given at one time?

D. STUDENT EVALUATION
1. How often and in what ways does the teacher evaluate student progress?

2. How are grades determined?

3. What types of tests are given?
   _____ essay              _____ matching         _____ simple recall
   _____ true/false         _____ completion       _____ fill in
   _____ multiple choice    _____ oral             _____ other

TABLE 6.2 (continued)

4. Does the teacher assign homework?
   a. What type?
   b. How much?
   c. How often?
5. Does the teacher assign special projects or extra-credit work? Please explain.

E.  CLASSROOM MANAGEMENT
   1. Does the teacher have a management system? Briefly describe it.

   2. What are the stated rules in the classroom?

   3. What are the unstated rules in the classroom?

   4. What are the consequences of following the rules? What are the consequences of not following the rules?

   5. In what ways and how often does the teacher reinforce the students?

   6. Does the teacher follow any special routines? What are they?

F.  SOCIAL INTERACTIONS
   1. How often are student interactions . . .　　　　% of time
      a. individualistic?　　　　　　　　　　_____
      b. cooperative?　　　　　　　　　　　　_____
      c. competitive?　　　　　　　　　　　　_____
   2. What are the student norms in this class concerning . . .
      a. dress?
      b. appearance?
      c. interests?
      d. acceptance of individual differences?
      e. other unique relevant characteristics? Please list.
   3. What are the students' attitudes toward the handicapped?

   4. What is the language and vocabulary level of the students?

TABLE 6.2 (continued)

---

    5.  What personality variables does the teacher exhibit that seem to affect the class?

G.  PHYSICAL DESIGN
    1.  What, if any, architectural barriers are in the classroom?

    2.  How does the design affect the students' . . .
        a.  academic performance?
        b.  social interactions?

---

*Note.*  From "Preparing Secondary Students for the Mainstream" by S. J. Salend and D. Viglianti, *Teaching Exceptional Children*, 1982, *14*(4), 138–139. Copyright 1982 by The Council for Exceptional Children. Reprinted by permission.

## SURFACE BEHAVIORS

When problems occur with mildly handicapped students, teachers often anticipate and fear long and involved management strategies, both time-consuming during the instructional period and lasting over months. However, not all behavior problems are that serious. Long and Newman (1980) have developed techniques for what they call surface behaviors—behaviors that merit attention but do not demand total management programs. Teachers should think of surface behaviors as minor infractions, those disruptive behaviors that occur but do not demand serious disciplinary measures. In fact, teachers probably already have the techniques developed by Long and Newman in their repertoire and merely need to remember a few "tricks" for coping with certain minor behavior problems. Before considering intervention, however, teachers should realize that some behaviors deviating from the norm should simply be tolerated.

TOLERATING BEHAVIORS    According to Long and Newman, teachers should tolerate some behaviors that under "normal" conditions would not be tolerated: learner's leeway, behavior symptomatic of a disability, and behavior reflecting a developmental stage.

Learner's leeway refers to the times a student tries to master a new academic skill or perhaps learn or practice a new social skill. Teachers cannot expect perfection the first, or even second or third time the student attempts to master the new skill or idea. At this stage, teachers tolerate mistakes and students understand that mistakes are normal and permitted.

Providing such leeway often eliminates the frustration felt by the mainstreamed student. Mildly handicapped students need many trials before they acquire skills, and teachers can relax the learning climate for the student by acknowledging that errors will occur and will be permitted while learning progresses. Teachers need to understand, in addition, that social skills often require learner's leeway just as academic skills do. Often mildly handicapped students simply do not pick up on social cues and therefore do not behave acceptably. For example, a teacher may correct a student for interrupting, and the remaining students learn not to interrupt from that example. But the mildly handicapped student may or may not learn through this incidental experience, and thus may continue to interrupt.

To tolerate behaviors symptomatic of a disability, teachers must become aware of what such behaviors are. Many teachers do not tolerate specific behaviors because they lack knowledge about handicaps. Thus, school systems need to provide ongoing training in recognizing and identifying disabilities and the behaviors associated with them. Some such behaviors are obvious: a student with asthma would certainly be exempt from strenuous physical exercises during days when the asthma was active. However, children with learning disabilities may behave impulsively, have the teacher misread their behavior as disruptive, and suffer unwarranted consequences. Also, children with emotional problems often display behaviors symptomatic of their disabilities, but these behaviors are considered inappropriate within the regular class environment. These behaviors, many times, must be tolerated, though not overlooked. The special class teacher, in conjunction with the regular class teacher, should deal with these overt behaviors within the objectives of the student's IEP.

Behavior reflecting a developmental stage refers to behavior typical of a special developmental or age level. For example, all teachers expect second grade students to behave impulsively at times; however, they may become upset when sixth graders act the same way. Knowing what behaviors are usual for a certain developmental level helps teachers overlook them. In addition, teachers need to know that handicapped students develop at a slower rate than normal students do and that developmental norms may vary for handicapped students. For example, mildly retarded students develop mentally at one-half to three-fourths the rate of a normal student. Developmentally, at age 10 the retarded student would not function in the same ways an average student at age 10 would. A normal child will usually pass through the impulsive developmental level by grade five, but the handicapped student at grade six may not have left it behind. Once teachers understand developmental differences, they can more easily tolerate a variety of behaviors.

INTERFERING WITH BEHAVIORS   Other times, however, the teacher cannot permit or overlook certain behaviors in the classroom. Then, the teacher needs a systematic plan for interfering with the appropriate behavior. Long and Newman discuss techniques they found successful in interfering with surface behaviors. These techniques can be used on a daily basis. The trick is to employ them immediately when a surface behavior occurs and to match the correct technique with the appropriate behavior.

FIGURE 6.2. Planned Ignoring

PLANNED IGNORING   A simple technique, requiring little training but a great deal of patience, is planned ignoring. Research psychologists refer to this technique as extinction, that is, eliminating a behavior by ignoring it. Planned ignoring means the teacher immediately rewards the student when he or she acts appropriately, and totally ignores the student as long as he or she behaves inappropriately. But the teacher must be patient. When a previously rewarded (with attention) behavior is suddenly ignored, the inappropriate behavior increases before it decreases because the student cannot understand why the teacher does not pay attention to the behavior that has always elicited a response. Teachers should keep calm, grit their teeth, and wait for the appropriate behavior.

SIGNAL INTERFERENCE   In signal interference, teachers use a nonverbal signal to let a student know that they see the inappropriate behavior occurring or about to occur. For examples, a teacher may use hand gestures to say, be quiet, sit down, come here, or give it to me. Teachers may also snap their fingers, use eye gestures, flick the light switch, or turn their backs to the group. Frequently, by using the technique of signal interference, teachers can stop the inappropriate behavior, or better yet, never let it start.

PROXIMITY CONTROL   Teachers can use proximity control and never interrupt the lesson merely by moving close to the student or students exhibiting inappropriate behavior. Often a teacher need only stand near the student or place a hand on the student's shoulder. This technique has a calming effect on some students and helps maintain control.

FIGURE 6.3. Signal Interference

DEFUSING TENSION THROUGH HUMOR  Everyone can remember humorous though inappropriate incidents. This technique employs humor to defuse a potentially explosive situation. For example, one teacher could have used humor during story time on Halloween. The teacher was reading a book about witches to a class of kindergarten students. One bright young boy looked up at the teacher and said, "You are a witch, aren't you?" The teacher immediately slammed the book down, had all the students return to their seats and put their

FIGURE 6.4. Proximity Control

FIGURE 6.5. Defusing Tension through Humor

heads on the desks for fifteen minutes. Instead, if the teacher had laughed and replied, "And you should see how fast I can ride my broom!" she would have eliminated the problem, and the story time would have gone uninterrupted.

SUPPORT FROM ROUTINE    A simple but effective technique for young children and mildly handicapped students involves providing support for the student's routine. Displaying a chart in a special place on the board to show the week's or day's schedule provides security for the student. Then the teacher can announce in advance whenever schedules need to change and what the new schedules will be. Such preparation gives the student consistency and avoids problems like the following. The school nurse appears at the door of a first grade class and tells all of the children to line up. A little boy begins to cry and nothing can calm him. At last the nurse says, "I'm only going to check your eyes." The young lad replies, "But I thought you were going to give me a shot!" Advance preparation for the change in the routine can prevent anxiety and save the teacher as well as the class from disruption.

INTEREST BOOSTING    This technique involves taking an interest in the student who may be off-task or on the verge of acting-out. Walk up to the student and mention one of the student's hobbies or interests. After a brief conversation, walk away. Often the student will go back to work and the inappropriate be-

FIGURE 6.6. Support from Routine

FIGURE 6.7. Interest Boosting

havior will not reoccur. Other times a student may become interested in only one aspect of a lesson or in a topic totally unrelated to the lesson. Then, the teacher can use interest boosting to channel the student's interest and get the student back to work. For example, a fourth grade class was studying prehistoric animals when one young student, becoming fascinated with dinosaurs, would not attend to any other class assignments. The teacher, realizing the problem, suddenly became greatly interested in dinosaurs and decided to do a unit on dinosaurs, placing the fascinated student in charge of the unit. Students could work on dinosaurs only during a selected period of the day and only after other work was completed. Thus, interest boosting encouraged the student to learn more but maintained the day's structure.

REMOVING DISTRACTING OBJECTS    Many a well-planned and well-intentioned lesson has gone astray because the teacher failed to remove distracting objects from the classroom. When using this technique, simply walk up to the student and remove the object from the desk or the student's hand. Or, begin the lesson, "I see some very tempting objects on some desks. I don't want to be tempted to stop our lesson to play with them, so please remove the objects when I count to three." The time teachers invest in removing such objects adds time to the instructional day.

FIGURE 6.8. Removing Distracting Objects

FIGURE 6.9. Antiseptic Bouncing

ANTISEPTIC BOUNCING    Antiseptic bouncing requires that the teacher remove the student from the class for a limited amount of time or until the inappropriate behavior diminishes. Teachers may ask the student who is out of control with uncontrollable giggles, for example, to run an errand or to get a drink of water. Once the student completes the task, the inappropriate behavior will usually stop.

## BEHAVIOR MANAGEMENT TECHNIQUES

When the mildly handicapped student may be the source of a classroom management problem, the teacher tries to prevent disruptive behavior through planning. Then teachers need to understand surface behaviors and simple ways to deal with them. Sometimes, however, teachers need to know about more complex behavior management processes. According to Sulzer-Azaroff (1977), teachers should implement a behavior management process when the student makes several independent requests for assistance; the student behaves differently from the comparison group; or an individual's behavior dramatically changes. If any of these conditions exist, the teacher should identify the target behavior first.

IDENTIFYING TARGET BEHAVIOR    Teachers identify target behaviors as those clearly needing change, but such behaviors must be explicitly defined, observed, and measured so that individuals administering the program agree the behaviors are detrimental to the student's social or academic development. When defining a target behavior, the teacher must refer to observable, unambiguous characteristics. For example, to state that Bobby misbehaves in class or that Joy is not doing well in science neither provides measurable data nor defines a specific behavior. However, if the teacher states that Bobby hits the other students in class, grabs their paper and pencils, and throws spitballs across the room, everyone knows exactly what behavior needs modifying. Similarly, a teacher who says that Joy is failing science, has difficulty grasping fifth grade concepts, cannot take class notes, and cannot focus on the important points of the lesson, has pinpointed Joy's specific behavioral weakness.

Once the target behavior has been clearly defined, the teacher must record or count how often the behavior occurs. Recording target behaviors is necessary, first, to determine the extent to which the target behavior occurs and second, to later evaluate the effectiveness of the technique used to change the target behavior. Once teachers establish that a student's behavior needs to be changed or modified, they can implement a behavior management program.

The teacher should become familiar with several behavior management techniques and select one best suited for the student. Many articles in the education field describe various behavior management techniques, but a few of the more common are positive reinforcement, token economy, contingency contracting, and free time.

POSITIVE REINFORCEMENT    Most people feel good when someone says, "Gee, you look nice today," when they get paid, or when they overhear a compliment. Educators call such examples positive reinforcement. Positive reinforcement means giving a reward to increase or maintain a behavior. In the classroom, for example, a teacher smiles at the student who has satisfactorily completed an assignment or tells a student he or she has shared nicely with a neighbor. When using positive reinforcement, teachers must be sure they have chosen the appropriate reinforcer, because what reinforces one student may not reinforce another. One way to find out what reinforces a student is to ask. In fact, some teachers develop a reinforcement menu for every student in their classes. The teacher has a card indicating all the items each student finds reinforcing. When it becomes obvious that a student has tired of a specific reinforcer, the teacher replaces it with another one. Students can even complete an interest inventory (See Table 6.3) so that the teacher knows what reinforces the student. Teachers can also observe students closely to find out what to use. Regardless of selection method, teachers must learn what type of reinforcer works the best for each student.

TABLE 6.3
Student Interest Inventory

---

These are the things I like:

My favorite school subject is _____.

The best reward anyone could give me is _____.

Three of my favorite things are:
   1. _____
   2. _____
   3. _____

My favorite TV show is _____.

I do not like to do _____.

Three things I would like to have are:
   1. _____
   2. _____
   3. _____

Three places I would like to go to are:
   1. _____
   2. _____
   3. _____

---

Reinforcers fall into three major categories: social reinforcers, tangible reinforcers, and activity reinforcers. Teachers should initially use tangible or activity reinforcers with a student and ultimately strive to transfer the student to a social reinforcer. Since society basically functions on social reinforcement, such as praise for a job well done, or a smile of acknowledgment, students need to learn to perform tasks related to their jobs or to behave in a socially acceptable manner without tangible or activity reinforcements. However, teachers should use tangible or activity rewards when beginning a behavior management program. Examples of the three groups of reinforcers and suggestions for rewards in each group follow:

☐ *Social*—Verbal, physical, or gestured stimulus with purpose of increasing or maintaining behavior:

   Teacher praise
   Smiles
   Getting personal time with teacher
   Playing with classmate of own choice
   Pat on back
   Sitting next to teacher at lunch

☐ *Token*—Tangible item given for performance of specified target behavior:
    Checks
    Points
    Happy faces
    Stars
    Rubber stamp marks
    Balloons
    Award buttons
    Award slips
    Magazines

☐ *Activity*—Activities earned for appropriate behavior:
    Dot-to-dot, word games, crossword puzzles
    Coloring books, getting free time
    Bingo, art activities, field trips
    Frisbees, reading with a friend
    Watching a film, watching TV
    Time in the library, play teacher
    Extra time to complete homework

After target behaviors have been identified and measured and the appropriate type of reinforcer selected, the implementation of a positive program should follow these guidelines: select appropriate reinforcements for the student; reinforce only those behaviors that need changing, modifying, or increasing; reinforce the appropriate behavior *immediately;* reinforce the desired behavior each time it occurs; once the student has learned, changed, or modified a behavior, reinforce only *intermittently,* i.e., on an alternating basis; if using a tangible or activity reinforcement, apply a social reinforcer simultaneously; and withdraw the tangible or activity reward slowly and keep reinforcing the student's behavior with a social reward.

Positive reinforcement has an important effect on the mainstreamed student. The mildly handicapped student usually enters the mainstreamed classroom with a very poor self-concept. Often the student has been in regular classes, unidentified as handicapped, struggling to succeed to no avail. Understandably, when previous failures to succeed condition the student to fear trying to learn, the student's self-concept will be low. Positive rewards are essential for students with a history of failure, because until they start to think they *can* succeed, they will not succeed. Thus, positive reinforcements in the mainstream lead to more self-assured handicapped students.

TOKEN ECONOMY   A token is a tangible item given to the student for performing a specified target behavior. It has no intrinsic value but acquires value when exchanged for a material reinforcer or reinforcing event. For example, a paycheck has no intrinsic value until the person cashes it in for money. And once someone receives cash, it is often exchanged for material items or reinforcing events.

Figure 6.10 shows the eight steps necessary to implement a token economy system within the classroom. As in any behavior management program, the first step involves identifying the target behavior. Once the behavior is identified, the student must understand what behavior must be exhibited to receive the tokens. Additionally, the teacher must clearly explain the tokens and what they may be exchanged for. The student should be capable of performing the desired behavior; otherwise, the token system will be marked for failure before it is initiated. The teacher can record the desired behavior on a wall chart or on a small chart on the student's desk. For younger students, draw pictures of the desired behavior on the behavior charts. Since secondary level students may resent having behaviors recorded on a wall chart, the teacher can keep them private by listing them in a small reward book.

The teacher must then select the back-up reinforcers for which the tokens will be exchanged. Back-up reinforcers may be small toys, candy, privileges, special activities, etc. Again, the reinforcer should appeal to the student. Teacher and student may choose an appropriate back-up reinforcer together. When the token system involves more than one student, the teacher should have a variety of back-up reinforcers. The student needs to clearly understand what a token is, how many tokens have to be earned before receiving the backup reinforcer, when the reinforcer will be received, and how the number of tokens will be recorded.

A well-designed token system will allow the teacher to gradually withdraw material reinforcers and replace them with social reinforcement. An effective token system should be implemented simply, function well, and not distract from the instructional process. The teacher should evaluate the token system's effectiveness, and as with any technique, change it when it loses its effectiveness.

CONTINGENCY CONTRACTS   With a contract, a student and a teacher agree to accomplish a specific objective. Contracts formally apply "Grandma's Law": "You get to do what you want to do after you do what I want you to do." To set up a contract, the teacher and student should choose the behavior, task, or skill to work on, agree on how many times the behavior should occur or how long the student should spend on the task, agree on how long the contract should be in effect, decide what the reinforcer should be if the student successfully completes the task, and sign the contract. Consequences of the contract should be realistic and understood—students should know what to expect if they meet the criteria of the contract and what to expect if they do not. Whether or not students meet the contract's criteria, they and the teacher should eventually evaluate the contract and decide if a new one is needed.

Contracts are fun to develop and design, and students should assist the teacher in designing and developing them. Contracting works well in main-

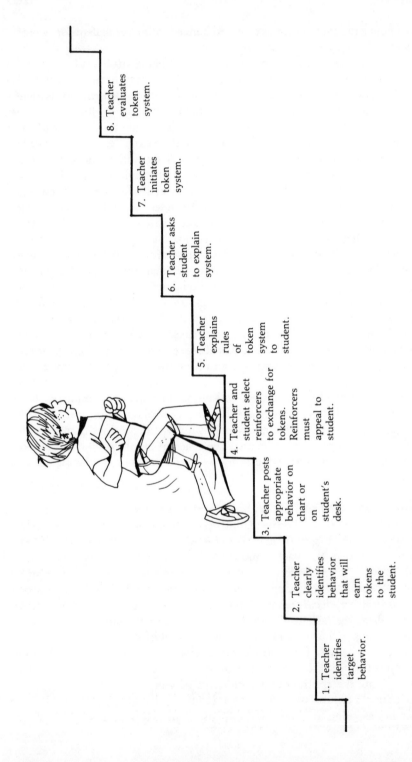

FIGURE 6.10. Steps to a Token Economy

1. Teacher identifies target behavior.

2. Teacher clearly identifies behavior that will earn tokens to the student.

3. Teacher posts appropriate behavior on chart or on student's desk.

4. Teacher and student select reinforcers to exchange for tokens. Reinforcers must appeal to student.

5. Teacher explains rules of token system to student.

6. Teacher asks student to explain system.

7. Teacher initiates token system.

8. Teacher evaluates token system.

streamed classes because contracts provide mildly handicapped students with structure—they know what is expected of them socially and academically. Also, the contract provides a visual and ongoing progress report for the mainstreamed student. Most important, the regular teacher and the special education teacher can develop the contract together, thus providing a bridge between two classrooms for the mainstreamed student.

FREE TIME  Free time is the time given to students as a reward for successfully completing their assignments or for doing something special. The student may use the free time to work on an art project, listen to a record, go to the library, or simply sit at the desk and choose an activity. The key phrase in the definition is "for successsfully completing their assignments." Students must earn free time. Teachers using free time should designate special areas in the room for it; place varied activities on different instructional levels in the free time areas; remember that activities too difficult for students are not rewards; and explain how the students can earn the free time privileges. Teachers may also want to try the following ideas for free time: use movable screens to divide the areas, making special places for the students; place an old-fashioned bathtub filled with pillows, books, and magazines in the back of the classroom; take the door off a closet and place a large bean bag in it for free time reading; use pieces of carpet for magic rides to free time; have areas for boys only; have areas for girls only; provide free time art areas; provide popular free time game areas; select one of the student's friends to share the free time area; provide free time library passes; and allow 10 minutes at the end of each period for free time winners.

## SUMMARY

Managing the classroom, an essential element in instruction, means managing the environment, analyzing one's own behavior, assessing the assignment, and observing the student. By looking at classroom management as a total process, not just as students' behavioral problems, teachers can cope with any problems that do occur.

Chapter 7 covers ways the teacher can evaluate mildly handicapped students. Even if the teacher has carefully implemented all other parts of the model, the continuum is incomplete until evaluation is also adapted. Working with mainstreamed students requires proper evaluation.

## REFERENCES

Cooper, J. M., Hansen, J., Martorella, P. H., Morine-Dershimer, G., Sadker, Sadker, M., Sokolve, S., Shostak, R., Ten Brink, T., & Weber, W. A. *Classroom teaching skills: A workbook.* Lexington, Mass.: D. C. Heath, 1977.

Long, N. J., & Newman, R. Managing surface behaviors of children in schools. In N. J. Long, W. Morse, & R. Newman (Eds.), *Conflict in the classroom: The education of emotionally disturbed children* (4th ed.). Belmont, Calif.: Wadsworth, 1980.

Purkey, W. *Inviting school success.* Belmont, Calif.: Wadsworth, 1978.

Salend, S. J., & Viglianti, D. Preparing secondary students for the mainstream. *Teaching Exceptional Children*, 1982, *14*(4), 137-140.

Sulzer-Azaroff, B., & Mayer, G. R. *Applying behavioral analysis procedures with children and youth.* New York: Holt, Rinehart and Winston, 1977.

Wilson, J. Selecting education materials and resources. In D. Hammil & W. Bartel (Eds.), *Teaching children with learning and behavior problems.* Boston: Allyn and Bacon, 1978.

# Chapter Seven

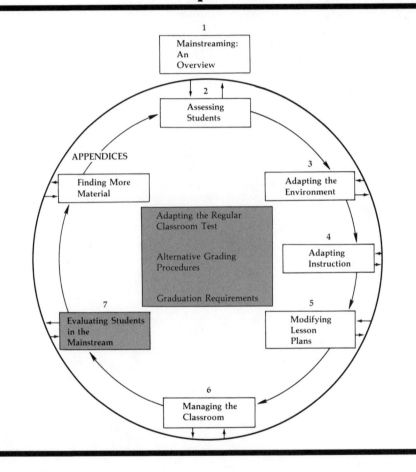

1
Mainstreaming:
An
Overview

2
Assessing
Students

APPENDICES

Finding More
Material

3
Adapting the
Environment

Adapting the Regular
Classroom Test

Alternative Grading
Procedures

Graduation Requirements

4
Adapting
Instruction

7
Evaluating Students
in the
Mainstream

5
Modifying
Lesson
Plans

6
Managing the
Classroom

# Evaluating Students in the Mainstream

Since the passage of Public Law 94-142, regular and special educators have been working together to modify curricula, adapt lesson plans, and alter classroom environments to meet the needs of mildly handicapped students. But considerably less attention has been given to the *evaluation* of such students. The term evaluation can cover test questions, grading systems, or graduation requirements and competency testing. Evaluation of mildly handicapped students in the mainstream has become controversial.

Since special education aims to foster student ability and potential by individualizing educational programming, both regular and special educators need to recognize the impact testing, grading, and graduation have on the achievement and self-concept of the handicapped student. Students need rewards for effort and for attaining goals; therefore, teachers must use evaluation methods that enable students to demonstrate mastery, and mastery must be based upon individual student ability or potential, not on the norm. After all, if handicapped students could achieve at standard levels, educators would not be serving them for handicaps. Robbins and Harway (1977) point out that "the school age period is crucial in the development of a child's view of himself" (p. 356). They further explain that the handicapped child experiences a wide variety of successes and failures that tend to interfere with the child's development of a sense of identity. In particular, Robbins and Harvey demonstrate that if teachers give learning disabled students positive feedback, those students gradually set more realistic goals for themselves. But since they have encountered a great many failures in school, they may need constant reinforcement before they are convinced that they *can* achieve.

Therefore, as teachers evaluate the mildly handicapped student's progress in the regular classroom, they need to consider the student's cognitive *and* affective development. To ensure student progress, teachers should select the most appropriate and nondiscriminatory method of evaluation. Educators can meet the needs of mildly handicapped students by using alternative evaluation techniques. This chapter focuses on adapting classroom testing for mildly handicapped students, the benefits and deficits of several grading systems presently in use, and the obstacles confronting teachers as they devise graduation requirements for special students.

# ADAPTING THE REGULAR CLASSROOM TEST

If the primary goal of most teachers is *concept mastery*, teachers must find ways to give mildly handicapped students the opportunity to demonstrate proficiency to regular classroom teachers, doubting and unaccepting peers, and themselves. If teachers persist in using traditional testing techniques, they further handicap the very students the law attempts to protect. While modifications in curricula and instructional procedures are more prevalent today in regular elementary and secondary classrooms, many teachers still resist changing a test's construction, administration, and site. To many teachers, the traditional test is sacred and thus the *only* instrument of evaluation. These same teachers feel that if the mildly handicapped student cannot demonstrate mastery via this one instrument under the same conditions as everyone else in the classroom, then that student has not achieved and does not deserve a passing grade. However, these teachers do not realize that the student may indeed have mastered the concept but cannot show the teacher that mastery unless certain modifications are made in the test. What the student lacks are the skills necessary to succeed in a traditional setting. While it is true that some handicapped students may not reach the same goals as their nonhandicapped peers, others will surpass these same peers through hard work, determination, and perseverance. As John Dewey commented in 1937, each child is "equally an individual and entitled to equal opportunities of development of his own capacity, be they large or small in range" (Dewey, 1937, pp. 458–459).

Before adapting a test, the teacher should evaluate test objectives to see whether or not the test is appropriate. To evaluate test objectives, the teacher should ask the following questions: Is content validity present in the test? Does the test measure what it is intended to measure? Does the test evaluate the skills taught? (Be sure it does not cover more complex skills or concepts than were discussed.) Is the test designed to reflect student *knowledge* rather than speed, ability to follow complicated directions, or vocabulary? Does the test test in the same way retention was taught? (For example, if the teacher teaches for recognition of facts—retention for recognition—the test should not require recall—retention for structured recall.)

## A MODEL FOR ADAPTING THE CLASSROOM TEST

Adapting classroom tests for mainstreamed students requires following a three-part model, shown in Figure 7.1. By adapting test construction, altering test administration, and changing test sites, the teacher helps mainstreamed students succeed in the regular classroom. Teachers can make a few simple alterations and allow some flexibility in actually giving the test. They can also provide different physical environments for taking the test. Before constructing a test, however, the teacher needs to understand the problems mildly handicapped students often encounter when taking tests. Once aware of these problems, the teacher can more equitably evaluate the mildly handicapped student.

POOR COMPREHENSION   Comprehension means the ability to clearly understand what is said or explained. Often mildly handicapped students do not understand verbal directions, and when the teacher gives a series of directions, these students cannot recall each step correctly. Without a clear understanding of what to do or how to proceed, they either proceed incorrectly or turn papers in with only their names at the top. Certainly, the responses obtained do not accurately indicate the student's knowledge. Similarly, written directions are often too lengthy and complicated for the mildly handicapped student. The

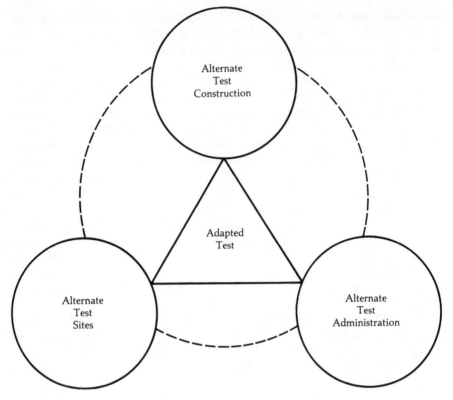

FIGURE 7.1. Model for Adapting Classroom Test

reading level alone may be above the student's instructional level. Directions may contain words or phrases that the student does not know, may instruct the student to perform several operations, or may ask the student to follow more than one procedure. For example, a mildly handicapped student with poor comprehension would have difficulty following and understanding these directions:

1. Write a sentence containing a gerund.
2. Draw a circle around the gerund.
3. Indicate whether the gerund is the subject, direct object, predicate nominative, or object of the preposition by writing S., D.O., P.N., or O.P. above the gerund.

A related difficulty involves abstractions. Mildly handicapped students do well recalling facts and dealing with concrete ideas, but they do not respond well to evaluative questions or those requiring inferences or deductive reasoning. For example, the student may understand how to write a paragraph, but would have trouble writing several paragraphs on this topic: ecology in action in our community.

PERCEPTUAL PROBLEMS: AUDITORY-TEACHER VARIABLES    Students with perceptual auditory problems cannot process auditory information quickly and easily. The student can hear, but problems in learning occur when he or she tries to process what is heard. Auditory problems associated with teacher variables, however, can be avoided. The teacher administering tests orally, for example, greatly penalizes students with auditory deficits. Even simple spelling tests pose problems. Some teachers proceed too fast; then the student does not have time to sound out the word and transfer these sounds into their written forms. Secondly, some teachers simply call out the words without clearly delineating each syllable or sound distinctly. The student may experience only minor difficulty with spelling tests, but major trouble occurs when the teacher administers quizzes or chapter tests orally. The student must process the question through the auditory system, a giant undertaking and also transfer the information to paper, sometimes virtually impossible. In addition, the auditorally handicapped student simply cannot recall previously asked questions. Thus, a good traditional technique prevents the student from demonstrating concept mastery.


PERCEPTUAL PROBLEMS: AUDITORY-ENVIRONMENTAL VARIABLES    Whereas teachers can determine the percentage of information presented verbally and the number of tests administered orally, they may have little control over certain environmental auditory distractions inside and outside the classroom. Frequently, teachers have grown accustomed to a reasonable amount of background noise or sounds and are oblivious to these distractions. Students with auditory problems, however, are not as fortunate. A variety of environmental variables may distract these students from their classwork or from verbal information being presented by the teacher: noise outside a window; conversations in an adjoining classroom; learning module distractions; announcements from the P.A. system; and incidental noise arising from peers, such as students asking the teacher a question, students whispering among themselves after completing assignments or tests, and teachers reprimanding students for talking at unauthorized times. Since many of these auditory distractions cannot be eliminated or modified, the teacher should realize that for a few seconds, these conditions create an environment hostile to learning and not ideal for testing. The teacher must guard against assuming that if students would just "pay attention," they would be able to understand or if they would just "concentrate" more, they could complete the assigned task or test. Students with auditory perceptual problems often find it difficult to discriminate the sounds coming from the front of the classroom (i.e., instructions from the teacher) from sounds filtering into the room from elsewhere. Also, for other students, concentrating and remaining "on-task" becomes virtually impossible in a clasroom with normal environmental sounds. For students experiencing auditory difficulties, alternative instructional methods may be needed but alternative testing sites may prove more helpful.

PERCEPTUAL PROBLEMS: VISUAL-TEACHER VARIABLES  Many students experience problems when they receive information visually. Again, the student does not have a problem seeing, but a problem processing information received visually. Teacher variables often contribute to the mildly handicapped student's visual problem.

Visual distractions abound in the typical classroom, but for the student with visual perceptual problems, some distractions are worse than others. For example, most teachers use blackboards as an instructional tool. Teachers invariably post spelling words, homework assignments, and other reminders on the board for students to copy into their notebooks. A number of teachers even write tests on the board, while others require students to work math problems, diagram sentences, or complete other tasks at the blackboard. All these teachers assume that information written correctly on the board will be copied correctly into notebooks. Although true for the majority of students in the class, the one or more with visual perceptual difficulties may have all kinds of problems. Primarily, they have trouble transferring information from the board to their paper or notebooks: transposing numbers, as in page numbers assigned for homework, or interchanging letters in spelling words or in the key terms for a new unit. Then students memorize the information copied incorrectly, leading to a misrepresentation of their ability and poor test scores. Similarly, copying homework assignments incorrectly leads to additional confusion. At night, students open their books to unfamiliar pages and problems they may not know how to solve; the following day, the teacher is suspicious of the student's explanation for not completing the assignment. The student with visual perceptual problems encounters some of the same difficulties when attempting to take a test written on the board—difficulty transferring information to paper, understanding written directions or questions, and copying correctly. As if these problems were not enough, visual distractions on or near the blackboard clutter the student's field of vision—homework assignments on the same board as the test, spelling words in another corner, and bulletin boards adjacent to the blackboard, for example. And although the majority of teachers keep clean boards, not all of them do.

The teacher's handwriting also affects how a student responds to any test. Although most teacher's printing or cursive handwriting ranges from average to excellent, not all teachers can claim such a distinction. Of course typed tests are better than handwritten ones, but teachers cannot always have their tests typed. Although a good test does not require typing, legibility is a must. Teachers with unusual cursive styles should print. If printing also presents problems, the teacher should ask someone else to write the test. Also important is legibility after duplicating. Not all schools possess the newest or most efficient duplicating equipment, but unreadable copies are inexcusable. Students should at least be able to decipher the questions.

Probably most teachers use written tests in one form or another—multiple choice, true-false, matching, fill-in-the-blank, completion, essay, or others. Once again, the student with visual perceptual problems encounters obstacles. For example, a teacher may hand secondary students a matching test with lengthy columns of answer choices and an equally lengthy column of descriptive statements. Although students may know the answer to the first descriptive statement, they must peruse the column of answer choices, up and down, up and down, to ascertain whether the answer is A, B, F, or H. The student spends unnecessary time searching for letter equivalents to answers, sometimes to the extent that often the student is unable to complete the test. Even more common, mildly handicapped students, oblivious to time, spend the allotted period on just the matching section and do not even attempt the remaining sections.

Length can also become a psychological barrier to success on written tests. Mildly handicapped students have usually failed repeatedly; therefore, to the majority of these students, tests mean unpleasantness. If teachers questioned them about previous tests, or about their ability to pass tests, their responses would probably be negative. When confronted with a lengthy test (three or more pages), mildly handicapped students, especially those with visual problems, may become discouraged, attempt the first page and stop when they realize they cannot finish, or feel defeated upon first examining the test. Teachers may overhear remarks such as, "I know I don't know the answers to that many questions," or "I know I'll never finish, so why should I even begin?" even among high school students. The number of questions on a particular page or the number of problems per page may visually overwhelm other students. Their eyes busily scan and rescan the page so that they cannot focus on individual questions or problems and thus cannot proceed.

Other students with visual problems have difficulty identifying, recognizing, or decoding symbols and/or abbreviations. Simple mathematical symbols, such as $+$ , $-$ , $>$ , $<$ , or $=$ , may cause visual turmoil for students with visual perceptual problems. They may confuse one symbol with another, or they may have trouble associating the symbol with its written equivalent—for example, plus $=$ $+$ . Students with pronounced visual difficulties usually experience extreme anxiety when attempting to solve algebraic equations:

$$\frac{(2x + 4)}{2} - 4 = (2x + 6) + 3(2x + 3x)$$

Of course, not all mildly handicapped students will take algebra, but some learning disabled students with normal to above normal IQs will need to complete algebra if their goals include a college degree. Other mildly handicapped students may not take algebra but will continue to encounter basic mathematical symbols throughout their academic years.

PERCEPTUAL PROBLEMS: VISUAL-ENVIRONMENT VARIABLES    Visual distractions and stimuli abound, both inside and outside the classroom. The degree to which these factors distract students, of course, varies from student to student.

For some students, most visual distractions are momentary, but for others, a distraction can completely disrupt their present visual field, their ability to concentrate, and their ability to keep working. Whether the distraction originates outside a classroom window or inside (as a result of movement of peers at their desks, motions or gestures from neighbors, movement as peers turn in their papers, or from visitors entering the classroom), these disruptions cause the student with minor visual problems to become temporarily nonfunctional and the student with more serious visual problems to remain nonfunctional indefinitely.

TIME CONSTRAINTS   Teachers generally strive to develop a test to fit the time frame for giving it. And most teachers attempt to allow extra time for students who work more slowly than others. However, for mildly handicapped students, time often plays a *major* role in taking a test. Within the group of mildly handicapped students, individuals have auditory perceptual problems, visual perceptual problems, motor coordination difficulties, and frequently, reading problems. These students are not necessarily slow or lazy, and they do not mean to aggravate the teacher or disrupt the test; rather, they have real problems caused by identified *learning* modality deficits. Therefore, the teacher needs to remember, for example, that students with auditory problems may not be able to answer oral questions in the same time frame as students without such a disability can. Similarly, students with visual perceptual problems, motor coordination problems, or reading problems will probably not complete most tests designed for the nonhandicapped student. Thus, teachers must try to avoid discriminating against students with recognized exceptionalities, students who are penalized, not because they lack knowledge, but because they lack an opportunity to demonstrate their proficiency.

ANXIETY   Most teachers have experienced test anxiety at least once during their academic lives. Most, then, can admit that test anxiety exists and is very real to the individual experiencing it. Teachers need to understand further, however, that the degree of test anxiety varies considerably from student to student. When anxiety makes a student nonfunctional, it should be recognized as a handicap similar to those in comprehension, visual and auditory perception, and motor coordination. This disability differs from the others, however, because it is usually temporary. Years of failure and negative responses from teachers, peers, and parents result in measurably lower self-concepts for mildly handicapped students. Because many automatically associate taking a test with failure, they become anxiety ridden even at the thought. For a few, fear and anxiety, along with a history of previous failures, cause test phobias. These students, for all practical purposes, simply cannot function in a traditional test setting. Others feel anxiety, but not to the same extent. These students may, for example, be extremely hesitant at the beginning of a test because they lack self-confidence, or they may stop midway through because they encounter one or two questions they do not know. Others stop working when they realize that their peers have finished and are turning in their papers. Such students want to be "normal" or at least appear "normal." They do not want to be the last ones working or to be called "dummies." Still other students allow their initial impression of the length or scope of the test to overwhelm them, and like the students with test phobias, become nonfunctional for a while. Anxiety, although difficult to measure, influences a student's ability to take and pass a test; thus, a teacher should consider a student's anxiety level when evaluating that student's performance. And a teacher should attempt to reduce that level as much as possible by adapting the test.

EMBARRASSMENT   Perhaps what most mildly handicapped students want is to be like everyone else. Identifying with, and being accepted by, one's peers is important to any student, but for the mildly handicapped student, it becomes essential. And as students mature into adolescence and young adulthood, this desire for peer acceptance and approval becomes even more pronounced. Thus, handicapped students, so acutely aware of their academic inabilities, will sometimes sacrifice a passing grade rather than ask the teacher a question in front of their peers and risk possible embarrassment. Over the years, students learn to hide and disguise their handicaps, becoming specialists in looking busy or in presenting an "I don't care" attitude rather than admitting they do not understand how to do the work. In addition, a high percentage of mildly handicapped students turn their test papers in simply because nearly everyone else in the class has done so—they cannot risk the embarrassment of being the last ones working. When teachers grade such papers and see so few questions answered, they assume, incorrectly, that the mildly handicapped students did not study.

Mainstreamed students are also sensitive about taking different tests from their peers. Although they realize they are receiving individualized programming, these students understandably want to maintain the appearance of doing the same work as their peers do. Some high school mildly handicapped students insist on taking the "regular" test along with their friends although they know it will not be scored and an individualized test will be administered to them in their resource class. Other handicapped students willingly take a modified test in the regular classroom as long as it closely resembles the one being taken by everyone else. The regular teacher must remember that, although mildly handicapped students certainly need to receive praise from parents and special education teachers, they also need to maintain their pride and self-esteem in the presence of peers.

## ALTERNATIVE TEST CONSTRUCTION

Once teachers clearly understand the problems mildly handicapped students encounter as they take tests, they can implement the three-part model for adapting tests: adapting the test itself, altering the test's administration, and changing the test's site. Wood and Englebert (1982) make the following suggestions for adapting the content of tests.

1.  Construct test sentences using only the most important words and use simple as opposed to complex sentence structure (noun-verb-object).
    *Original Construction:*
    In 1492, America was discovered by _____,
    a famous Italian explorer searching for a shorter
    route to India.
    a.  DeGama
    b.  Magellan
    c.  Amerigo Vespucci
    d.  Columbus
    *Alternative Construction:*
    _____ discovered America.
    a.  DeGama
    b.  Magellan
    c.  Amerigo Vespucci
    d.  Columbus

2.  Identify key words in math reading problems by circling them in red.
    Joey's mother gave him one dollar to go to the corner
    store to buy apples. Apples cost five cents each and
    oranges cost ten cents each. How many apples can Joey
    buy?

3.  Also, place the numerical value of numbers in parentheses.
    Joey's mother gave him one dollar ($1.00). Each apple
    cost five cents (5¢).

4.  For students with problems recognizing arithmetic symbols ($+$, $-$, $\times$, $-$), write the name of the symbol above or beside the sign.
    (plus)                                    (times—multiply)
    $\frac{1}{4} + \frac{3}{4} = $ _____           $\frac{3}{4} \times \frac{2}{3} = $ _____

5.  For students with figure-ground difficulties, place a minimum number of words and/or math problems on each page and space them appropriately.

6.  Since matching tests often present problems for special students, try the following alternatives:
    a.  Offer fill-in-the-blank or multiple choice questions instead.
    b.  Shorten the choice column, using a minimum of responses.

7.  Avoid spelling tests with scrambled letters to be decoded. As an alternative, provide the word and leave out some letters for the student to fill in.

*Original Construction:*
   nautputec
*Alternative Construction:*
   p _ _ c t u _ _ e

8. Many times phrasing and vocabulary make tests difficult for special students. The teacher should either clarify the questions orally or modify the question when making up the test. Change phrasing to eliminate unnecessary words and present alternative vocabulary in parentheses.

**Phrasing**
*Original Construction:*
   Why did the percentage of the population living
   in cities increase rapidly after 1880?
*Alternative Construction:*
   Why did more people move to the cities after
   1880?

**Vocabulary**
*Original Construction:*
   Why have American blacks had to face obstacles
   not faced by other Americans?
*Alternative Construction:*
   Why have American blacks had to face obstacles
   (hardships) not faced by other Americans?

9. Special students perform better on tests constructed in a logical, sequential order. For example, construct math tests from the simple to the complex. And a history test should proceed in chronological order.

10. Concentrate on concrete facts and avoid abstractions.
   *Original Construction:*
      What effect did *Uncle Tom's Cabin* have on the
      slavery dispute?
   *Alternative Construction:*
      What is the name of a famous book written by
      Harriet Beecher Stover that describes the suffering
      of slaves and the cruelties of their
      masters? (Wood & Englebert, 1982, p. 65)

Teachers adapting tests for their mildly handicapped students can also do the following:

1. Write simple directions at the top of the page and use simple words.
2. Shorten the length of directions.
3. Evaluate the vocabulary of questions and use simpler terms whenever possible.
4. Decrease the number of test questions altogether.
5. Space questions and problems appropriately on the page.
6. Write legibly.
7. Be sure the test is clearly printed.

## ALTERNATIVE TEST ADMINISTRATION

To administer tests fairly to mildly handicapped students, teachers should consider the following alterations.

1. Administer a lengthy math test by cutting it into strips consisting of only a few problems. As the student completes one strip, add another one.
2. For students who have difficulty with left to right orientation, place a green dot (go) at the beginning of the question or sentence and a red dot (stop) at the end.
3. Cut "window frames" the size of the problem or sentence out of construction paper. This technique reduces visual stimuli and helps students concentrate.
4. For students easily distracted, place colored construction paper behind the test. It provides a solid border that helps maintain the student's attention.
5. Lengthy tests penalize special students, especially at the secondary level when tests increase in both number of pages and difficulty. Two possible ways to shorten tests follow:
   a. Administer one-half of the test on one day and the other half on the next day, or allow the special student to take one-half of the test in the regular classroom and one-half in the resource room.
   b. Require special students to do fewer problems or questions. If the teacher does not have time to develop a separate test, circle only the odd or even questions for the special student.
6. Allow students to use calculators and multiplication tables after they understand the basic process but still have difficulty memorizing facts. (Wood & Englebert, 1982, p. 65)

Teachers might also do the following:

1. Administer directions both orally and in written form.
2. Administer *tests* orally and in written form.
3. Remove unnecessary visual distractions from blackboard.
4. Place directions on blackboard and make copies for mildly handicapped students to use at their desks.

## ALTERNATE TEST SITES

Allowing mildly handicapped students to take their tests in an alternate environment, such as the resource room, poses a number of problems for regular teachers. First, teachers need to make out and duplicate their tests the day *before* the test so that they can get copies of the test to the resource teacher. Those teachers with the habit of making out tests at the last minute and running them off in the office beween classes may find this new procedure inconvenient at first. Teachers must also match resource teachers to mainstreamed students (assuming that there are two or more special education teachers on staff) so that they can give copies of tests to the appropriate teacher. Keep such information in the grade book or keep separate lists of resource students by resource teacher. Some regular teachers, in addition, think they have sole responsibility for transmitting copies of tests to resource teachers, when actually, regular and special education teachers should share this responsibility.

A second potential problem involves teachers' feelings about someone else administering and/or modifying their tests. As mentioned earlier, some teachers consider their tests sacred, and therefore, they want ultimate authority over developing and administering them. Part of the problem stems from academic training before passage of Public Law 94-142 and part from habit: "I've always done it this way." Also, a few teachers believe that there is only one correct way to test students. Of course, it would be more convenient for all educators if all students possessed similar abilities, learned in the same way, and could be tested with a single instrument under similar conditions. However, students are individuals with diverse abilities and equally diverse needs; as professionals, teachers should attempt to meet those needs and evaluate those abilities by using whatever method is the most appropriate and by using *all* available resources, whether these resources be classroom materials, special education personnel, or alternate learning or testing environments. Regular and special educators should work together, not separately, for the common good of the child, and if regular teachers have doubts about a resource teacher's administration of a test, they should visit the resource room and observe. See Table 7.1 for some advantages of testing in the resource room.

Modifying tests for resource students is primarily the responsibility of the regular classroom teacher since the regular teacher is more familiar with the material presented to the student. However, since the special education teacher knows the individual student's unique strengths and weaknesses, it is best if the regular and special education teachers combine their talents.

To work together to modify any test, regular and special education teachers must find opportunities to meet, either during the school day or after school. Since elementary teachers do not generally have planning periods, they have only one option: after school. However well-intentioned both regular teachers and special teachers may be, though, faculty meetings, school activities, family commitments, and parent conferences frequently prevent such joint work sessions. Similarly, regular and special teachers on the secondary level rarely share identical planning periods. And planning periods and after school hours often fill up with conferences and other school and family responsibilities. Also, the regular teacher has a load of 130 to 150 students, whereas the special education teacher has a load of 18 to 20 students. Alternatives to frequent meetings after school might include the following:

1. Regular and special teacher work together to familiarize the regular teacher with each student's needs, the ultimate goal being the regular teacher's assuming full responsibility.
2. Regular and special teacher work together to familiarize the regular teacher with ways the special education teacher modifies tests and to acquaint the special education teacher with the desired goals for the course, the ultimate goal being the special teacher's assuming full responsibility.
3. Regular and special education teacher work together for a longer period of time, the ultimate goal being the creation of a test bank from which both could draw throughout the year, and then make minor modifications depending on the amount of material covered.

Regular teachers also fear that peers may resent it when mildly handicapped students make better grades than nonhandicapped students do when they take tests in the resource room. This fear is based on the assumption that mildly handicapped students will, in fact, make better grades than nonhandi-

TABLE 7.1
Advantages of Testing in Resource Room[a]

| Specific Problem | Potential Solution |
|---|---|
| Reading difficulties<br>  Slow reader<br>  Low vocabulary<br>  Low comprehension | Oral tests<br>  More time<br>  Questions can be clarified<br>  New vocabulary can be explained<br>  Less pressure<br>  Record test on tape recorder |
| Student embarrassed by taking<br>  a test different from one given<br>  to peers in regular class. | Student has acceptable setting<br>  for completing test |
| Student easily confused by<br>  verbal or written directions | Student has more opportunity<br>  to ask questions and may feel<br>  less frustrated |
| Student distracted by<br>  activity within regular<br>  classroom | Student has a more structured<br>  setting that contains fewer<br>  distractions |
| Student experiencing test<br>  anxiety, frustration | Anxiety reduced<br>  No longer competing with peers<br>  Can work at own pace<br>  Has support of resource teacher |

[a]Although many resource rooms administer regular class tests, not all of them do.

*Note.* From "Mainstreaming Minimanual" by J. Wood and B. Englebert, *Instructor,* 1982. *91*(7), 63–66. Copyright 1982 by *Instructor.* Used by permission of The Instructor Publications, Inc.

capped students because their tests are "easier." However, although some handicapped students do score significantly higher, others do well to pass. And when questioned, regular students usually do not resent their peers who take their tests in a resource setting. Quite the contrary. Regular students sometimes exhibit more compassion than teachers do: they are pleased when their friends can pass and do well; they realize that their friends have problems in school; and they often understand that their peers function below grade level, take different tests, and have reasons for being tested in resource. Usually, when teachers handle resource programming and testing appropriately, students, regular and special, view the program positively. Even average to above average students sometimes ask to attend resource for temporary assistance or to complete a test, and the majority of slow learners not eligible for special education services would gladly attend resource.

The whole dilemma revolves around equality of evaluation. Just as teachers traditionally evaluate by testing, they similarly express the results of their evaluation via the use of letter (A, B, C, D, F) or numerical (95, 90, 85, 80) grades. To teachers, students, parents, and the general public, these symbols generally represent a certain standard, and when students do not take the same tests as peers but receive traditional grades, some teachers believe a standard has been violated. This issue has not been resolved; however, the following points should be noted:

1. Mildly handicapped students do have definite learning problems as attested to by their placement in special education.
2. Authorities do recommend alternate site testing.
3. School systems across the nation do use alternate grading systems.

For the present, then, regular and special educators should strive to develop equitable grading policies that will reward handicapped students for their efforts and encourage all students to work toward their potential.

# ALTERNATIVE GRADING PROCEDURES

Evaluation in the mainstream includes three components: classroom testing, grading, and graduation. Because teachers often overlook grading, they may once again subject mildly handicapped students to discriminatory practices and unnecessary embarrassment. Since Public Law 94-142 calls for individual programming to meet the needs of special students, educators must also develop more appropriate grading policies and procedures to adequately reflect student achievement. As Vasa (1980) reports, "the traditional system of comparing the individual with the rest of the class is no longer appropriate" (p. 1). But, as Marsh and Price (1980) point out, an estimated 82 per cent of junior high schools and 84 per cent of senior high schools use a letter grading system to evaluate the performance of students, citing letter grades as good predictors of college performance. Certainly some mildly handicapped students will attend college, but many others will need to select more appropriate goals. Therefore, the rationale given for traditional grading may not fit the mildly handicapped student's situation.

Regular and special teachers often experience difficulty developing effective and appropriate alternative grading procedures for mildly handicapped students. To date, regular teachers use a variety of approaches. Kinnison, Hayes, and Acord (1981) discuss seven alternatives often used in elementary and secondary classrooms.

**The Individualized Education Program** bases grading on the student's attaining goals and objectives specified in the IEP. The IEP also establishes minimum acceptable levels of competence for specific skills and/or knowledge, such as 80 per cent accuracy. Programming for the IEP requires that teachers consider the student's learning style and use multiple activities as part of the total instructional program. Teachers usually give grades on the basis of the school district's criteria for acceptable performance. Thus, if the IEP requires 80 per cent accuracy and 80 on the local scale equals a C, then the student receives a C.

**Mastery level or criterion systems** generally divide content into various subcomponents and require pre- and posttest measures for each step. Students earn credit, therefore, after their proficiency or mastery reaches an acceptable level. Problems with this approach include teachers needing additional time and students being rewarded or passed for minimum performance.

In **student self-comparison,** students evaluate themselves on a strictly individual basis in terms of whether or not they have met the goals and objectives of the instructional program. In **contracting,** the student and the teacher agree on specified activities or assignments required for a certain grade. Generally, teachers who use contracts consider the individual student's ability.

**Multiple grading** rewards the student in several areas (i.e., ability, effort, and achievement). The teacher usually determines the student's final grade by averaging all three grades. Some teachers use letter grades with subscript numbers to indicate level (above grade level, on grade level or below grade level). **Shared grading** means that two or more teachers determine a grade. This system is especially effective when students receive assistance in the resource room. And the **point system** assigns points to activities and assignments that add up to the six- or nine-week grade. Because teachers can give equal weight to activities other than tests, they can individualize their instruction and evaluation much more easily. (pp. 97–99)

On the secondary level, grading practices for mildly handicapped students vary from school to school. In a survey of junior and senior high schools, Vasa (1980) identifies 30 different grading practices or variations of grading practices. Six of the most common of these grading and reporting practices appear in Table 7.2.

Vasa discusses the advantages and disadvantages of several grading practices. In the **pass/fail system,** the teacher need only determine minimum

TABLE 7.2
Six Common Grading Practices in Secondary Schools

| Grading Practice | Description |
| --- | --- |
| Letter or Numerical | Traditional system of giving the student a mark of A, B, C, D, and F or 1, 2, 3, 4 or 5 to demonstrate relative level of performance on unit or course of study. |
| Pass/Fail Credit/No Credit | Criterion-based measurement system permits individual teacher to indicate that the student has either met or not met previously determined standards. |
| Checklists | Criterion-based measurement system that has the instructor check student's progress against a predetermined list of needed skills or completion of specific tasks. |
| Contracts | Student and teacher agree to assign a mark based on predetermined goals and objectives that student will reach during the instructional period. Such goals may be written in conjunction with the special education teacher/consultant. |
| Letters to Parents | A written report provided to student or parents to give narrative information about student's performance. |
| Blanket Grades | All students receive a predetermined grade at end of marking period. |

*Note.* From "Alternative Procedure for Grading Handicapped Students in the Secondary Schools" by S. F. Vasa. In *Integrating Secondary Handicapped Students in General and Vocational Curriculum.* Des Moines, Iowa: Midwest Regional Resource Center, Drake University, 1980, 2. Copyright 1981 by S. F. Vasa. Reprinted by permission.

competencies for the course or for individuals. Students meeting those standards receive a "P" or pass and students not meeting the minimum standards receive an "F" or fail. The pass/fail system has the following advantages:

☐ students feel less pressure to compete;
☐ students feel less anxiety;
☐ students need not cheat or "butter up" the teacher;
☐ students know what the teacher expects of them and work toward a goal;
☐ the teacher can increase a student's achievement or aspiration level;
☐ the teacher can carefully examine the student's relative abilities and disabilities; and
☐ the teacher does not have to compare students' work. (p. 12–13)

Disadvantages of the pass/fail systems are:

☐ the teacher may not provide corrective feedback in weak areas;
☐ the passing grade does not distinguish between students of differing abilities;
☐ some students do less work when freed of traditional grade pressures;

☐ students close to failing feel the same pressures they do with traditional grades; and
☐ teachers sometimes find minimum standards arbitrary and difficult to define. (p. 12–13)

**Checklists** provide teachers with a way to evaluate student progress through developmentally sequenced academic courses. This method has several advantages. It gives

☐ more value than a grade alone and thus means more to the student;
☐ more information to parents and future employers;
☐ more detailed information about the student's performance;
☐ more information to the school about weaknesses in the instructional program; and
☐ more information about which skills have priority over others. (p. 12–13)

On the other hand, checklists

☐ may be time-consuming for the teacher;
☐ increase the amount of paperwork for the teacher;
☐ may be misunderstood by parents;
☐ may require extensive revising every time instructional objectives are changed; and
☐ tend to focus on weaknesses. (p. 12–13)

Educators want to find some method of evaluation that most realistically reflects the progress and effort of the mildly handicapped student. But selecting a single method of grading mildly handicapped students is difficult. Perhaps the desirable alternative, then, is for teachers to use more than one procedure depending on students' individual needs and to evaluate in terms of the individual. For example, mildly handicapped students often experience difficulty on tests and on written assignments. Teachers, then, need to include other evaluative procedures to deal with those particular difficulties. Vasa suggests that teachers use class interaction and discussion, class projects, papers, verbal reports, student interviews, and daily logs of activities as ways to supplement traditional assignments and tests. (p. 10)

Although grading is beneficial in terms of identifying students for promotion and honors, identifying those who should go to college, communicating with parents and others, and accounting to the public, it can be detrimental if it does not appropriately reflect the student's progress and if it serves only to discourage and defeat the already handicapped student. Self-esteem is very important to each of us, but to the mildly handicapped student it is critical. Therefore, if mildly handicapped students are to experience success and positive reinforcement in the classroom, they must be graded in appropriate ways.

# GRADUATION REQUIREMENTS

Assessing student progress leads eventually to evaluating students in terms of graduation requirements. The traditional method of awarding diplomas, the earning of a prescribed number of carnegie units, often prevents the special student from receiving a diploma. Although some mildly handicapped students do not have the ability to earn a regular high school diploma, they do possess certain abilities, and they have reached the goals established for them in their individualized programs. Therefore, educators need to determine the policies and procedures for awarding diplomas and/or certificates to these students for what they *have* accomplished. Schools currently use a number of approaches. Weintraub and Ross (1980) identify five of the most widely used: pass/fail, certificate of attendance, IEP, special education diploma, and curricular.

Of these methods, the curricular approach seems the most viable because it provides all students with curricula to meet their individual needs. For example, curricula could focus on, "college preparation, vocational education, basic skills, or life management" (Weintraub & Ross, p. 203). Teachers can establish requirements and include competency tests, if appropriate, within each curriculum. Weintraub and Ross point out the advantages and the disadvantages of the curricular approach. Since all students have access to a program leading to a diploma, the policy secures the doctrine of equality of educational access. Educators can use a minimum competency test or other standards within each curriculum to set levels of achievement for all students. And a handicapped student can reasonably expect to receive a diploma, indicating successful completion of his or her curriculum. On the other hand, educators have to develop and validate competencies for each curriculum. Handicapped students may be placed in a particular curriculum rather than receive an education appropriate to their unique educational needs. And the policy might lower the standards of certain curricula by focusing more on getting students into the program than on evaluating their performance once admitted to the program. (p. 203) Although educators have to validate competencies for the different curricula, the curricular approach offers alternatives to all students rather than to only a designated percentage of those students.

Other authorities agree that alternatives are needed. Wimmer (1981), for example, points out that entire portions of curricula are inappropriate for handicapped students. She recommends that a curriculum for some mildly handicapped students include social and vocational preparation with an emphasis on career development. She further advocates the waiving of carnegie units for some students and believes the answer lies in an equivalent high school diploma.

The issues involved in graduation requirements and the emerging problems associated with competency testing have yet to be resolved. The emphasis on equality of opportunity and the focus on the rights of handicapped individuals means that discriminatory practices will continue to be challenged. But if special

educators, regular educators, and parents work together, appropriate evaluation measures for mildly handicapped children will emerge.

## SUMMARY

Instructional planning for the mildly handicapped student must also include
planning for evaluation. To accurately assess the mainstreamed student's acquisition of skills, the teacher must adapt the evaluation process, i.e., adapt
the regular classroom test. Many mildly handicapped students have reached
the instructional objective but need special consideration in testing so that they
can show what they know. When teachers modify test construction, test administration, and test site, they have a framework for assessing the student's learning. Although many alternatives for grading procedures and graduation requirements now exist, the balance between maintaining standards for all students
and establishing appropriate standards for mildly handicapped students has not
yet been attained.

## REFERENCES

Dewey, J. Democracy and educational administration. *School and Society*, April 1937,
    pp. 458–459.

Kinnison, L. R., Hayes, C., & Acord, J. Evaluating student progress in mainstreamed
    classes. *Teaching Exceptional Children*, 1981, *13*(3), 97–99.

Marsh, G. E., & Price, B. J. *Methods for Teaching the Mildly Handicapped Adolescent.*
    St. Louis, Mo.: C. V. Mosby, 1980.

Robbins, R. L., & Harway, N. I. Goal setting and reactions to success and failure in
    children with learning disabilities. *Journal of Learning Disabilities*, 1977, *10*(6),
    356–362.

Vasa, S. F. Alternative procedures for grading handicapped students in the secondary
    schools. *Education Unlimited*, 1981, *3*(1), 16–23.

Weintraub, F. J., & Ross, J. W. Policy approaches regarding the impact of graduation
    requirements on handicapped students. *Exceptional Children*, 1980, *47*(3), 200–203.

Wimmer, D. Functional learning curricula in the secondary schools. *Exceptional Children*,
    1981, *47*(8), 610–616.

Wood, J. W., & Englebert, B. Mainstreaming Minimanual. *Instructor*, 1982, *91*(7), 63–66.

# Appendices

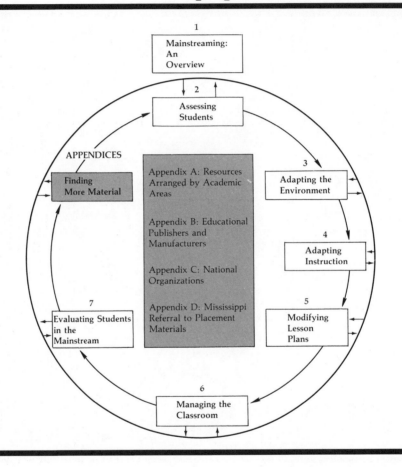

1
Mainstreaming:
An
Overview

2
Assessing
Students

APPENDICES

Finding
More Material

Appendix A: Resources
Arranged by Academic
Areas

Appendix B: Educational
Publishers and
Manufacturers

Appendix C: National
Organizations

Appendix D: Mississippi
Referral to Placement
Materials

3
Adapting the
Environment

4
Adapting
Instruction

7
Evaluating Students
in the
Mainstream

5
Modifying
Lesson
Plans

6
Managing the
Classroom

# Finding More Material

# APPENDIX A
# RESOURCES ARRANGED BY
# ACADEMIC AREAS

## READING

### BOOKS

Carnine, D., & Silbert, J. *Direct instruction reading.* Columbus, Ohio: Charles E. Merrill, 1979.

Cook, J. E., & Earlly, E. C. *Remediating reading disabilities: Simple things that work.* Germantown, Md.: Aspen System Corporation, 1979.

Ekwall, E. E. *Locating and correcting reading difficulties* (3rd ed.). Columbus, Ohio: Charles E. Merrill, 1981.

Gillespie-Silver, P. H. *Teaching reading to children with special needs.* Columbus, Ohio: Charles E. Merrill, 1979.

Hargis, C. H. *Teaching reading to handicapped children.* Denver: Love Publishing Company, 1982.

Kirk, S., Kliebhan, J. M., & Lerner, J. W. *Teaching reading to slow and disabled learners.* Boston: Houghton Mifflin, 1978.

Moseley, C., & Moseley, D. *Language and reading among underachievers: A practical review.* Atlantic Highlands, N.J.: Humanities Press, 1977.

Otto, W., & Smith, R. J. *Corrective and remedial teaching* (3rd ed.). Boston: Houghton Mifflin, 1980.

### ARTICLES

Berger, N. S. Why can't Johnny read? Perhaps he's not a good listener. *Journal of Learning Disabilities,* 1978, *11,* 633–638.

Cohen, S. B., & Plaskon, S. P. Selecting a reading approach for the mainstreamed child. *Language Arts,* 1978, *55,* 966–970.

Hirst, L. T., & O'Such, T. Using musical television commercials to teach reading. *Teaching Exceptional Children,* 1979, *11,* 80–81.

Ivarie, J. J. Programming for individualization in the junior high school. *Journal of Reading, 20,* 295–300.

Lehman, K. A. Teaching reading to special education students. *Reading Improvement,* 1981, *18*(1), 81–95.

Samuels, S. J. The method of repeated readings. *The Reading Teacher,* 1979, *32,* 403–408.

Sartain, H. W. Instruction of disabled learners: A reading perspective. *Journal of Learning Disabilities,* 1976, *9,* 489–497.

### MATERIALS

*Diagnostic reading for your classroom* (guide). Drier.

*Edmark reading program* (kit). Edmark Associates.

*Informal reading inventory* (Tips For Teachers). National Education Association.

*125 Motivators for reading* (activities). Fearon Publishers.

*Reading incentive program* (kits). Bowmar.

*Remedial reading drills* (exercises). George Wahr Publishing.

*Specific skills series* (books). Barnell Loft, Ltd.

*Survival reading* (cards). New Readers Press.

*Teaching reading to handicapped children* (Tips for Teachers). National Educational Association.

*Troubleshooter II* (workbook). Houghton Mifflin Company.

## MEDIA

*How to read . . . for everyday living* (5 cassettes and 10 activity books/dittos). Educational Activities.

*Phonics from symbol to sound* (3 sets of filmstrips and cassettes). Kimbo Educational.

*Phrase training filmstrips* (12 filmstrips). Educational Activities.

*Tell me a story library* (4 filmstrips and 2 cassettes). Garrard Publishing Company.

# LANGUAGE ARTS

## BOOKS

Canfield, S. et al. *Educable mentally handicapped (EMH): Language arts—Level IV.* Louisville, Ky.: Jefferson County Public Schools, 1976.

Canfield, S. et al. *Educable mentally handicapped (EMH): Reading and language arts—Level V.* Louisville, Ky.: Jefferson County Public Schools, 1977.

Greenburg, J. C., Vernon, M., DuBois, J. H., & McKnight, J. *The language arts handbook: A total communication approach.* Baltimore: University Park Press, 1981.

*Language arts core of basic skills.* Ocala, Fla.: Marion County Public Schools, 1977.

## ARTICLES

Aaron, R. L. et al. A language arts program for disturbed adolescents. *Journal of Reading,* 1975, *19,* 208–213.

Abbott, R. E. The newspaper as a teaching tool. *Pointer,* 1976, *20*(3), 52–55.

Kauffman, J. M., Hallahan, D. P., Haas, K., Brame, T., & Boren, R. Imitating children's errors to improve their spelling performance. *Journal of Learning Disabilities,* 1978, *11,* 217–222.

Lloyd, J. et al. Direct instruction: Effects on oral and written language comprehension. *Learning Disabilities Quarterly,* 1980, *3*(4), 70–76.

Stowitscheck, C. E., & Jobes, N. K. Getting the bugs out of spelling—Or an alternative to the spelling bee. *Teaching Exceptional Children,* 1977, *9,* 74–76.

## MATERIALS

*Helping young children develop language skills: A book of activities.* Council for Exceptional Children.

*Improving spelling skills in handicapped learners: Why isn't fish spelled "ghoti"?* (activity manual). National Education Association.

*Sparks for learning: Ideals for teaching reading and language arts* (activity book). ESN Press.

*Spelling our language* (workbook). Scott, Foresman and Company.

*Spelling word power laboratory* (kit). Science Research Associates.

## MEDIA

*Demon spelling words* (record/cassette). Educational Activities.

*Listening and responding to sounds and language* (3 records). Kimbo Educational Company.

*Sentences that work* (4 filmstrips and cassettes). Kimbo Educational Company.

*The wordplay vocabulary program* (filmstrips and storybooks). Kimbo Educational Company.


# MATHEMATICS

## BOOKS

Johnson, S. W. *Arithmetic and learning disabilities: Guidelines for identification and remediation.* Boston: Allyn and Bacon, 1979.

Reisman, F. K. *Teaching mathematics to children with special needs.* Columbus, Ohio: Charles E. Merrill, 1980.

Reisman, F. K. *Teaching mathematics: Methods and content* (2nd ed.). Boston: Houghton Mifflin, 1981.

Underhill, R. G., Uprichard, A. E., & Heddens, J. W. (Eds.). *Diagnosing mathematical difficulties.* Columbus, Ohio: Charles E. Merrill, 1980.

## ARTICLES

Frank, A. R. Teaching money skills with a number line. *Teaching Exceptional Children,* 1978, *10*(2), 46–47.

Frank, A. R., & McFarland, T. D. Teaching coin skills to EMR children: A curriculum study. *Education and Training of the Mentally Retarded,* 1980, *15*, 270–278.

Sander, M. Getting ready for arithmetic: Prerequisites for learning to add. *Teaching Exceptional Children,* 1981, *13*(2), 54–57.

Watkins, M. W., & Webb, C. Computer assisted instruction with learning disabled students. *Educational Computer,* 1981, *1*(3), 24–27.

## MATERIALS

*Fun and games with mathematics: Primary* (activity book). Prentice-Hall Learning Systems, Incorporated.

*Fundamental skills and concepts 2: Arithmetic lessons for grades 1–3* (teacher's manual). Fearon Publishers.

*Money makes sense* (high-interest low-level reader). Fearon Publishers.

*Pacemaker arithmetic program* (series). Fearon Publishers.

*Teacher-made materials for math: Patterns for primary teachers.* Fearon Publishers.

## MEDIA

*Addition and subtraction* (record). Educational Activities.

*Countdown cassette tape program.* Bowmar/Noble.

*Fractions as a tool* (5 cassette and 10 activity books/dittos). Educational Activities.

*Math for everyday living* (5 cassette and 10 activity books/dittos). Educational Activities.

*Singing multiplication tables* (record). Educational Activities.


# SOCIAL STUDIES

## BOOKS

Adams, A. H. et al. *Mainstreaming language arts and social studies: Special ideas and activities for the whole class.* Santa Monica, Calif.: Goodyear, 1977.

Herlihy, J. G., & Herlihy, M. T. (Eds.). *Mainstreaming in the social studies: Bulletin 62.* Washington, D.C.: National Council for the Social Studies, 1980.

Ochoa, A. S., & Shuster, S. K. *Social studies in the mainstreamed classroom K–6.* Boulder, Colo.: Social Science Educational Consortium, 1980.

Singleton, L. R. *Social studies for the visually impaired child: MAVIS sourcebook 4.* Boulder, Colo.: Social Science Education Consortium, 1980.

## ARTICLES

Curtis, C. K., & Shaver, J. P. Slow learners and the study of contemporary problems. *Social Education,* 1980, *44,* 302–309.

Lawrence, S. L. Motivating poor readers in social studies. *Georgia Social Science,* 1981, *12*(2), 18–21.

Smith, A. Are they alike? History textbooks for poor readers. *Social Studies,* 1980, *71*(5), 199–204.

Tyo, J. An alternative for poor readers in social science. *Social Education,* 1980, *44,* 312–317.

## MATERIALS

*America's story—Book 1 and 2* (high-interest low-level readers). Steck-Vaughan Company.

*Color me American* (workbook). Lawson Book Company.

*Skills for understanding maps and globes* (lesson book). Follett Publishing Company.

*World history and you—Book 1 and 2* (high-interest low-level readers). Steck-Vaughn Company.

## MEDIA

*Alice in consumerland* (5 filmstrips and cassettes). Educational Activities, Incorporated.
   *When there's a hole in your pocket*
   *And this little bottle went to market*
   *Fables and labels*
   *Catch a commercial*
   *When things don't work*

*Geography* (2 filmstrips and cassettes or records). Educational Activities, Incorporated.
   *What is geography?*
   *Maps and globes*

*Rules we live by* (5 filmstrips, cassettes, and workbooks). Educational Activities, Incorporated.
   *"I know it's here, somewhere"*
   *"But, we agreed that"*
   *"Do not pass go . . ."*
   *"Who needs law?"*
   *Order and the pursuit of happiness*

# SCIENCE

## BOOKS

Jennings, F., & Metro, P. M. *Ecology for the exceptional child, grades 7–12 EMR*. Rocky River, Ohio: Rocky River Public Schools, 1977.

Jennings, F., & Metro, P. M. *Ecology for the exceptional child*. Rocky River, Ohio: Rocky River Public Schools, 1977.

Leavy, M. B., & Hollifield, J. H. *Teacher's manual: Using teams–games–tournament (TGT) in your life science classroom*. Baltimore: Johns Hopkins University, 1980.

Leavy, M. B., & Hollifield, J. H. *Teacher's Manual: Using teams–games–tournament (TGT) in your physical science classroom*. Baltimore: Johns Hopkins University, 1980.

## ARTICLES

Danglade, R., & Ball, D. W. Science for someone special. *Science and Children*, 1978, *16*(3), 23–24.

Keller, W. D. Science for the handicapped. *Focus on Exceptional Children*, 1981, *13*(5), 1–11.

Phillips, D. Piaget's perspective on science teaching. *Science Teacher*, 1976, *43*(2), 30–31.

## MATERIALS

*Biology of man* (high-interest low-level reader). Quercus Corporation.

*Biology of plants and animals* (high-interest low-level reader). Quercus Corporation.

*Creative science experiences for the young child* (activities). Incentive Publications.

*Earth science* (high-interest low-level reader). Quercus Corporation.

*Physical science* (high-interest low-level reader). Quercus Corporation.

*Probe: A handbook for teachers of elementary science* (activities). Educational Services.
*Solar Safari* (games). Incentive Publications.

## MEDIA

*Heat* (2 filmstrips and cassette/record). Educational Activities.
    *What is heat?*
    *How heat travels*
*Light* (2 filmstrips and cassette/record). Educational Activities.
    *What is light?*
    *How light travels*
*What is science?* (filmstrip and record/cassette). Educational Activities.

# VOCATIONAL/CAREER EDUCATION

## BOOKS

Brolin, D. E. *Vocational preparation of persons with handicaps* (2nd ed.). Columbus,
    Ohio: Charles E. Merrill, 1982.

Brolin, D. E., & Kokasak, C. *Career education for handicapped children and youth.*
    Columbus, Ohio: Charles E. Merrill, 1982.

Palomaki, M. K. (Ed.). *Teaching handicapped students vocational education: A resource
    handbook for K–12 teachers.* Washington, D.C.: National Education Association,
    1981.

Phelps, L. A., & Lutz, R. J. *Career exploration and preparation for the special need
    learner.* Boston: Allyn and Bacon, 1977.

Weisgerber, R. (Ed.). *Vocational education: Teaching the handicapped in regular classes.*
    Reston, Va.: The Council for Exceptional Children, 1978.

## ARTICLES

Brolin, D. E., & D'Alonzo, B. Critical issues in career education for handicapped students.
    *Exceptional Children,* 1979, *45,* 246–253.

Hoyt, K. B. Why Johnny and Joann can't work. *Occupational Outlook Quarterly,* 1977,
    *21*(2), 1–3.

Richter-Stein, C., & Stodden, R. A. Simulated job samples: A student-centered approach
    to vocational exploration and evaluation. *Teaching Exceptional Children,* 1981,
    *14*(3), 116–119.

Schweich, P. D. The development of choices—An educational approach to employment.
    *Academic Therapy,* 1975, *10,* 277–283.

Sitlington, P. L. Vocational and special education in career programming for the mildly
    handicapped adolescent. *Exceptional Children,* 1981, *47,* 592–598.

## MATERIALS

*Be informed on finding a job* (booklet). New Readers Press.
*Career guidance* (catalog of materials). Careers Incorporated.

*Career series* (10 booklets/cassettes). Occupational Awareness.

*Get that job!* (high-interest low-level reader). Quercus Corporation.

*Pacemaker vocational readers* (10 high-interest low-level readers). Pitman Learning, Incorporated.

*Success at work* (high-interest low-level reader). Steck-Vaughn.

*The job boxes* (70 booklets). Fearon Publishers.

*The way to work* (high-interest, low-level reader). Quercus Corporation.

*Work attitudes* (10 booklets). Occupational Awareness.

## MEDIA

*Community helpers* (2 records/cassettes). Kimbo Educational.

*Winning the job game* (4 filmstrips and cassettes). Educational Activities.
> *It's your life*
> *The job hunt from A to Z*
> *Selling yourself with a résumé and cover letter*
> *The paper puzzle*

# MOTOR DEVELOPMENT/
# PHYSICAL EDUCATION/HEALTH

## BOOKS

Allen, L. et al. *Health education for special children: Primary ED–LD.* Homer, N.Y.: Cortland-Madison Board of Cooperative Educational Services, 1976.

Brodie, P. et al. *Health education for special children: Junior High EMR.* Homer, N.Y.: Cortland-Madison Board of Cooperative Educational Services, 1976.

Chambless, J. B. et al. *Mastery learning of stunts and tumbling activities for the mentally retarded.* Oxford: Mississippi University, 1980.

Jansma, P., & French, R. *Special physical education.* Columbus, Ohio: Charles E. Merrill, 1982.

Morris, G. S. D. *Elementary physical education: Toward inclusion.* Salt Lake City, Utah: Brighton Publishing Company, 1980.

Upton, G. (Ed.). *Physical and creative activities for the mentally handicapped.* Cambridge, Mass.: Cambridge University Press, 1979.

## ARTICLES

Marlowe, M. Games analysis: Designing games for handicapped children. *Teaching Exceptional Children*, 1980, *12*(2), 48–51.

Mori, A. A. Children in the mainstream—Implications for the health educator. *Journal of School Health*, 1981, *51*, 119–122.

Movement for mentally handicapped children. *Parents Voice*, 1976, *26*(2), 10–12.

Roswal, G., & Frith, G. H. The children's developmental play program: Physical activity designed to facilitate the growth and development of mildly handicapped children. *Education and Training of the Mentally Retarded*, 1980, *15*, 322–324.

Schworm, R. W. Walking in rhythm, moving in style, teaching fundamental movement patterns to children with learning problems. *Teaching Exceptional Children,* 1977, *9*(2), 52–53.

## MATERIALS

*About drugs* (high-interest low-level reader). Fearon Publishers.

*Health and you* (high-intererst low-level reader). Steck-Vaughn.

*Movement games for children of all ages.* Sterling Publishing Company.

*Physical activities for the mentally retarded: Ideas for instruction.* American Association for Health, Physical Education, and Recreation.

*Safe and sound* (workbook). Lawson Book Company.

## MEDIA

*Learning basic skills through music—Health and safety* (record). Educational Activities.

*Nutrition for little children* (filmstrip and cassette/record). Educational Activities.

*Nutrition for you* (2 filmstrips and cassette/record). Educational Activities.
    *What is nutrition?*
    *You are what you eat*

*Perceptual-motor rhythm games* (record). Educational Activities.

*Special exercises for exceptional children* (record). Kimbo Educational Company.

*VD: Kids get it too* (film). ACI Films, Incorporated.


# SELF-CONCEPT DEVELOPMENT

## BOOKS

Campbell, J. H. *It's me! Building self-concepts through art.* Hingham, Mass.: Teaching Resources Corporation, n.d.

Canfield, J., & Wells, H. C. *100 ways to enhance self-concept in the classroom.* Englewood Cliffs, N.J.: Prentice-Hall, 1976.

DiFrancesca, S. *The step method: Learning and practicing thinking skills.* New York: The Psychological Corporation, 1979.

Rodriquez, A. M., & Baptiste, H. P., Jr. *Me, you, and us—Affective education module.* Houston: University of Houston, Texas College of Education, 1980.

## ARTICLES

Gable, R. A., Strain, P. S., & Hendrickson, J. M. Strategies for improving the status and social behavior of learning disabled children. *Learning Disabilities Quarterly,* 1979, *2,* 33–39.

Silverman, R., Zigmond, N., & Sansone, J. Teaching coping skills to adolescents with learning problems. *Focus on Exceptional Children,* 1981, *13*(6), 1–20.

Smith, M. D. Prediction of self-concept among learning disabled children. *Journal of Learning Disabilities,* 1979, *12,* 30–35.

## MATERIALS

*Consequences: In other people's shoes* (cards). Argus Communications.

*Getting it together* (reader). Science Research Associates.

*Holt impact series* (reader). Holt, Rinehart and Winston, Inc.

*People need each other* (activities book). Incentive Publications.

*Social learning curriculum* (kit). Charles E. Merrill Publishing Company.

## MEDIA

*Being you* (4 filmstrips). Kimbo Educational Company.
> *Your wonderful body*
> *Your very own feelings*
> *Liking yourself*
> *Your special place*

*Depression, blahs, blues, better days* (film). American Educational Films.

*Developing self-respect* (4 filmstrips). Kimbo Educational Company.
> *Doing your share*
> *Doing what you think is right*
> *Liking and respecting others*
> *Liking and respecting yourself*

*I like myself* (record). Kimbo Educational Company.

*Understanding differences* (4 filmstrips). Kimbo Educational Company.
> *I can't read*
> *People say I'm slow*
> *What's so great about being smart?*
> *How can I run?*

*What would you do?* (4 filmstrips). Kimbo Educational Company.
> *Finders, keepers?*
> *To tell or not to tell*
> *The easy way out*
> *I wish I hadn't said that*

# ADDITIONAL BOOKS ABOUT HANDICAPS

Anderson, R. M., Greer, J. G., & Odle, S. J. (Eds.). *Individualizing educational materials for special children in the mainstream.* Baltimore: University Park Press, 1978.

Charles, C. M., & Malian, I. M. *The special student: Practical help for the classroom teacher.* St. Louis, Mo.: C. V. Mosby, 1980.

Coburn, P., Kelman, P., Roberts, N., Snyder, T., Watt, D., & Weiner, C. *Practical guide to computers in education.* Reading, Mass.: Addison-Wesley, 1982.

Fairchild, T. N. (Series Ed.). *Mainstreaming series.* Hingham, Mass.: Teaching Resources Corporation, n.d.

Hart, V. *Mainstreaming children with special needs.* New York: Longman, 1981.

Justen, J. E., III, Reichard, C. L., & Cronis, T. G. *Creative teaching of the mentally handicapped.* Denver: Love Publishing Company, 1982.

Larsen, S. C., & Poplin, M. S. *Methods for educating the handicapped: An individualzied education program approach.* Boston: Allyn and Bacon, 1980.

Marsh, G. E., & Price, B. J. *Methods for teaching the mildly handicapped adolescent.* St. Louis, Mo.: C. V. Mosby, 1980.

*1983 classroom computer news directory of educational computing resources.* Watertown, Mass. Intentional Educations, 1983.

Pasanella, A. L., & Volkmor, C. B. *Coming back . . . or never leaving; Instructional programming for handicapped students in the mainstream.* Columbus, Ohio: Charles E. Merrill, 1977.

Payne, J. S., Polloway, E. A., Smith, J. E., Jr., & Payne, R. A. *Strategies for teaching the mentally retarded* (2nd ed.). Columbus, Ohio,: Charles E. Merrill, 1981.

Rich, H. L. *Disturbed students: Characteristics and educational strategies.* Baltimore, Md.: University Park Press, 1982.

Stowitschek, J. J., Gable, R. A., & Hendrickson, J. M. *Instructional materials for exceptional children: Selection, management, and adaptation.* Germantown, Md.: Aspen Systems Corporation, 1980.

Taber, F. M. *Microcomputers in special education.* Reston, Va.: Council for Exceptional Children, 1983.

Torres, S. (Ed.). *A primer on individualized education programs for handicapped children.* Reston, Va.: Council for Exceptional Children, 1977.

# APPENDIX B
# EDUCATIONAL PUBLISHERS AND
# MANUFACTURERS

ACI Films Incorporated
35 West 45th Street
New York, New York 10036

American Alliance for Health, Physical
    Education, Recreation, and Dance Pro-
    grams for the Handicapped
1900 Association Drive
Reston, Virginia 22091

American Education Films
P.O. Box 5091
Beverly Hills, California 38210

American Guidance Service
Publisher's Building
Circle Pines, Minnesota 55014

Argus Communications
7440 Natchez Avenue
Niles, Illinois 60648

Barnell-Loft
958 Church Street
Baldwin, New York 11510

Bell and Howell
Audio-Visual Products Division
7100 McCormick Road
Chicago, Illinois 60645

Bobbs Merrill Company
College Division
4300 West 62nd Street
Indianapolis, Indiana 46206

Bowmar/Noble
4563 Colorado Boulevard
Los Angeles, California 90039

Brighton Publishing Company
P.O. Box 6235
Salt Lake City, Utah 84106

Careers, Incorporated
P.O. Box 135
Lago, Florida 33540

The Council for Exceptional Children
Department 5506
1920 Association Drive
Reston, Virginia 22091

Cuisenaire Company of America
12 Church Street
New Rochelle, New York 10805

Developmental Learning Materials
One DLM Park, P.O. Box 4000
Allen, Texas 75002

Drier
300 Raritan Avenue
Highland Park, New Jersey 08904

ESN Press
85 Main Street
Watertown, Massachusetts 02172

Edmark Associates
13241 Northup Way
Bellvue, Washington 98005

Educational Activities
P.O. Box 392
Freeport, Long Island
New York 11520

Educational Services
P.O. Box 3787
Thousand Oaks, California 91359

Fearon Publishers
6 Davis Drive
Belmont, California 94002

Follett Publishing Company
1010 West Washington Boulevard
Chicago, Illinois 60607

Garrard Publishing Company
1607 North Market Street
Champaign, Illinois 61820

Holt, Rinehart and Winston
521 Fifth Avenue, Sixth floor
New York, New York 10175

Houghton Mifflin Company
One Beacon Street
Boston, Massachusetts 02107

Incentive Publications
Box 120189
Nashville, Tennessee 37212

Kimbo Educational Company
P.O. Box 477
Long Branch, New Jersey 07740

Lawson Book Company
9488 Sara Street
Elk Grove, California 95624

Love Publishing Company
1777 South Bellaire Street
Denver, Colorado 80222

Macmillan Publishing Company
100A Brown Street
Riverside, New Jersey 08370

McGraw-Hill
1221 Avenue of the Americas
New York, New York 10020

Charles E. Merrill Publishing Company
1300 Alum Creek Drive, Box 508
Columbus, Ohio 43216

Mosby
11830 Westline Industrial Drive
St. Louis, Missouri 63141

National Council for Social Studies
3615 Wisconsin Avenue, NW
Washington, D.C. 20016

National Education Association
1201 16th Street, NW
Washington, D.C. 20036

New Readers Press
P.O. Box 131
Syracuse, New York 13210

Occupational Awareness
P.O. Box 948
Los Alamitos, California 90720-0948

J. H. Pence Company
5105-07 Lakeside Avenue
Richmond, Virginia 23228

Pitman Publishing Company
P.O. Box 741
Belmont, California 94002

Prentice-Hall Publishing Company
P.O. Box 47X
Englewood Cliffs, New Jersey 07632

The Psychological Corporation
757 Third Avenue
New York, New York 10017

Quercus Corporation
2768 Pineridge Road
Castro Valley, California 94546

Research Press
Box 317760
Champaign, Illinois 61820

Science Research Associates, Incorporated
259 South Erie Street
Chicago, Illinois 60611

Scott, Foresman & Company
1900 East Lake Avenue
Glenview, Illinois 60025

Silver Burdett Company
250 James Street
Morristown, New Jersey 07960

Social Science Education Consortium
855 Broadway
Boulder, Colorado 80302

Special Child Publications
4525 Union Bay Place, NE
Seattle, Washington 98105

Special Education Materials
484 South Broadway
Yankers, New York 10705

Steck-Vaughn
P.O. Box 2028
807 Brazos
Austin, Texas 78767

Sterling Publishing Company, Inc.
2 Park Avenue
New York, New York 10016

Teaching Resources Corporation
50 Pond Park Road
Hingham, Massachusetts 02043

University Park Press
300 North Charles Street
Baltimore, Maryland 21201

George Wahr Publishing Company
304½ South State Street
Ann Arbor, Michigan 48104

Zaner-Bloser
612 North Park Street, P.O. Box 589
Columbus, Ohio 43215

# APPENDIX C
# NATIONAL ORGANIZATIONS

Alexander Graham Bell Association for
the Deaf, Inc.
3417 Volta Place
Washington, D.C. 20007

American Association for Gifted Children
15 Gramercy Park
New York, New York 10003

American Association on Mental
Deficiency
5201 Connecticut Avenue, NW
Washington, D.C. 20015

American Foundation for the Blind
15 West Sixteenth Street
New York, New York 10011

American Printing House for the Blind
P.O. Box 6085
Louisville, Kentucky 40206

American Psychological Association
1200 Seventeenth Street, NW
Washington, D.C. 20036

American Speech and Hearing
Association
9030 Old Georgetown Road
Washington, D.C. 20014

Association for the Aid of Crippled
Children
345 East 46th Street
New York, New York 10017

Association for Children with Learning
Disabilities
5225 Grace Street
Pittsburgh, Pennsylvania 15236

Association for the Education of the
Visually Handicapped
919 Walnut, Fourth Floor
Philadelphia, Pennsylvania 19107

Association of Rehabilitation Facilities
5530 Wisconsin Avenue
Washington, D.C. 20015

Braille Circulating Library
2823 West Grace Street
Richmond, Virginia 23221

Clearinghouse on Programs and Research
in Child Abuse and Neglect
Herner and Company
2100 M Street, NW, Suite 316
Washington, D.C. 20037

Closer Look
National Information Center for the
Handicapped
1201 Sixteenth Street, NW
Washington, D.C. 20037

The Council for Exceptional Children
1920 Association Drive
Reston, Virginia 22091

Division for the Blind and Physically
Handicapped
Library of Congress
Washington, D.C. 20542

Gifted Child Society, Inc.
59 Glen Gray Road
Oakland, New Jersey 07436

Muscular Dystrophy Association
810 Seventh Avenue
New York, New York 10019

National Association for Creative Children and Adults
8080 Spring Valley Drive
Cincinnati, Ohio 45236

National Association for Retarded Citizens
2709 Avenue E East
Arlington, Texas 76011

National Association for the Visually Handicapped
3201 Balboa Street
San Francisco, California 94121

National Association of the Deaf
814 Thayer Avenue
Silver Springs, Maryland 20910

National Braille Press
88 St. Stephen Street
Boston, Massachusetts 02115

National Center on Educational Media and Materials for the Handicapped
The Ohio State University
Columbus, Ohio 43210

National Easter Seal Society for Crippled Children and Adults
2023 West Ogden Avenue
Chicago, Illinois 60612

National Foundation
March of Dimes
Division of Health Information and School Relations
1275 Mamaroneck Avenue
White Plains, New York 10605

National Rehabilitation Association
1522 K Street, NW
Washington, D.C. 20005

National Society for Autistic Children
169 Tampa Avenue
Albany, New York 12208

National Society for Autistic Children
Information and Referral Service
306-31st Street
Huntington, West Virginia 25702

Orton Society, Inc.
8415 Bellona Lane
Baltimore, Maryland 21204

United Cerebral Palsy Association
Program Department
66 East 34th Street
New York, New York 10016

We Are People First
P.O. Box 5208
Salem, Oregon 97304

# APPENDIX D
# MISSISSIPPI REFERRAL TO
# PLACEMENT MATERIALS

## PARENT INFORMATION PAMPHLET

Dear Parents:

Because we want to give your child the best education possible, we feel that your child needs to be tested. This testing will be done to give us more information about your child so that we can better meet any special needs that your child might have. As we work together to meet your child's needs, we want you to know about your rights as a parent.

You have the right to:

☐ Ask that your child be tested to find out his/her strengths and weaknesses for learning.

☐ Agree or disagree with the school about any testing that the school wants to do with your child.

☐ Have what you think about your child's strengths and weaknesses be included in the results of your child's testing.

If your child has been tested and has a handicap, you have the right to:

☐ Help decide what kind of class is best for your child.

☐ Agree or disagree with the class offered for your child by the school.

☐ Have what you want your child to learn considered for his/her special educational plan. This special plan is called an Individualized Educational Plan (IEP) and is made up each year.

☐ Disagree with any part or all of the IEP if you wish.

☐ Meet with people from the school to talk about your child's IEP at the time or place you both agree on.

☐ Talk about how your child is doing in school with the teacher at any time in the school year (check with your school for the time they have set aside for this meeting).

If you are not exactly sure what your child needs, you have the right to:

☐ Look at your child's records at the school.

☐ Get a copy of any of your child's records (you may be charged for the actual cost of the copies and the cost of stamps if the data is to be mailed).

☐ Have someone of your choosing look at your child's records and represent you and your child.

If you and the school cannot agree on what your child needs, you have the right to:

☐ Ask that someone else besides people at the school test your child if you do not agree with the first test results.

☐ Ask for a hearing (you must write your district school superintendent to ask for this hearing).

From State of Mississippi Referral to Placement Guidlines, 1982. Reprinted with permission.

## PROCEDURAL SAFEGUARDS SIMPLIFIED (PARENTS' RIGHTS)

As the parent of a child who may be evaluated to determine the need for special education services or who is already receiving special education services, you and your child are guaranteed certain rights with regard to the provision of a free appropriate public education (FAPE). These rights, mandated by law, are outlined in regulations adopted by your local school board. We want you to know about them. Therefore, this brief outline of these rights has been prepared for you. If you do not understand any part of this or if you would like more information, contact the Superintendent of Education, _____ , or the District Supervisor of Special Education, _____ , at _____ (phone number).

### DUE PROCESS

You may see any of your child's records which relate to referral, identification, evaluation, educational placement, or the provision of FAPE. The information in these records will be explained to you and any questions you have will be answered.

If you disagree with the evaluation done by your school district, you may have your child tested by another examiner not employed by the school district. Results of this evaluation will be used when making a decision about your child's eligibility for special education and placement in a special education program. School district personnel will give you information about where you may get this evaluation and will pay for it unless they decide to ask for a hearing to show that their first evaluation was correct.

You will be given, or sent, a notice before the school district decides to take (or not to take) any action about the identification, evaluation, or change of placement or program of your child or provision of a FAPE. This notice, written so that it is understandable by the general public, will be in your native language or other means of communication (unless it is clearly not practical to do so). It will describe what is being considered and why, all information about testing that was used in deciding what the district is proposing, and any other choices that were considered and why they were not taken. The notice that is given to you before the first evaluation will include information about your rights and a copy of the Parent Information Pamphlet. This Pamphlet will be explained *orally* before you are asked to give your permission in writing for the initial testing. Prior to the first placement of your child in a special education program, you will be asked to give your permission in writing for that placement.

You may ask for an impartial due process hearing if you and school district personnel cannot reach an agreement about the identification, evaluation, placement or provision of free appropriate public education for your child. If you ask, school district personnel will let you know of any free or low-cost legal and other services that are available. You have the right to have the hearing at a time and place that has been agreed upon by you and the district; to have a hearing officer who is not partial to either party (not an employee of the school district or a member of the school board or does not have an interest in the outcome of the hearing); to have and be advised by an attorney or other individuals with special knowledge of handicapped children; to give evidence or to stop the introduction of evidence that has not been given to you at least five days before the hearing; to require the attendance of and to question witnesses; to have a record of the hearing; to have your child at the hearing; to open the hearing to the public; to have the written findings and the decision of the hearing officer within 45 days of the date you asked for the hearing; to ask for a review; and to disagree and appeal the decision in court. During the hearing your child may stay in his present classroom or in a mutually-agreed upon class unless this placement presents a danger to the child or other children (in which case he shall remain at home until the hearing is completed).

The law provides for a process where a surrogate parent can be appointed if no parent can be found or identified or if the child is a ward of the state. However, since you are available, this will not apply to you or your child unless that situation should change.

## PROTECTION IN EVALUATION (NONDISCRIMINATORY TESTING)

Your child's evaluation will be conducted by a qualified examiner(s) who will give a complete and individual evaluation in your child's native language or other means of communication. The district will use more than a single test to decide to recommend that your child be ruled eligible for a special education program. Your child will be tested in all areas related to the suspected problems. More than one person will interpret test information and make placement decisions. This group of people in your child's school district is the Local Survey Committee. For more protection in evaluation, a second group of professional people, those on the Screening Team, will review the information and make an eligibility ruling. If your child is ruled ineligible, you will be informed of this decision and, if further testing is needed, you have the right to withdraw your consent for that testing. Your child will have a complete reevaluation every three years or more often if you or your child's teachers request it.

## LEAST RESTRICTIVE ENVIRONMENT

As much as is possible, your child will be educated and take part in nonacademic and other school activities with nonhandicapped children of about the same age. Your child will not be taken out of a regular education program if he/she can make average progress when extra aids and services are provided. Different types of placement will be available as needed and indicated on your child's Individual Education Program (IEP). Classroom placement will be reconsidered at least once a year or when your child's IEP is reviewed/revised.

If your child is in a private school or an institution, the placement there will meet the above criteria unless this is in conflict with other regulations or court orders.

## CONFIDENTIALITY

All of your child's records will be kept confidential by this school district and will be provided to other agencies only in accord with the Family Rights and Privacy Act and the Education of All Handicapped Children Act. No unauthorized person may see your child's records unless you give your consent in writing. You will be told before information in your child's folder is to be destroyed and you will be given the opportunity to get a copy of this information before it is destroyed.

You or your representative may see your child's records which relate to referral, identification, evaluation, educational placement, or the provision of a FAPE. You will be allowed to see them no later than 45 days from the time of your request. In most cases, copies of the records will be provided if you need them; however, you may be expected to pay for the costs of making the copies.

A record will be kept of those people other than district personnel who see your child's records. If you want to know what information is on file about your child and where it is kept, you may ask for such a list.

If you believe that any of the information in your child's record is wrong, you may request school district personnel to change the record. If the district agrees with you, they will change the record. If they do not agree, a hearing may be held to determine whether the information should be taken out of the record. If the hearing indicates that the information is okay, you may put a statement in the record indicating that you think the information is wrong. This statement will stay with the record.

When your child reaches the age of majority (18), he/she will have the same rights that you have unless there is a severe or profound handicap.

The school district will ask for your permission in writing before the first testing is done and before your child's first placement in special education. You may give your consent, refuse to give consent, or change your mind and withdraw consent at any time. If you refuse or withdraw consent, however, the district may ask for a hearing to settle the disagreement.

As parents of a child who may be evaluated to see if he/she needs special education services or of a child who is now enrolled in a special education program, you have many rights. Along with these rights there are responsibilities, too . . . both for you, as parents, and for your school system. The school system is responsible for guarding your rights and providing an appropriate education for your child. You, in turn, have the *responsibility* to keep in touch with us and to help with your child's education by coming to the conference that is held at least every year to develop or to review/revise your child's Individual Education Program (IEP).

Feel free to contact us at any time about your child. If you are unhappy with your child's education, it is important to tell your school principal or the supervisor of special education services. If you need further help, you can also contact the State Department of Education or any of the organizations listed in the Parent Information Pamphlet you received before your child was evaluated. But first and foremost, *please* talk to your child's teacher, your principal, or other school administrators. Schools are there to help children grow and develop into capable adults, but schools need the help and cooperation of parents, too.

## EXAMPLES OF INTERVIEW QUESTIONS FOR PARENTS

The following are questions in various areas that would yield information useful for the assessment. These questions should not be asked verbatim, but in a conversational fashion so as to gather a more complete picture of the child.

Student's name _____ Birthdate _____

Date _____ Relationship to student _____

Information gathered by _____

### BIRTH HISTORY

1. Did the mother have any illnesses or complications during her pregnancy with this child? If yes, explain.

2. Was childbirth normal? If no, explain.

   How much did the child weigh?

3. Was the child kept in an incubator over twelve hours? If yes, why?

   Did the child have a blue or yellow color after birth? If yes, for how long?

4. If the child was adopted, what age was the child when you adopted and what previous history do you know about the child?

### DEVELOPMENTAL HISTORY

1. Did the child have adequate reflexes (startle reflex) when an infant?

2. As compared to other children, did your child sit up, crawl, and/or walk early, late, or at the same approximate time as peers?

3. Was the child active as a toddler?

4. Was feeding the child a problem? If yes, explain.

5. Was the child a picky or fussy eater?

6. Did the child require a special diet prescribed by a physician? If yes, explain.

7. At about what age did the child dress without help?

8. At about what age did the child learn to tie his shoes without help?

9. Did the child fall frequently?

10. With which hand does the child eat? Draw or write? Throw a ball?

### MEDICAL HISTORY

1. What childhood diseases has the child had?

2. Has the child had other illnesses or serious accidents which required treatment by a physician? If yes, describe.

3. Has the child ever fainted or passed out? If yes, how long before the child regained consciousness?
   Has the child ever had convulsions? If yes, how many times?

4. Has the child complained of frequent headaches, stomachaches, earaches, or leg cramps?

5. Has the child had frequent ear infections?
   Has the child ever had a hearing problem and/or worn a hearing aid?

6. Has the child ever had surgery? If yes, explain.

7. Has the child ever had visual problems?
   Has the child ever worn glasses or had them prescribed?

8. Does the child take any type of medication regularly? If yes, explain.

9. Has the child had high fever? If yes, how high and for how long?

## LANGUAGE/SPEECH DEVELOPMENT
1. At what age did the child begin to babble?

2. When did the child say his first word?
   Two or three word sentences?

3. Does the child understand what is said to him?

4. Does the child respond to commands?
   At what age did the child begin responding?

5. Does the child initiate a conversation?

6. Can you understand the child's speech? Can others?

7. To what extent does the child use gestures in place of speech?

## EDUCATIONAL BACKGROUND
1. Did your child attend nursery school, day care and/or kindergarten? At what age? Were there any problems with peers, teachers, or learning activities? If yes, explain.

2. If your child did not attend nursery school and/or kindergarten, who took care of your child?

3. Does the child like school now? If no, explain.

4. What does the child like best about school?

5. Do you help the child complete homework assignments?

6. Does your child enjoy books?

## INTERPERSONAL RELATIONSHIPS

1. How would you describe your child's personality or behavior?

___ very active    ___ inactive          ___ leader        ___ follower

___ happy         ___ sad             ___ quiet         ___ loud

___ even-          ___ moody       ___ independent    ___ dependent

     tempered                            ___ attentive      ___ daydreams

___ friendly      ___ unfriendly    ___ likes to be    ___ likes to be

___ patient       ___ easily              with others        alone

                       frustrated

___ easy to      ___ hard to      ___ no problems    ___ problems

     discipline        discipline         sleeping          sleeping

___ affectionate    ___ unaffectionate    ___ secure          ___ insecure

2. Describe any of the child's behavior that is a problem.

 How do you deal with the child's behavior problem?

3. How does the child play at home? Alone? With younger children? With children his own age? With older children? With brothers and sisters?

## FAMILY

1. Have there been situations or circumstances in your family life that would adversely affect the child?

2. Do you have other children and what are their ages?
 Do they all live at home?

3. Are there persons who live at home in addition to the parents and children?

4. Is a language other than English spoken at home?

## OTHER

1. Does your child enjoy T.V.? Which shows?

 Does your child enjoy talking on the telephone?

 Does your child enjoy games? Which ones?

2. What does your child enjoy doing most?

3. What are some things your child does well?

4. What are some things you like best about your child?

5. Comments by parents:

# INDIVIDUALIZED EDUCATIONAL PLAN

Child's Name _____

School _____

Summary of
Present Levels of Performance _____

Annual Goals: (Correlate with Present Level of Performance) _____

| Short Term Instructional Objectives | Beginning and Ending Date | Objective Criteria and Evaluation Procedures for Short Term Instructional Objectives |
|---|---|---|
| | | |

Special Education Services

Name/Position of Individual Providing these Services

Related Services

Name/Position of Individual Providing these Services

Regular Classroom Participation (Subject and amount of time each day)

| Projected Date(s) for Reassessment | Committee Members Present |
| --- | --- |
| | Name _____ Special Ed. Teacher |
| | Name _____ Agency Representative |
| | Name _____ Parent(s) |
| | Name _____ Other |
| | Name _____ Other |
| | Name _____ Other |
| | Name _____ Other |

My rights and those of my child regarding confidentiality and procedural safeguards have been fully explained and I hereby give consent for my child to be placed in a _____ special education program based on his eligibility determination and his individualized education plan.

_____     _____
Parental Signature                Date

Other

# Index

**221**

## About the Author

Judy W. Wood was reared in Center, Texas, and has taught in public schools in regular and special education in numerous states. She received her Ph.D in special education from the University of Southern Mississippi in Hattiesburg. Prior to teaching at Virginia Commonwealth University, she taught at the University of Southern Mississippi. Her interests lie in training teachers to adapt intact instruction for mildly handicapped students. Judy has consulted with school divisions and has conducted in-service workshops for both regular and special education teachers throughout the nation.